Criminal Justice
Recent Scholarship

Edited by
Marilyn McShane and Frank P. Williams III

A Series from LFB Scholarly

The Misuse of Information Systems
The Impact of Security Countermeasures

John P. D'Arcy

LFB Scholarly Publishing LLC
New York 2007

Library of Congress Cataloging-in-Publication Data

D'Arcy, John P., 1975-
  The misuse of information systems : the impact of security
countermeasures / John P. D'Arcy.
      p. cm. -- (Criminal justice: recent scholarship)
  Includes bibliographical references and index.
  ISBN 978-1-59332-243-4 (alk. paper)
  1. Computer security. 2. Computer networks--Security measures. I.
Title.
  QA76.9.A25D335 2007
  005.8--dc22

2007035028

ISBN 978-159332-243-4

Printed on acid-free 250-year-life paper.

Table of Contents

Acknowledgements

The study presented in this book would not have been possible without the assistance of several faculty and staff from the Fox School of Business and Management at Temple University. Chief among these is Dr. Anat Hovav, who was instrumental in conceptualizing the theoretical underpinnings of the study from the outset. Other important contributors include Dr. Dennis Galletta, Dr. Robert Giacalone, Dr. Gerald Zeitz, and Dr. Munir Mandviwalla.

Thanks to the State Farm Companies Foundation for providing partial funding for this research. Thanks also to the managers from the eight participating organizations for their overall support of this project and for facilitating the survey data collection.

I cannot name, but nonetheless do greatly appreciate, the voluntary participation of the hundreds of employees and MBA students who completed surveys for this research project. Finally, this acknowledgement cannot be complete without a thank you to the following individuals who in some way assisted in the data collection efforts for this study: William Aaronson, Norman Baglini, Sondra Barbour, Joanne Bibik, Michael Carey, Thomas Daymont, Fred Dellva, Terry Halbert, Robert Hamilton, Kim Kerr, Jim Lammendola, Wyman Lewis, Devi Mahadevia, David McGettigan, Karen Moran, Carey O'Donnell, Troy Pappas, and Michael Stalbaum.

Preface

As organizational reliance on information systems has increased over recent decades, so has the number of security breaches and their impact on organizations. Computer viruses, worms, spyware, and other forms of cyber attack are almost daily occurrences. These attacks have resulted in financial losses amounting to hundreds of millions of dollars to companies and organizations in the U.S. and possibly billions of dollars worldwide. The frequency and magnitude of computer security breaches are expected to grow due to an increasingly sophisticated population of computer abusers armed with the latest software attack tools, combined with the expanding complexity of network-based organizational information systems.

Interestingly, while organizations continue to focus on external security threats, industry surveys suggest that a substantial proportion of computer security incidents are due to the intentional actions of legitimate users. Moreover, research suggests that insider attacks are more costly and that more successful attacks come from inside the organization than from external sources. Firewalls and intrusion detection systems can stop a number of attacks from the outside. However, no security technology can stop an employee who has authorized access to a computer system from obtaining confidential company information and selling it to competitors. Many security experts agree that the insider threat to information systems represents the single greatest source of risk to organizations.

Considering the number of security breaches that involve insider misuse of IS resources, it is important to understand how to reduce such behavior. Information security researchers and practitioners recommend that organizations implement various countermeasures as a strategy for combating IS misuse. This book reports on a study that examined the effectiveness of four such countermeasures (security policies, security awareness program, computer monitoring, and preventative security software) in deterring IS misuse in an organizational setting. Using the criminological theory of general deterrence as a foundation, a research model was developed and empirically tested using survey responses from 507 employed professionals. Based on extensive analysis of three separate datasets, strong support was found for the effectiveness of security policies, security awareness programs, and computer monitoring in deterring IS misuse. The analysis also suggests that the impact of these countermeasures is not uniform across all individuals. From a theoretical perspective, the results confirm the applicability of general deterrence theory to the IS security domain while providing support for the differential deterrence hypothesis as it pertains to security countermeasures. From a practical perspective, the results suggest several approaches for improving information security management programs in organizations.

The following chapters describe the aforementioned study in detail. The purpose of *The Misuse of Information Systems: The Impact of Security Countermeasures* is to contribute to the existing body of computer crime-related literature by exploring the misuse of information systems in an organizational context. Several avenues for future research remain and I hope that this book will stimulate others to extend this line of inquiry.

CHAPTER 1

Introduction

INFORMATION SYSTEMS MISUSE AND ITS IMPACT ON BUSINESS AND SOCIETY

Rapid advances in electronic networks and computer-based information systems have given businesses enormous capabilities to process, store, and transmit digital data. Consequently, use of information systems (IS) has proliferated to the point where many organizations are now dependent upon IS for operational, strategic, e-commerce, and e-business activities. Increased organizational reliance on IS has led to a corresponding increase in the impact of IS misuse (Kankanhalli et al. 2003). Prior research has shown that IS misuse can be either accidental or intentional and happen as a result of both internal and external unauthorized activity (Hoffer and Straub 1989; Im and Baskerville 2005; Loch, Carr, and Warkentin 1992; Magklaras and Furnell 2002). This study focuses upon intentional insider IS misuse, defined as "unauthorized, deliberate, and internally recognizable misuse of assets of the local organizational information system by individuals" (Straub 1986, p. 27).

IS misuse[1] represents a very real and costly threat to organizations. Industry surveys indicate that between one-half and three-quarters of all security incidents originate from within the organization, with a substantial proportion due to the intentional actions of legitimate users (Berinato 2005; CSO Magazine 2006; InformationWeek 2005). A recent study of the world's leading financial institutions reported that

---

[1] The term IS misuse, as used hereafter, refers to intentional insider misuse of information systems.

more organizations experienced internal attacks on information systems than external attacks over a twelve month period (Deloitte and Touche 2005). There is also evidence that insider attacks are potentially more costly. A study by Vista Research found that 70 percent of security breaches that involved losses of more than $100,000 were internal, often perpetrated by disgruntled employees (Standage 2002). Besides financial losses, other negative consequences of IS misuse include negative publicity, competitive disadvantage, reduced organizational viability, loss of customer confidence, and legal liability (Dutta and Roy 2003; Foltz 2000; Kankanhalli et al. 2003; Pierce and Henry 2000; Sindell 2002). Researchers expect that the frequency of IS misuse and the amount of losses associated with it will continue in the future due to better computer literacy, increased computer user sophistication, and the availability of advanced software tools (Kankanhalli et al. 2003; Lee and Lee 2002; Straub and Nance 1990).

PRIOR RESEARCH

Prior research has examined many aspects of IS misuse, such as classifications of misuse behaviors, individual motivation to commit misuse, and determinants of misuse (e.g., Banerjee, Cronan, and Jones 1998; Cronan and Douglas 2006; Cronan et al. 2005; Leonard and Cronan 2001; Magklaras and Furnell 2002; Parker 1976; Peace, Galletta, and Thong 2003; Straub and Widom 1984). In addition, a number of studies have attempted to find ways to reduce IS misuse. The primary work in this area has focused on applying the criminological theory of general deterrence to computer abuse and computer crime (e.g., D'Arcy and Hovav 2007; Foltz 2000; Harrington 1996; Straub 1990; Wiant 2003). General deterrence theory (GDT) predicts that "disincentives" or sanctions dissuade potential offenders from illicit behavior and that as the certainty and severity of sanctions increase, the level of illicit behaviors should decrease (Gibbs 1975). Within the context of IS security, GDT provides a theoretical basis for the use of certain technical and procedural countermeasures as a means to limit the incidence of IS misuse in organizations by convincing potential offenders that there is too high a certainty of getting caught and getting punished severely (Straub and Welke 1998). Straub (1990) applied GDT to the IS environment and found that organizational use of security countermeasures such as policy statements that specify conditions for proper system use and preventative security software was associated with lower levels of computer abuse. Similarly, Kankanhalli et al. (2003) found that greater organizational deterrent and preventative efforts were associated with improved IS security effectiveness. However, other studies that have assessed the effectiveness of IS security countermeasures have produced conflicting results. Doherty and Fulford (2005) and Wiant (2003) both found that use of security policies was not associated with lower incidence of computer abuse. In addition, a number of studies that have examined the impact of different security countermeasures (i.e., codes of ethics, security policies, security software) on individual IS misuse intentions and behaviors have found that such techniques have little or no deterrent effect (Foltz 2000; Harrington 1996; Kreie and Cronan 2000; Lee, Lee, and Yoo 2004; Pierce and Henry 1996).

UNANSWERED CONCERNS

Despite the strong theoretical basis for the use of security countermeasure as a means to deter IS misuse, empirical studies that have assessed the effectiveness of such techniques have produced mixed results. Hence, there is a need for further investigation. A review of the deterrence literature from the field of criminology reveals the following limitations with existing IS deterrence studies:

1. Organizational-level IS deterrence studies have relied on aggregate misuse statistics gathered from victimization surveys. These studies reveal little about actual IS misuse behavior or the extent to which security countermeasures impact such behavior. In addition, victimization surveys introduce the possibility of bias, as respondents (i.e., IS managers) have a vested interest in reporting a lower frequency and magnitude of IS misuse incidents within their organizations in an effort to increase the perceived effectiveness of the IS function's deterrent efforts. Further, it is unlikely that the aggregate statistics reported in organizational-level IS deterrence studies represent the actual level of IS misuse occurring within organizations, as only a small percentage of IS misuse is actually discovered (Hoffer and Straub 1989; Parker 1998; Straub and Nance 1990; Whitman 2003).

2. IS deterrence studies have not assessed the impact of security countermeasures on individual perceptions of punishment certainty and severity, which, according to GDT, have a direct impact on misuse intentions. Instead, these studies have assumed that the actual level of security countermeasures employed in an organization represent how potential abusers perceive risk.

3. IS deterrence studies have not considered several individual factors that may influence punishment perceptions and therefore impact the effectiveness of security countermeasures. The differential deterrence hypothesis (Mann et al. 2003) suggests that the impact of security countermeasures will not be uniform across all persons due to individual and situational differences. Hence, it is possible that certain security countermeasures that deter some people may be perceived as only a minor threat by others. Failure to account for individual factors may explain the inconsistent findings of prior IS deterrence studies. Moreover, failure to consider the specific conditions under which security countermeasures are likely to be important influences on behavior may explain why organizations continue to have difficulties preventing IS misuse. Several authors have called for further research to better understand what factors influence the effectiveness of IS security countermeasures (Banerjee, Cronan, and Jones 1998; Gattiker and Kelley 1999; Harrington 1996; Ives, Walsh, and Schneider 2004).

An additional concern comes from the apparent lack of management awareness of several deterrent tools available for controlling IS misuse. Straub and Welke (1998) found that managers relied on a combination of technical preventatives (e.g., access controls) and remedial actions (e.g., fines, prosecution, suspensions) to combat IS misuse and were generally unaware of procedural security countermeasures such as security awareness programs and acceptable use policies. Industry statistics are consistent with these findings, as 82 percent of organizations have reported using some sort of advanced access control technology while only 28 percent reported that they have security awareness programs in place (InformationWeek 2005). Moreover, there is evidence that organizations are shifting resources away from procedural security measures to security technologies. In a recent survey by PricewaterhouseCoopers (CIO Magazine 2006), security awareness training dropped from second to tenth (compared to the previous year) on the priority list for IT executives, while data backup and network firewalls were listed as the number one and two priorities, respectively. This disproportionate focus on technical security countermeasures is one viable explanation why losses from IS misuse remain uncomfortably large despite ongoing attempts to deal with the problem (Straub and Welke 1998). Straub and Welke's (1998) Security Action Cycle posits that both procedural and technical security countermeasures are necessary components of an effective security management program. However, there is very little empirical research that has examined the impact of a combination of procedural and technical security countermeasures on individual IS misuse behavior. Additional research is needed in order to provide managers with a better understanding of the full range of tools available for controlling IS misuse.

THE CURRENT RESEARCH STUDY

The purpose of the study presented in this book is to address the aforementioned concerns by (1) assessing the impact of a combination of technical and procedural security countermeasures (i.e., security policies, security awareness program, monitoring practices, preventative security software) on individual perceptions of punishment associated with IS misuse, and (2) testing the differential deterrence hypothesis by exploring the moderating impact of computer self-efficacy, risk propensity, and virtual status[2] on the effectiveness of security countermeasures. In other words, are security countermeasures more/less effective in deterring IS misuse for certain people depending on these individual differences?

Research from the fields of criminology, organizational behavior, and social psychology suggests that computer self-efficacy and risk propensity influence one's perceived risk of punishment for engaging in IS misuse. However, neither of these individual factors has been included in prior studies that have assessed the effectiveness of IS

---

[2] Virtual status is defined as "the degree to which an employee operates from traditional offices or from dispersed locations (via telecommunications equipment)" (Wiesenfeld, Raghuram, and Garud, 1999, p.780). Further discussion of virtual status is presented in Chapter 3.

security countermeasures. In addition, there is no empirical research that has examined the impact of virtual status on IS misuse. An understanding of the influence of virtual status on the effectiveness of IS security countermeasures is of increasing importance to modern organizations, given the rise in telecommuting and other virtual work arrangements. Recent estimates indicate that nearly twenty-nine million U.S. workers (approximately 30 percent of the workforce) currently spend at least a portion of their workweek in virtual mode and this number is expected to increase to more than forty million by 2010 (Potter 2003).

Research Questions

This study of the impact of IS security countermeasures addresses the following two research questions:

- Do security countermeasures increase the perceived threat of punishment associated with IS misuse and therefore decrease IS misuse intentions?
- Do individual differences moderate the impact of security countermeasures on punishment perceptions and therefore impact IS misuse intentions?

To answer these questions, a theoretical model is developed and tested. The model expands on the framework of general deterrence theory and proposes a relationship between security countermeasures, sanction perceptions, individual differences, and IS misuse intention. Specific hypotheses that identify relationships between each of the variables are empirically tested. Data were collected using a survey instrument consisting of scenarios that depict common IS misuse behaviors.

CHAPTER 2

IS Security, IS Misuse, and Security Countermeasures

HISTORICAL ACCOUNT OF INFORMATION SYSTEMS SECURITY

Information systems (IS) security has been a concern of management since computers were first introduced in business. Early studies by Allen (1968) and Wasserman (1969), for example, discussed security and audit controls for electronic data processing activities involving punched cards, magnetic tapes, and disks. However, the business computing environment of the 1960s and 1970s consisted of standalone mainframe computers with security requirements that were relatively easy to satisfy (Dhillon 2001; Thomson and von Solms 1998). These early mainframe computers were extremely large and therefore had to be housed in completely separate facilities (i.e., computer centers). Anyone needing access to the computer had to be admitted into the building in which it was being kept through physical access controls. Further, the type of systems in use allowed for only one user at a time to work on the machine and electronic access to the data did not exist. Hence, it was very difficult for unauthorized users to gain access to any data. The major threats to this form of computing were of an environmental nature (e.g., floods, earthquakes, fires, civil disorders) and effective physical precautions could be taken to minimize them to an acceptable level (Loch, Carr, and Warkentin 1992; Thomson and von Solms 1998). As the use of computers evolved to a multi-user computing environment, new security threats needed to be countered. Specifically, the following (Thomson and von Solms 1998): (1) more people were able to work on the same machine at the same time, and not always within the confines of the computer center;

(2) physical access control to the computer center was no longer adequate to determine the validity of users because workstations were now situated in the user's work environment; (3) users were allowed access to computer systems electronically; and (4) many components were shared (e.g., memory, databases, printers, etc.). These security threats were largely eliminated by security controls embedded within mainframe operating systems. Mainframe security management products such as IBM's RACF (Resource Access Control Facility) were used to identify and verify users to the system (via user id and password, terminal id, and physical location), control the means of access to protected resources, and log and report unauthorized access to protected resources. The workstations in use at this time were dumb terminals (all intelligence resided on the central computer) and so it was relatively easy to restrict users to work in certain areas. Thus, at this phase of business computing, a combination of mainframe operating system controls and physical security measures were adequate to ensure effective information security (Thomson and von Solms 1998).

The introduction of end user computing (EUC) brought a number of new security concerns for organizations. Bostrom, Olfman, and Sein (1988) defined an end user as "one who does not rely directly on the IS department in order to use the computer on the job" (p. 225). The EUC environment allowed end users to develop, maintain, and use their own information systems from their own workstations. In contrast to the standalone computing environment that was historically controlled by a small group of knowledgeable IS professionals in a centralized batch processing mode (Loch, Carr, and Warkentin 1992), EUC shifted much of the burden of computer security to the end users themselves. Several researchers acknowledged the increased security threats posed by the spread of computer technology in the form of EUC (Alavi and Weiss 1985; Benson 1983; Boockholdt 1989; Rockart and Flannery 1983; Wybo and Straub 1989). Alavi and Weiss (1985) cited data integrity and data security as the major risks associated with EUC. They also cautioned that the user-friendliness and ease of access provided through end-user tools increased the risk of unauthorized access to data. Further, EUC placed significantly more moveable hardware resources within the organization. Bostrom, Olfman, and Sein (1988) and Sein, Bostrom, and Olfman (1987) argued that end users needed to be trained on systems security techniques in order to minimize the risks associated with EUC. Empirical results seemed to validate these security concerns. Rockart and Flannery (1983) studied the EUC environment in seven organizations and found that control policies for computer usage were largely nonexistent and those that did exist were developed based on the older standalone computing environment. Benson (1983) found that end users were not aware of security policies regarding the use of IS tools and that security and information assurance procedures such as backing up data and locking up floppy disks were not followed. Benson (1983, p. 43) concluded that "security and integrity" and "database access for microcomputers" were critical issues that needed to be resolved through increased user training and education.

Despite the increased threats to information systems brought on by the growth of EUC, managers seemed to have a low regard for IS security during this time period. In a 1981 survey of IS professionals, security ranked as the fourteenth most important information management topic (Ball and Harris 1982). By 1985, it had moved to fifth place (Hartog and Herbert 1986) but a 1986 study (Brancheau and Wetherbe 1987) reported IS security in eighteenth place. By 1989, IS security had dropped to nineteenth place on the list of key issues in MIS (Niederman, Brancheau, and Wetherbe 1991). In addition, in one study general managers did not even rank security among the top twenty critical management issues in the IS domain (Brancheau and Wetherbe 1987). Even more telling, Hoffer and Straub (1989) reported that through 1986, only 60 percent of all organizations had initiated IS security as a functional area and nearly half of those dedicated less than nine hours a week to the function. These results suggest that both IS and non-IS executives believed that either security was not an important issue, or that they had implemented enough controls to sufficiently address the problem.

The advent of the network-centric computing environment, and the Internet and e-commerce in particular, has brought about new challenges in the area of IS security. Networking has further facilitated what can be seen as the decentralizing of computer power that has progressed through the multi-user and EUC computing environments. LANS (local area networks), WANS (wide area networks), and more recently the Internet, extranets, and intranets have all accelerated this process. With this increased flexibility comes a cost: decreased control. Today's almost unlimited access to organizational information systems by a large, knowledgeable community of end users from desktop and network facilities has created an extremely vulnerable computing environment (Loch, Carr, and Warkentin 1992). Users are increasingly getting access to data on a "must have now" basis due to the competitive nature of business. In many instances, this situation has resulted in people gaining access to or modifying data that they are not supposed to, whether it be intentional or accidental (Im and Baskerville, 2005; Parker 1998; Thompson and von Solms 1998). In addition, as the use of information systems continues to proliferate, the computer literacy of organizational staffs increases, creating sophisticated users of technology. An undesirable side effect of this increased sophistication is that users are becoming adept at committing various types of computer abuse (Straub and Nance 1990).

As connectivity among computing resources has increased, so has the likelihood of intrusion, theft, viruses, defacement, and other forms of security breaches from both internal and external sources. Moreover, as organizations become increasingly dependent on information systems for successful daily operations, communication failures (i.e., network or Internet connection failures) represent a growing security concern. Depending on the industry, a security breach involving the disruption of an organization's computer networks can cause outcomes ranging from inconvenience to catastrophe (Loch, Carr, and Warkentin 1992). Pure e-commerce companies are particularly at risk to IS security threats as they have complete reliance on information technology (IT) for such fundamental business operations as buying and selling of goods. An interruption of service can literally cease operations for a period of time, which can be damaging to the financial performance of these companies (Hovav and D'Arcy 2003). In June 1999, online auction company e-Bay was shut down for a twenty-two hour period due to operating system problems and over a two-day period the company lost 25 percent of its stock price, or $6 billion (Glover, Liddle, and Prawitt 2001).

Industry statistics indicate the legitimacy of the various threats to information systems, as reports of serious security breaches have become frequent in today's network-centric computing environment. The 2006 CSI/FBI Computer Crime and Security Survey indicated that approximately 65 percent of respondents (primarily large corporations and government agencies) detected some type of computer security breach within the twelve months preceding the study, with losses averaging $168,000 among the 51 percent of respondents willing and able to estimate losses (Gordon et al. 2006). Another study by CompTIA Research (2002) reported that nearly one-third of respondents suffered one-to-three major security breaches (i.e., resulting in financial damage, confidential information compromised, and/or interrupted business) during the previous six months. A United Nations (2005) report describes "tens, if not hundreds of billions of dollars per year" of worldwide economic damage caused by compromises in information security. Besides actual and potential financial losses, other negative consequences of IS security breaches that have been reported include negative publicity, loss of competitive advantage, reduced organizational viability, loss of customer confidence, and legal liability (Dutta and Roy 2003; Foltz 2000; Kankanhalli et al. 2003; Pierce and Henry 2000).

These reported losses have spurred increased interest in IS security among researchers and practitioners. Security and privacy was ranked as the number two most important IT management issue in a survey of Society of Information Management (SIM) member IT executives (Luftman et al. 2006). Research by Ernst and Young (2004) indicates that 93 percent of organizations view information security as highly important for achieving their overall objectives. Further, organizations continue to invest in IS security. Organizations responding to the 2006 E-Crime Watch survey (CSO Magazine 2006) spent an average of $20 million on IT security. A survey by PricewaterhouseCoopers (CIO Magazine 2006) indicated that large organizations spend nearly 17 percent of their overall IT budgets on security, an increase of 54 percent over figures reported in 2003.

In summary, the evolution of business computing from standalone mainframes to the current network-centric environment has greatly increased the risk of information security breaches. In addition, the meaning and scope of IS security has evolved from mostly physical controls of internal and closed systems to what is now termed information assurance of distributed and open systems (Schou and Trimmer 2004).

DEFINITION OF INFORMATION SYSTEMS SECURITY

A variety of definitions and meanings have been associated with the term information systems security. Some authors use the terms information systems security and information security interchangeably, while others distinguish between the two. Schweitzer (1990) viewed IS security as a necessary subset of information security. Information security encompasses all forms of information storage and processing including electronic, paper, and mental (i.e., the employee knowledge base). IS security is defined more narrowly as "the protection of the operations and data in process in an organization's computing systems" (Schweitzer 1990, p. 62). This information is created during company business operations including engineering, manufacturing, marketing, and other processes. Hill and Pemberton (1995) described information security as encompassing systems and procedures designed to protect an organization's information assets from disclosure to any person or entity not authorized to have access to that information, especially information that is considered sensitive, proprietary, confidential, or classified. Parker (1998) defined IS security in terms of its goals. According to Parker, the goal of IS security is to meet the owners' needs to preserve the desired security elements of their information from intentional and accidental acts of abusers and misusers (and from physical forces) that would cause losses. This is to be done by applying safeguards and practices that are selected by standards of due care and from special needs to achieve desired objectives.

Other descriptions of IS security extend the boundaries to include the security of the physical information system itself, in addition to the information contained within the system. Cronin (1986) offered a comprehensive definition of IS security that includes any and all threats to information systems and information stored within those systems:

> Security assumes the safe and continuous operation of your computer system performed by trained, authorized personnel. The computer system itself must be protected as well as the integrity of all programs and data. Finally, security means that any entered data can be retrieved at any future time, without alteration by accident or deliberate intent (p. 2).

Similarly, Denning et al. (1984) viewed IS security as "that body of technology, techniques, procedures, and practices that provides the protective mechanisms to assure the safety of both the systems themselves and the information within them, and limits access to such information solely to authorized users" (p. 315). Landwehr (2001) suggested that IS security should have three main foci: (1) securing the data that are received, stored, and retransmitted; (2) securing the processes that are performed on these data; and (3) securing the physical system properties such as backup tapes, hard-copy output, and laptops. Landwehr (2001) warned that failure to account for each of these elements substantially increases an organization's vulnerability to a security breach.

While the wording and scope may vary, each of the previous definitions of IS security involves the protection and preservation of four key aspects of information: availability, integrity, authenticity, and confidentially. Parker (1998) referred to these as the elements of IS security. Definitions for these elements are presented in Table 2.1.

Table 2.1. Elements of IS Security

Security Element	Description
Availability	Usability of information for a purpose.
Integrity	Completeness, wholeness, and readability of information and quality being unchanged from a previous state.
Authenticity	Validity, conformance, and genuineness of information.
Confidentially	Limited observation and disclosure of knowledge to only authorized individuals.

OVERVIEW OF IS SECURITY LITERATURE

The importance of information security in a computer-based environment has resulted in a large body of research that can be grouped into three categories: (1) technical aspects of IS security; (2) economic and financial aspects of IS security; and (3) behavioral aspects of IS security.

Technical IS Security Research

The focus of most research in IS security has been on the formal automated part of an information system (Dhillon and Backhouse 2001). This literature views IS security as a technical issue that can be effectively managed by selecting appropriate hardware and software components and designing an architecture to protect the information assets of the organization (Dutta and Roy 2003). One of the primary topics of technical IS security research has been the development of technological solutions for fundamental information security problems such as how to restrict information resource access to authorized individuals, how to transmit and receive information in a secure manner, and how to keep information accurate and available in the face of internal and external threats (Stanton et al. 2003). This body of work includes studies on (1) secure identification and verification technologies such as passwords and personal identification numbers (PINs) (e.g., Irakleous et al. 2002; Zviran and Haga 1999), access controls (e.g., Osborn, Ravi, and Qamar 2000; Sandhu et al. 1996), smart cards (e.g., Giampaolo 2003; Plouffe, Hulland, and Vandenbosch 2001; Venter and Eloff 2003), and biometric controls (e.g., Freeman 2003; Jain and Lin 2000; Jain and Ross 2004; Sherman 1992); (2) encryption and secure communications (e.g., Denning and Branstad 1996; Gupta, Tung, and Marsden 2004; Lou and Liu 2002; Poore 2003; Rubin 2003; Simmons 1994; Venter and Eloff 2003); and (3) protective devices such as firewalls (e.g., Frolick 2003; Kamara et al. 2003; Venter and Eloff 2003), intrusion detection systems (e.g., Axelsson 2000; Frincke 2000; Liao and Vemuri 2002; Rosenthal 2002; Vigna and Kemmerer 1999), and anti-virus software (e.g., Post and Kagan 1998; Wen 1998).

Another topic of technical IS security research has been the incorporation of security into the design of information systems. In one of the earliest studies to address security controls in information systems design, Conway et al. (1972) introduced a security matrix that allowed system designers to specify the conditions under which a user could access a particular data structure and the action that a user could perform upon the data structure. Their matrix also considered the costs of security controls in terms of decreased flexibility for system users. Wang and Wang (2003) discussed security-related risks and threats that need to be considered during the design phase of the software development process. They presented a taxonomy of security risks and threats that included three layers: application layer, platform layer, and network layer. Wang and Wang argued that software designers must consider security risks at each of these layers prior to system construction in order to avoid negative impacts on software quality due to security flaws. Johnston, Eloff, and Labuschagne (2003) applied usability criteria from human computer interface (HCI) research to the interface of Windows XP's Internet Connection Firewall. They concluded that HCI research has the potential to improve security interface design which should increase use of security features and ultimately improve the security of information systems. Sarathy and Muralidhar (2002) introduced an evaluation method to assist in the design of security controls for organizational databases. Their evaluation method was based on canonical correlation analysis and focused on the security of confidential numerical data contained within databases. Payne (2002) discussed security issues associated with the design of open source software. Results of an earlier empirical study were presented in which open source software was found to be more secure than proprietary software. Payne argued that these results were due to the fact that open source code is "regularly and purposefully examined with the explicit intention of finding and fixing security holes" (p. 76).

A related stream of technical IS security research has examined risk analysis methods for the design of secure information systems. This body of work is quite substantial and can arguably be considered a separate category of IS security research. However, the current study classifies risk analysis as a subset of technical IS security research because risk analysis is concerned with the design of security controls in the formal, automated part of an information system. Risk analysis methods suggest that negative IS security events can be prevented and information systems can be made more secure if security controls are developed and implemented within information systems in a logical and sequential manner (Birch and McEvoy 1992; Dhillon and Backhouse 2001). Birch and McEvoy (1992) presented a risk analysis methodology called Structured Risk Analysis (SRA) that involves the creation of a risk catalogue of threats and vulnerabilities to information systems. A risk exists where there is a threat and vulnerability that coincide within the risk catalogue. Appropriate security controls (either technical or procedural) are then implemented into the information system depending on the nature of the risk. Similarly, Fisher (1984) developed a risk-based methodology for the design of data security that includes the following sequential steps: (1) define the data inventory, (2) identification of exposures, (3) assess risk, (4) design controls, and (5) analyze cost effectiveness. Several other risk analysis methodologies that follow similar steps in designing technical security controls for information systems have also been studied (e.g., Ekenberg, Oberoi, and Orci 1995; Parker 1981; von Solms et al. 1994).

Baskerville (1988, 1993) discussed the weaknesses of risk analysis techniques in his comprehensive review of three generations of systems security development methodologies. He pointed out that systems security design methods that utilize risk analysis assume that a largely similar set of controls can be used effectively across a wide dissimilar population of information systems. In contrast, Baskerville (1988) argued that security controls must be specifically designed for each information system. He asserted that structured security analysis and design can be carried out in much the same way as a structured systems analysis. According to Baskerville, "the best approach to the development of security analysis and design methodology, both for office use and for practice in general, would essentially be to nest it as a component part of an existing, established, successful overall information systems analysis and design methodology" (Baskerville 1988, p. 88). Baskerville (1988) used DeMarco's structured systems analysis and specification approach and implemented security controls, by developing formal heuristics, in its logical design phase. Interestingly, Baskerville (1991) later defended the use of risk analysis techniques in practice. However, he argued that risk analysis is more useful as a communication channel between security and management professionals than as a control selection technique (Baskerville 1991).

In addition to technical IS security research that has focused on the security of information systems themselves, there is also work that has explored the technical details of various threats to information systems. Cohen (1984) discussed the technical aspects of computer viruses and conducted a series of experiments that demonstrated the feasibility of a viral attack against unprotected systems. Spafford (1989) detailed the technical functioning of the Robert Morris worm, which is the first known viral attack against the Internet. More recent studies include technical accounts of the Code Red (Berghel 2001), LoveLetter (Hinde 2000), Slammer (Panko 2003), and Blaster worms (Chen 2003) as well as categorizations of various virus/worm types (Chen 2003; Nachenberg 1997). Bagchi and Udo (2003) analyzed the growth patterns of many different technical computer and Internet security breaches and found that breaches grow at different rates. Voelker, and Savage (2001) examined the spread of denial-of-service (DOS) attacks over a three week period using a technique called "backscatter analysis." The researchers observed over twelve thousand DOS attacks against approximately five thousand websites worldwide and concluded that DOS attacks represent a growing threat to well-known Internet companies (e.g., Amazon.com) as well as small and foreign companies.

Economic and Financial IS Security Research

There is a growing body of literature that has explored the economic and financial aspects of IS security. This literature includes a diverse set of topics such as IS security investment decisions, economic analyses of software piracy and intrusion detection systems, and the financial impact of IS security breaches. Cavusoglu, Cavusoglu, and Raghunathan (2004) discussed four important elements that organizations should consider while managing the security function from an economic perspective. The four elements are: estimation of a security breach cost, a risk management approach, cost effective technology configuration, and value deployment of multiple technologies. Gordon and Loeb (2002) developed an economic model to determine the optimal amount that organizations should invest in information security. They found that optimal expenditures for protecting information assets did not always increase with the level of vulnerability of a firm's information. Gordon and Loeb's (2002) results suggest that firms may be better off concentrating their security efforts on information sets with midrange vulnerabilities since extremely vulnerable information sets may be too expensive to protect. Cavusoglu, Mishra, and Raghunathan, (2004) presented an economic model based on game theory to evaluate the return on IS security investments. Their model improved upon earlier IS security evaluation approaches by incorporating the costs and benefits of multiple security technologies. Gopal and Saunders (1997) used an economic model to determine the effect of deterrent and preventative antipiracy efforts on software developers' profits. Their empirical results suggest that preventative controls (e.g., special codes in the software that make copying more difficult for users) decrease profits and deterrent controls (e.g., distributing information concerning the illegality of software piracy) can potentially increase profits. Anderson (2001) used economic analysis (i.e., network externalities, asymmetric information, moral hazard, adverse selection) to explain several IS security problems. He argued that insecure systems result from perverse economic incentives in which the party who is in a position to protect the information system is not the party who suffers the negative results of a security failure. Cavusoglu, Mishra, and Raghunathan (2005) utilized an economic model to assess the value of intrusion detection systems. They found that an improperly configured intrusion detection system can encourage hacking behavior, resulting in a higher cost for the firm. A properly configured intrusion detection system can create value by deterring hacker activities through increased detection.

Research on the financial aspects of IS security has focused on assessments of financial damage caused by various types of security breaches. This research is of interest to organizations trying to decide where to spend their information security budgets as well as for insurance companies that provide cyber-risk policies (Gordon, Loeb, and Sohail 2003). McAfee and Haynes (1989) studied the financial impact of the Robert Morris worm. The worm infected sixty-two hundred individual machines (7.3 percent of the Internet's computers at the time) and caused eight million hours of lost access. McAfee and Haynes (1989) estimated the total dollar loss due to the infestation was $98 million. Coursen (1997) investigated several computer virus outbreaks in large organizations and concluded that a single virus incident costs organizations approximately $50,000. The estimate included costs for employee lost time, recovery coordination, virus scans and installations, and data recovery.

Several studies have attempted to quantify the financial impact of IS security breaches using the event study methodology. The event study methodology examines the impact of a public announcement of a particular event on the stock price of the affected firm(s) (McWilliams and Siegel 1997). Ettredge and Richardson (2003) assessed the spillover effect of a series of DOS attacks against several well-known Internet firms (e.g., E-bay.com, Amazon.com, E*TRADE.com) on the stock prices of similar Internet firms that were not attacked. Results showed that the DOS attacks had a negative spillover effect on the stock prices of Internet firms that were not attacked, both within Internet industries in which some firms were attacked and within industries in which no firms were attacked. In addition, the DOS attacks had a positive effect on the stock prices of developers of Internet security products. Garg, Curtis, and Halper (2003) studied the impact of the same DOS attacks on the stock prices of the attacked companies. They found that the DOS attacks had a negative impact on the stock prices of attacked companies for a period of three days after the public announcement of the attacks. Consistent with Ettredge and Richardson's (2003) results, Garg, Curtis, and Halper (2003) also found that the DOS attacks had a positive impact on the stock prices of security technology vendors. Hovav and D'Arcy (2003) studied the impact of DOS attacks that occurred over an extended period (i.e., 4.5 years) on the stock prices of attacked companies and found little overall impact. However, the DOS attacks did have a larger impact on Internet-specific companies than on other companies. Hovav and D'Arcy (2004) also assessed the impact of computer virus announcements on the stock prices of attacked companies and found no significant effects. Cavusoglu, Mishra, and Raghunathan (2004a) assessed the impact of a variety of security breach types on the stock prices of attacked companies. Results indicated that announcements of Internet security breaches were negatively associated with the stock prices of attacked firms. Similar to other studies, there was also a positive relationship between security breach announcements and the stock prices of security technology developers. Campbell et al. (2003) found evidence that the stock market discriminates across types of IS security breaches when accessing their economic impact on affected firms. Specifically, they found a highly significant negative market reaction for security breaches involving unauthorized access to confidential data (e.g., access to customer credit card data, access to pricing or other firm proprietary data), but no significant reaction for breaches that did not involve confidential information. Finally, Hovav and D'Arcy (2005) found that companies that produce vulnerable IT products that render virus attacks rarely suffer negative market returns.

Behavioral IS Security Research

Research on the behavioral aspects of IS security has become an increasingly important component of the IS security literature. Stanton et al. (2003) defined behavioral information security as "the complexes of human action that influence the availability, confidentiality, and integrity of information systems" (p. 3). Behavioral IS security research has been driven by the results of academic studies and industry statistics that indicate that technological countermeasures alone do not provide adequate security of information resources. Many researchers now agree that the success of IS security appears to depend in part upon the effective behavior of the individuals involved in its use. This view is expressed in the following quote from Parker (1981):

If any single conclusion is to be drawn from the 11 years of research and consulting, it is that computer security is not primarily a technological subject. It is a subject of psychological and sociological behavior of people. As I have said repeatedly in my worldwide lecturing, computers do not commit errors, omissions, or crimes; only people can do these things that may subsequently be manifested in computers. Solutions to these problems also must come from people, their actions and their attitudes (p. xi).

Existing behavioral IS security research has explored appropriate as well as improper use of information systems. From an IS security perspective, appropriate and constructive computing behaviors are considered security compliance. Inappropriate, destructive, and illegal computing behaviors are a form of computer abuse. Such behaviors are referred to as IS misuse throughout this study.

Thomson and von Solms (1998) discussed the use of techniques from social psychology as a strategy for improving security compliance. They argued that incorporating techniques such as social learning, persuasion, and attribution into security awareness and training programs can improve user attitudes toward IS security, which in turn will increase compliant behavior. Siponen (2000) also asserted that behavioral models from social psychology may be useful in understanding the factors that influence individual intentions to comply with security policies and procedures. Parker (1995) proposed that organizations include security accountability as a specific objective in every job description in order to improve security compliance. He suggested peer evaluations, managers' evaluations, absence of security violations, and attendance at training sessions as options for measuring security accountability. Lee (1995) conducted an empirical study that examined the factors that influence employees' willingness to adhere to IS security procedures in financial institutions. He found that the following factors had a positive impact on security compliance: affirmative attitudes toward IS security from management, responsive and reasonable disciplinary actions toward security violators, frequent communications between management and employees toward IS security issues, and pleasant and friendly work environment. Magklaras and Furnell (2005) examined the influence of end user sophistication in predicting inappropriate use of IS resources by internal users. Aytes and Connolly (2004) studied secure computing practices among college students and found that computer expertise and perceived probability of negative consequences were positively associated with the following security behaviors: regularly backing-up data, scanning unknown e-mail attachments for viruses, changing passwords, and not sharing passwords. Stanton et al. (2005) found that secure password behavior among end users was associated with training, awareness, monitoring, and motivation.

In contrast to the security compliance research, the body of work on IS misuse is much larger and includes studies on the determinants of misuse behaviors as well as the impact of organizational responses such as procedural and technical security countermeasures. IS misuse is the focus of the current study and therefore a comprehensive review of relevant literature is presented in the remaining sections of this chapter.

THE PROBLEM OF IS MISUSE

The misuse of information technology resources is not a new problem. The first recorded computer abuse incident occurred in 1958 (Parker 1976). By 1975, Donn Parker and his research team at Stanford University had compiled a database of 374 computer misuse and crime incidents. However, IS misuse did not receive much attention from managers until the mid-1980s, when valid and reliable statistics became widely available. A 1984 study by the American Bar Association reported total dollar losses from computer misuse of approximately $5 billion per year in only seventy-two firms (American Bar Association 1984). In nearly all cases, the perpetrators were employees. Another study by the Research Institute of America (1983) reported monetary losses suffered from computer misuse in the U.S. at billions of dollars per year.

The frequency and cost of IS misuse continued to increase throughout the 1990s, as organizations shifted to network-centric computing environments. Anthes (1996) reported that the frequency of loss caused by IS misuse increased by 323 percent between 1992 and 1996, with estimated monthly costs of $2 billion in the U.S. The evidence from this study also makes it clear that IS misuse is primarily caused by insiders, as almost 75 percent of incidents were attributed to employees.

Recent industry statistics indicate that IS misuse continues to be a very real and costly threat for organizations. Surveys reveal that between one-half and three-quarters of all security incidents originate from within the organization, with a substantial proportion due to the intentional actions of legitimate users (Berinato 2005; CSO Magazine 2006; InformationWeek 2005). A recent study of the world's leading financial institutions reported that more organizations experienced internal attacks on information systems than external attacks over a twelve month period (Deloitte and Touche 2005). Vista Research estimated that over 70 percent of security breaches that involve losses of more than $100,000 are perpetrated internally, often by disgruntled employees (Standage 2002). In addition, as indicated by a variety of studies, the IS misuse problem is international in scope (Baskerville 1993; Dhillon 1999; Kankanhalli et al. 2003; Lee, Lee, and Yoo 2004; Warren 2002).

Reports of the frequency and severity of IS misuse have not gone unnoticed by industry professionals. According to an Information Security Magazine survey (Savage 2006), IT security practitioners view the insider threat as a top concern for IT security management. In another study by Mehta and George (2001), IS managers identified insider abuse of network access and unauthorized access by insiders as two of the most severe threats to information systems. Whitman (2003) also included several IS misuse behaviors in his ranking of the top threats to information security. The frequency of IS misuse and the amount of losses associated with it are expected to grow due to highly sophisticated and educated abusers armed with the latest information technology (Lee and Lee 2002; Straub and Nance 1990).

RESEARCH ON IS MISUSE BEHAVIOR

There is a large body of research that has explored "negative" or improper computing behaviors. These studies use terms such as unethical computing acts, immoral computing acts, computer abuse, computer misuse, IS misuse, computer crime, and insider attacks. While the names and severity of the behaviors vary, each can be considered a form of IS misuse and therefore represents an example of an internal IS security breach.

Classifications of IS Misusers

Straub and Widom (1984) developed a classification of computer abusers based on the strength of their motivation. Type I computer abusers are borderline abusers that are motivated by ethical ignorance. They may not intentionally abuse computing resources, but they are nonetheless violating the intentions of the asset owner. Type I abusers lack knowledge that their use of the computer is not acceptable to the owner of the information asset. Type II computer abusers are those individuals that are motivated to abuse computing assets for personal gain. These individuals are aware of the fact that they are doing something wrong or illegal but continue in spite of this knowledge. Fear of punishment is overridden by inducement for professional or personal gain. Type III computer abusers are individuals that are aware that their behavior is socially unacceptable but still proceed in spite of all sanctions. The actions of Type III abusers may be reinforced by the antisocial values of their subculture. Finally, type IV computer abusers are motivated by corruption. These individuals have a clear sense of wrongdoing but believe they will escape the consequences of their actions by their mastery of the situation. Corrupt persons in high positions can dictate terms to lower ranking members of their organization, thereby making prevention of corruption-motivated abuse almost impossible.

Magklaras and Furnell (2002) classified misusers of information technology according to three dimensions: system role, reason of misuse, and system consequences. The system role dimension is concerned with the actual role of a particular person with reference to a specific computing system. System role consists of three categories based on the type and level of system knowledge a person possesses: system master, advanced users, and application users. System masters pose a substantial threat to IS security because of the increased level of access and trust they are given. Advanced users do not have the same level of system privileges as system masters, but their substantial knowledge of system vulnerabilities makes them a serious threat. Application users represent the rest of legitimate users that utilize certain standard applications, such as Web browsers, e-mail, and database applications. These users have no additional access to system resources and therefore are only likely to misuse the specific applications they normally access. Reason of misuse includes both intentional and unintentional misuse. Intentional misusers can be subdivided based on their motives which include trying to access sensitive data (data theft), taking revenge against a particular person or an entire organization (personal differences), or deliberate ignorance of a particular regulation of the information security policy. The system consequences dimension considers the system level at which the misuse activity takes place. IS misuse can involve operating system components, network data, system hardware, or some combination of the three.

Determinants of IS Misuse

The rationale behind studying the determinants of IS misuse behavior is that an understanding of the underlying individual and situational causes of IS misuse should assist organizations in predicting this behavior (Banerjee, Cronan, and Jones 1998; Cronan and Douglas 2006; Pierce and Henry 2000; Schultz 2002; Shaw, Ruby, and Post 1998). Shaw, Ruby, and Post (1998) argued that the failure of management to understand the personality and motivation of an at-risk employee is a contributor to insider computer abuse incidents. Moreover, several researchers have suggested that individual and situational characteristics of personnel who act unethically may be an overlooked deterrent that is effective as well as lead to the formation of more effective future deterrent efforts (Banerjee, Cronan, and Jones 1998; Shaw, Ruby, and Post 1998). Such knowledge facilitates the identification of which organizational policies and procedures will or will not be accepted by most users (Gattiker and Kelley 1999).

Parker (1998) developed a general model of computer abuse and computer crime that applies to both insider and outsider attacks. The model includes skills, knowledge, resources, authority, and motives as factors that influence computer abuse. Shaw, Ruby, and Post (1998) conducted research on the psychological makeup of convicted perpetrators of insider computer violations and developed a list of risk factors that increase an individual's vulnerability toward illegal or destructive computing behavior in organizations. The risk factors consist of employee work context (i.e., full-time/part-time, contractors/partners/consultants/temporary workers, current/former) as well as the following personal and cultural characteristics: introversion, social and personal frustrations, computer dependency (i.e., "computer-addicted" individuals), a loose ethical culture, reduced loyalty, a sense of entitlement, and lack of empathy. Shultz (2002) developed a framework of insider computer abuse that includes indicators of future abuse behavior. The indicators are meaningful markers, meaningful errors, preparatory behaviors, correlated usage patterns, verbal behavior, and personality traits. Shultz argued that from these set of indicators, clues can be pieced together to predict and detect an attack. Willison (2000) applied situational crime prevention concepts to the domain of computer abuse and argued that computer abuse behaviors are a function of the opportunities to commit them within the organization. Such opportunities include inappropriate controls and changing organizational structures.

While each of the previously discussed models offers insights into the determinants of IS misuse behaviors, none has been empirically validated. In addition, both Parker's (1998) and Schultz's (2002) models are very general (e.g., personality traits, motives) while Shaw, Ruby, and Post's (1998) risk factors apply only to IS specialists who "design, maintain, or manage critical information systems" (p. 3).

There are a number of empirical studies that provide stronger evidence of the individual and situational factors that affect IS misuse using both IS and non-IS samples. Many of these studies have incorporated models of behavioral intentions from the field of social psychology along with other individual and situational factors to predict unethical computing behavior. Two well-known theoretical models of behavioral intentions that have been utilized in prior IS misuse studies are the theory of reasoned action and the theory of planned behavior. The theory of reasoned action (TRA) was developed by Ajzen and Fishbein (1969) and proposes that a person's intention toward a specific behavior is a factor in whether or not that individual will carry out that behavior. The TRA depicts two factors that affect behavioral intention – attitudes toward the behavior and subjective norms. Ajzen (1991) extended the TRA model and called the new model the theory of planned behavior. The theory of planned behavior (TPB) adds perceived behavioral control as another factor that influences behavioral intention. Much support has been found for the predictive ability of both the TRA and the TPB in explaining a wide variety of positive and negative behaviors (Ajzen 1991; Foltz 2000; Sheppard, Hartwick, and Warshaw 1988).

Eining and Christensen (1991) used the TRA as a base theory to develop a model to explain software piracy behavior. Their model incorporates computer attitudes, material consequences, norms, socio-legal attitudes, employment status, and affective factors as variables that contribute to intentions, which in turn predict software piracy behavior. Empirical results showed that all variables, except socio-legal attitude, were significant in explaining software piracy behavior. Peace, Galletta, and Thong (2003) studied software piracy behavior using the TPB. They found that that attitude, subjective norms, and level of perceived behavioral control were significantly associated with software piracy intentions. In addition, belief in punishment certainty, belief in punishment severity, and software cost were shown to have a strong relationship with attitude. Belief in punishment certainty also affected perceived behavioral control. Galletta and Polak (2003) used the TPB to study Internet abuse in the workplace. They found strong support for subjective norms and moderate support for attitudinal factors (i.e., job satisfaction, Internet addiction) as predictors of Internet abuse intention, along with gender and computer experience. However, none of their perceived behavioral control variables were significant. Foltz (2002) applied the TPB to the broader domain of IS misuse and found that the theory could predict and explain many forms of computer abuse and computer crime intentions. Related IS misuse behaviors were grouped into two categories: (i) modifying, stealing, or destroying software and, (ii) modifying, stealing, or destroying data. Consistent with the theory, the correlations between attitudes and intentions, between subjective norms and intentions, and between perceived behavioral control and intentions were significant for both categories of misuse.

Loch and Conger (1996) used an extended version of the TRA to study differences in ethical decisions involving the use of computers between men and women. In their model, deindividuation, computer literacy, and self-image are directly related to attitudes, which influence behavioral intentions. Social norms also have a direct influence on behavioral intentions. The results showed partial support for deindividuation, computer literacy, and social norms as predictors of ethical behavior intentions and full support for attitudes and gender. These results, while statistically significant, are not very meaningful since the model did not explain more than 14 percent of intention variance over three different IS ethical scenarios (stealing application documentation, reading others' e-mail, running a program at work for a friend). Therefore, the authors concluded that the TRA is inadequate to explain ethical behaviors in the context of IS.

Banerjee, Cronan, and Jones (1998) proposed and tested a TRA-based IT ethics model using a series of ethical scenarios (i.e., using computing resources for personal use after hours, accessing others' e-mail, using software without a license, unauthorized modification of employee records). Their model included attitude and personal normative beliefs as predictors of unethical behavior of IS personnel. In addition, moral judgment, ego strength, locus of control, and organizational ethical climate were included as variables that affect ethical behavioral intention. Only personal normative beliefs, organizational ethical climate, and organization-scenario (an indicator variable controlling for scenario and company) were found to be significant. These results do not support the attitude-intention relationship predicted by the TRA and suggest that the organizational environment may be a more powerful predictor of ethical behavior intention. Banerjee, Cronan, and Jones (1998) cautioned that these results could be due to their small sample size and the fact that their sample consisted of only IS personnel. Leonard and Cronan (2001) tested the Banerjee, Cronan, and Jones (1998) IT ethics model using a much larger sample of both IT and non-IT future professionals (i.e., university students). They also added gender as an additional variable in the model. Results were much more supportive of the TRA, as attitude toward ethical behavior and personal normative beliefs were both significant. In addition, ego strength, scenario (situation), gender, and moral reasoning were all significant characteristics of ethical behavioral intention. Leonard, Cronan, and Kreie (2004) further enhanced the original Banerjee, Cronan, and Jones (1998) IT ethics model by adding perceived importance of the ethical situation and age as predictors of ethical behavioral intention. They tested the model and found that perceived importance and age had a significant impact on the intent to behave ethically/unethically. As in previous findings, attitude, personal normative beliefs, ego strength, gender, and moral judgment were also significant influences on behavioral intention. Cronan, Leonard, and Kreie (2005) tested a similar IT ethics model and found that perceived importance and gender had significant influences on ethical judgment and behavioral intention.

Additional studies have explored IS misuse behavior outside of the framework of either the TRA or the TPB. Kreie and Cronan (1998) examined the impact of the environment, personal values, characteristics of the individual, moral obligation, and awareness of consequences on ethical judgments involving the following behaviors: making unauthorized program modifications, keeping software that was not paid for, using company IT resources after hours, using a program without paying for it, and illegally copying data. They found that gender, moral obligation, and awareness of consequences were significant indicators of whether an act was judged as acceptable or unacceptable. The significant influence of moral obligation is consistent with findings by Leonard and Cronan (2001) but inconsistent with Banerjee, Cronan, and Jones (1998). Gattiker and Kelley (1999) studied users' moral assessments of three ethical dilemmas involving the use of computers and the Internet (i.e., uploading computer viruses, distribution of a violent, sexual, and racial game, and installing encryption software) and tested whether individual differences influenced their judgments. They found that age and gender influenced moral judgments of ethical behavior while prior computer use and socioeconomic status did not. Specifically, older people and women were more cautious regarding certain moral and immoral acts involving computers. Moores and Chang (2006) tested an ethical decision making model for software piracy. They found that software piracy was determined by buying pirated software, which was determined by intention, and intention was determined by moral judgment. Eining and Lee (1997) found evidence that culture influences computer abuse behaviors. They studied attitudes toward IT ethical issues involving information privacy, property, accuracy, and access and reported significant differences between U.S. students and students of Chinese descent. Specifically, U.S. students assessed ethical scenarios based on rules and legal issues (i.e., whether or not an individual had authorized access to data) while Chinese students' assessments were based on relationships between the individual and the organization. Skinner and Fream (1997) used social learning theory to study computer misuse among college students. They found that associating with peers who participated in computer misuse (i.e., software piracy, guessing passwords to gain unauthorized access, accessing another's account without his/her permission) was a significant predictor of misuse behavior. However, the influences of other sources of imitation such as family, teachers, and media were inconsistent across the different misuse behaviors studied. In another study of computer misuse among college students, Hollinger (1993) found that software piracy was predicted by gender, influence of peers, and perceived consequences and that unauthorized account access was predicted by gender and influence of peers.

In summary, prior research suggests that there are various individual and situational factors that influence IS misuse. However, as evidenced in the preceding discussion, the predictive ability of many of these factors has not been consistently strong over a variety of misuse behaviors. Hence, this research suggests that simply relying on knowledge of individual and situational factors as effective deterrents may not be an appropriate strategy for lowering many forms of IS misuse. However, researchers have suggested that combining knowledge of individual and situational influences with other deterrent interventions could assist organizations in managing IS misuse (Banerjee, Cronan, and Jones 1998; Harrington 1996).

SECURITY COUNTERMEASURES AND THEIR IMPACT ON IS MISUSE

In addition to research that seeks to understand the underlying individual and situational causes of IS misuse, there is a body of work that focuses on ways to reduce IS misuse through organizational interventions. Researchers have suggested that organizations implement a combination of procedural and technical controls as a strategy for deterring IS misuse (Dhillon 1999; Dutta and Roy 2003; Parker 1998; Straub 1990; Straub and Welke 1998). Following Straub (1990), this study uses the term "security countermeasures" to refer to such controls.

The foundation for the use of security countermeasures to manage and control IS misuse dates back to Parker's (1976) studies of computer crime. Based on his interviews with computer abusers and years of data on computer crime, Parker suggested that organizations adopt procedural countermeasures, such as guidelines and policy statements, to lower computer abuse. More recently, researchers have suggested that organizations adopt a mix of procedural and technical security countermeasures (Dhillon 1999; Parker 1998; Straub and Welke 1998). Dhillon (1999), for example, discussed technical and informational interventions that organizations can put in place to manage and control misuse. Technical interventions include controls to limit access to buildings, rooms or computer systems, such as a simple access control mechanism. Informational interventions include implementing security guidelines and procedures and increasing awareness of security issues throughout the organization through education and training programs.

A number of studies have examined the impact of security countermeasures on IS misuse from a theoretical perspective, utilizing the criminological theory of general deterrence (D'Arcy and Hovav 2007; Foltz 2000; Gopal and Sanders 1997; Harrington 1996; Kankanhalli et al. 2003; Lee, Lee, and Yoo 2004; Peace, Galletta, and Thong 2003; Straub 1990; Wiant 2003). General deterrence theory (GDT) predicts that "disincentives" or sanctions dissuade potential offenders from illicit behavior and that as the certainty and severity of sanctions increase, the level of illicit behaviors should decrease (Gibbs 1975). Within the context of IS security, GDT provides a theoretical basis for the use security countermeasures as a means to limit the incidence of IS misuse in organizations by convincing potential offenders that there is too high a certainty of getting caught and getting punished severely (Straub and Welke 1998).

Straub (1990) used a GDT-based theoretical framework to empirically test the effectiveness of deterrent and preventative security countermeasures in lowering computer abuse. Survey responses from IS personnel in 1,211 randomly selected organizations indicated that higher levels of deterrent (e.g., number of information sources, number of security staff hours per week) and preventative (e.g., screen access to a system to admit authorized users only, use of specialized security software) security controls was associated with lower levels of computer abuse. In addition, the use of more comprehensive preventative security software was found to be associated with a greater ability to identify perpetrators of abuse and to discover more serious computer abuse incidents. Kankanhalli et al. (2003) also tested the impact of deterrent and preventative measures on IS security effectiveness. Consistent with GDT, the researchers found that greater organizational deterrent efforts (in the form of person-hours expended on IS security purposes) and preventative efforts (in the form of more advanced security software) were associated with higher perceived IS security effectiveness. In contrast to Straub's (1990) and Kankanhalli et al.'s (2003) studies, Wiant (2003) did not find evidence of the effectiveness of security countermeasures in deterring IS misuse. Wiant (2003) used a modified version of Straub's (1990) GDT-based theoretical framework to assess the impact of information systems policies on the level of computer abuse in hospitals. Survey responses from IS managers in 140 U.S. hospitals were collected and results indicated that use of information security policies was not associated with lower incidence or severity of computer abuse incidents. Doherty and Fulford (2005) also investigated the effectiveness of security policies, using a sample of large organizations in the United Kingdom. The researchers found no statistically significant relationships between the adoption of IS security policies and the incidence or severity of security breaches.

In addition to organizational-level studies, several studies have assessed the effectiveness of security countermeasures at the individual level of analysis. These studies have focused on the impact of deterrent techniques on individual IS misuse behavior. Foltz (2000) performed an experiment to investigate the before and after effects of a university computer usage policy on computer misuse intentions and self-reported misuse behaviors. Results showed that the implementation of the computer usage policy had no effect on misuse intentions and behaviors involving (i) modifying, stealing, or destroying software and, (ii) modifying, stealing, or destroying data. Pierce and Henry (1996) surveyed a sample of 356 IS professionals and asked them to rate the effectiveness of formal codes of computer ethics in deterring unethical behavior in their organizations. Respondents reported moderate confidence (mean of 2.7 on a scale of 1-5) in the influence of formal codes of computer ethics as a deterrent to unethical behavior. Harrington (1996) assessed the impact of general and IS-specific codes of ethics on computer abuse judgments and intentions among IS employees. Computer abuse was defined as cracking and copying software, computer sabotage, writing and spreading viruses, and fraudulent use of computers. Harrington found that general codes of ethics had no effect on computer abuse judgments and intentions while IS-specific codes of ethics showed a slight relationship with judgments and intentions for one of the computer abuse scenarios (computer sabotage). However, general codes of ethics did have a significant impact on computer abuse judgments and intentions among individuals high in a psychological trait called responsibility denial. Thus,

Harrington's (1996) results suggest that the impacts of security countermeasures are contingent on individual factors. Kreie and Cronan's (2000) results also suggest that individual differences influence the effectiveness of security countermeasures. They found that individuals are more likely to abide by company standards for acceptable systems usage and company codes of ethics when the given situation is not considered personally relevant.

Gopal and Sanders (1997) used an experiment to study the impact of security countermeasures on software piracy intentions and found that a deterrent treatment consisting of information about software piracy (i.e., current copyright laws, the consequences of being caught for violating copyright laws, actions taken by the Software Piracy Association to curtail piracy, and the negative effects of software piracy on software firms and users) resulted in lower piracy intentions among participants. Lee, Lee, and Yoo (2004) combined general deterrence and organizational trust factors and assessed their impact on IS security intentions (defined as intentions to install access control software and intrusion protection software) and computer abuse behaviors. They found that use of preventative security software was positively associated with IS security intentions while security awareness and security policies were not. In addition, preventative security software, security awareness, and security policies had no impact on computer abuse behaviors. D'Arcy and Hovav (2007) examined the influences of user awareness of security policies, security education, training, and awareness (SETA) programs, and computer monitoring on IS misuse intentions. Their results suggest that computer monitoring is effective in deterring more severe forms of IS misuse, while security policies and SETA programs are effective against numerous misuse types that vary in severity. A summary of the IS deterrence research is presented in Table 2.2.

Limitations of IS Deterrence Studies

Despite the theoretical basis for the use of security countermeasures as a means to deter IS misuse, empirical studies that have assessed the effectiveness of such techniques (see Table 2.2) have produced mixed results. These equivocal results suggest the need for further investigation. A review of the deterrence literature from the field of criminology reveals limitations with existing IS deterrence studies. These limitations focus upon the level at which the data were gathered, the distinction between actual and perceived sanctions, and the impact of individual differences on deterrent effectiveness.

Many early deterrence studies in the criminology literature utilized data gathered at the organizational or geographical level of analysis since individual-level data were unavailable or difficult to obtain (Blumstein, Cohen, and Nagin 1978; Klepper and Nagin 1989; Tittle 1980). Tittle (1980), for example, cited over three dozen deterrence studies that found negative relationships between sanction characteristics and crime rates. However, the use of aggregate data has been criticized in the literature. Manski (1978) argued that the crime rates examined in many deterrence studies are influenced by the interaction between criminals, victims, and the criminal justice system. The interaction between these factors is so complex and interdependent that the impact of deterrence policies upon aggregate crime rates is difficult or impossible to isolate. There is also evidence that official crime statistics and victimization surveys underrepresent the amount of criminal behavior that actually occurs (Tittle 1980; Nagin and Pogarsky 2001). Finally, aggregate studies reveal little about the kinds of persons who are deterrable or the extent to which different types of deviant behavior are influenced by sanctions or sanction threats (Anderson 1979; Tittle 1980). As a result of these criticisms, researchers have suggested using individual-level data in deterrence studies (Klepper and Nagin 1989; Manski 1978; Tittle 1980).

Despite the concerns mentioned above, Straub (1990), Kankanhalli et al. (2003), Wiant (2003), and Doherty and Fulford (2005) each used organizational-level data in their IS deterrence studies. Straub (1990) used IS personnel responses to a victimization survey to gather data on organizational use of deterrent and preventative security countermeasures (e.g., number of security hours worked, number of security staff, number of security software applications). Kankanhalli et al. (2003) used a similar procedure to collect information on organizational deterrent and preventative efforts used to increase IS security effectiveness. While both of these studies found strong support for the use of security countermeasures in deterring IS misuse, they fail to account for the impact of deterrents on potential abusers' behavior. Assessments of deterrent effectiveness are based on victim perspectives (i.e., IS managers) and not those of abusers or potential abusers. This introduces the potential for bias, as IS managers have a vested interest in reporting that their deterrent efforts were successful in controlling IS misuse within their organizations. In addition, both Straub's (1990) and Wiant's (2003) use of victimization surveys to gather data from IS managers limits their results to only those computer abuse incidents that came to the attention of the IS function. Research suggests that the number of actual IS security incidents far exceeds the number of reported and detected incidents (Hoffer and Straub 1989; Parker 1998; Straub and Nance 1990; Whitman 2003).

Another limitation of existing IS deterrence studies is that they have not assessed the impact of security countermeasures on individual perceptions of punishment certainty and severity, which, according to GDT, have a direct influence on abusive behavior. The deterrence literature argues that deterrence is a "state of mind" and that it is the perceptions of sanctions rather than the sanctions themselves that lead to deterrence (Anderson 1979; Bachman, Paternoster, and Ward 1992; Cole 1989; Gibbs 1975; Nagin and Pogarsky 2001; Richards and Tittle 1981; Tittle 1980). The impact of sanctions or sanctioning practices on criminal behavior works through perceived certainty and perceived severity of sanctions. Objective properties of sanctions influence perceived certainty and severity of sanctions, which in turn affect behavior (Richards and Tittle 1981). This suggests that the impact of security countermeasures on IS misuse behavior is dependent upon the countermeasures' ability to influence an individual's perceived risk of sanctions (i.e., getting caught and getting punished severely). Within the IS deterrence literature, only Straub (1990) and Kankanhalli et al. (2003) recognize the importance of sanction perceptions in their studies. However, neither study included measures of sanction perceptions as variables. Straub (1990) argued that objective measures of deterrents and preventatives serve as surrogates for perceived certainty and severity of sanctions since "deterrent security activities represent how potential abusers perceive risk" (p. 258). This is based on the assumption that potential offenders perceive risk of sanctions to be in direct proportion to efforts to monitor and uncover illicit behaviors. Similarly, Kankanhalli et al. (2003) asserted that "deterrent efforts correspond to certainty of sanctions because the amount of such efforts directly affects the probability that IS abusers will be caught" (p. 141). However, the deterrence literature suggests that objective measures may not serve as adequate surrogates for perceived certainty and severity of sanctions. Tittle (1980) argued that perceptions of sanction characteristics may vary independently of objective sanction characteristics. Other researchers suggest that perceptions of sanctions are more important than actual characteristics of sanctions, as people often misperceive reality and act on what they believe to be true regardless of whether it is actually true (Gibbs 1975; Tittle and Logan 1973). Therefore, individual perceptions of the threats imposed by IS security countermeasures may not be directly proportional to the actual level of countermeasures employed in an organization.

A third limitation of existing IS deterrence studies is that they have not accounted for several individual factors that may influence punishment perceptions and therefore impact the effectiveness of security countermeasures. With the exception of Harrington (1996) and Kreie and Cronan (2000), IS deterrence studies have implicitly assumed that the impact of security countermeasures is the same for all individuals. However, several researchers have argued that formal sanctions have different deterrence values for persons with different perspectives on the law, morality, and/or the threat of punishment itself and therefore the deterrent effect of various sanction practices will differ radically from individual to individual and from social group to social group (Bachman, Paternoster, and Ward 1992; Grasmick, Jacobs, and McCollom 1983; Silberman 1976; Tittle 1980). This argument is captured within the differential deterrence hypothesis, which posits that the impact of formal sanctions is not uniform across all persons due to individual and situational differences (Mann et al. 2003). Existing research from the fields of social psychology and criminology supports the differential deterrence hypothesis as variables such as age, gender, risk propensity, expertise, socioeconomic status, race, geographic mobility, and labor force status have all been shown to influence perceptions of sanctions and/or projected deviant and criminal behavior (Grasmick, Jacobs, and McCollom 1983; Hollinger and Clark 1983; Richards and Tittle 1981; Tittle 1980; Weaver and Carroll 1985). There is also support for the differential deterrence hypothesis within the IS literature. Harrington (1996) found that an individual personality trait, responsibility denial, influenced the effectiveness of IS codes of ethics in deterring computer abuse behaviors. Kreie and Cronan (2000) found that personal relevance of an issue was an important factor in whether or not individuals complied with IS usage policies. The differential deterrence hypothesis provides a possible explanation for the inconclusive results of previous IS deterrence studies by suggesting that the impact of security countermeasures is dependent upon individual factors (i.e., security countermeasures that deter some people may be perceived as only a minor threat by others). Researchers have called for a greater emphasis on understanding the factors that influence sanction perceptions in order to identify the conditions under which deterrent strategies are likely to be important influences on behavior (Grasmick, Jacobs, and McCollom 1983; Hollinger and Clark 1983; Tittle 1980). IS researchers have also called for additional research to better understand what factors influence the effectiveness of IS security countermeasures (Banerjee, Cronan, and Jones 1998; Gattiker and Kelley 1999; Harrington 1996; Ives, Walsh, and Schneider 2004).

Table 2.2. IS Deterrence Empirical Studies

Reference	Sample	Level of Analysis	Security Countermeasures	Results
Straub (1990)	IS managers	Organization	Security policies, security personnel, preventative security software	Policies, security personnel, and preventative software associated with lower levels of computer abuse.
Harrington (1996)	IS employees	Individual	General and IS-specific codes of ethics	General codes had no impact on misuse intentions, except for high responsibility denial people. IS-specific codes had small effect.
Pierce and Henry (1996)	IS employees	Individual	Computer codes of ethics	Moderate confidence in the effectiveness of codes as deterrents.
Gopal and Sanders (1997)	Graduate students	Individual	Software piracy laws and consequences of breaking the law	Participants who received the software piracy information reported lower software piracy intention.
Kreie and Cronan (2000)	Undergraduate students	Individual	IS codes of ethics and acceptable systems usage policies	Intention to follow codes and policies contingent upon whether the scenario was judged as personally relevant.
Foltz (2000)	Undergraduate students	Individual	Computer usage policy	Computer usage policy had no effect on misuse intentions or behaviors.

Table 2.2 (continued). IS Deterrence Empirical Studies

Reference	Sample	Level of Analysis	Security Countermeasures	Results
Kankanhalli et al. (2003)	IS managers	Organization	Deterrent (security personnel hours) and preventative (security software) efforts	Deterrent and preventative efforts were positively associated with perceived security effectiveness.
Wiant (2003)	IS managers	Organization	Security policy for medical records	Security policies were not associated with number or severity of computer abuse incidents.
Lee, Lee, and Yoo (2004)	IS managers and graduate students	Individual	Security policy, security awareness, preventative security systems	Security systems, security policies, and security awareness had no impact on computer abuse.
Doherty and Fulford (2005)	IS managers	Organization	Security policy	Security policy had no impact on the incidence or severity of security breaches.
D'Arcy and Hovav (2007)	End users and graduate students	Individual	Security policy, SETA program, computer monitoring	Monitoring had effect on modification intention. Security policy and SETA program had effect on several misuse intentions.

CHAPTER 3

A Deterrence-Based Model for Assessing Security Countermeasure Effectiveness

INTRODUCTION

The review of IS deterrence research presented in Chapter 2 indicates that this body of work has produced mixed results. Further investigation of the IS deterrence research reveals limitations. Specifically, the following: (1) use of aggregate misuse statistics in organizational-level IS deterrence studies, (2) failure to assess the impact of security countermeasures on individual punishment perceptions (i.e., assumption that the actual level of security countermeasures employed in an organization represent how potential abusers perceive risk), and (3) failure to account for several individual factors that may influence punishment perceptions and therefore impact the effectiveness of security countermeasures.

In addition to concerns with prior research, there is also evidence that managers have a disproportionate reliance on technical security countermeasures and are generally unaware of the benefits of procedural controls such as security awareness programs and acceptable use policies (CIO Magazine 2006; InformationWeek 2005; Straub and Welke 1998). As such, there is a need for additional research that examines the impact of a combination of technical and procedural security countermeasures on IS misuse behavior in order to assist managers in their security management activities.

The purpose of the current study is to address these issues by (1) investigating the impact of a combination of technical and procedural security countermeasures (i.e., security policies, security awareness program, monitoring practices, and preventative security software) on individual perceptions of punishment associated with IS misuse, and (2) testing the differential deterrence hypothesis by exploring the moderating impact of computer self-efficacy, risk propensity, and virtual status (i.e., the degree to which an employee operates from traditional offices or from dispersed locations via telecommunications equipment) on the effectiveness of security countermeasures. In other words, are security countermeasures more/less effective in deterring IS misuse for certain people depending on these individual differences? Two overall research questions are addressed:

- Do security countermeasures increase the perceived threat of punishment associated with IS misuse and therefore decrease IS misuse intentions?
- Do individual differences moderate the impact of security countermeasures on punishment perceptions and therefore impact IS misuse intentions?

To answer these questions, a theoretical model is developed and tested. The model (Figure 3.1) expands on the framework of general deterrence theory and depicts a relationship between security countermeasures, sanction perceptions, individual differences, and IS misuse intention. Specifically, the model proposes that security countermeasures impact sanction perceptions, which in turn predict IS misuse intention. In addition, the model proposes that computer self-efficacy, risk propensity, and virtual status moderate the relationship between security countermeasures and sanction perceptions.

Research from the fields of criminology, organizational behavior, and social psychology suggests that computer self-efficacy and risk propensity influence one's perceived risk of punishment for engaging in IS misuse. However, neither of these individual factors has been included in prior studies that have assessed the effectiveness of IS security countermeasures. In addition, there is no empirical research that has examined the impact of virtual status on IS misuse. An understanding of the influence of virtual status on the effectiveness of IS security countermeasures is of increasing importance to modern organizations, given the rise in telecommuting and other virtual work arrangements. Definitions for the three proposed moderator variables are provided in Table 3.1.

Table 3.1. Definitions of Moderator Variables

Variable	Definition
Computer self-efficacy	An individual judgment of one's ability to use a computer (Compeau and Higgins 1995).
Risk propensity	An individual's tendency to take or avoid risks (Sitkin and Weingart 1995)
Virtual status	The degree of work that an individual performs within traditional offices or from dispersed locations (via telecommunications equipment) (Wiesenfeld, Raghuram, and Garud 1999)

DEFINITION AND SCOPE OF IS MISUSE

Before discussing the research model and the proposed linkages among the model constructs, it is necessary to define IS misuse and delimit the scope of IS misuse to the behaviors that are examined in this study.

Definition of IS Misuse

Various terms have been utilized to describe inappropriate or illegal activities involving information systems. Within the literature, the terms computer abuse and computer crime are found often. Solarz (1987) used the term computer crime to include "every type of offense known to criminal law, so long as it is related to computerized information technology" (p. 52). Parker (1976) suggested that the term computer crime encompasses a variety of offenses including the use of the computer as a symbol to deceive or intimidate others and the utilization of the computer as a tool to plan or execute a crime. Saari (1987) defined computer crime as "any crime where the perpetrator has to have a technical knowledge of computer to engage in the crime" (p. 111). For purposes of this research, these definitions are too restrictive since they are limited to criminal activities that involve computers. The domain of the current study is the misuse of information technology, which may or may not be illegal. For example, inappropriate use of e-mail (e.g., sending a chain letter) may not violate local, state, or federal laws, but it may violate organizational policies for acceptable systems use and therefore can be considered IS misuse.

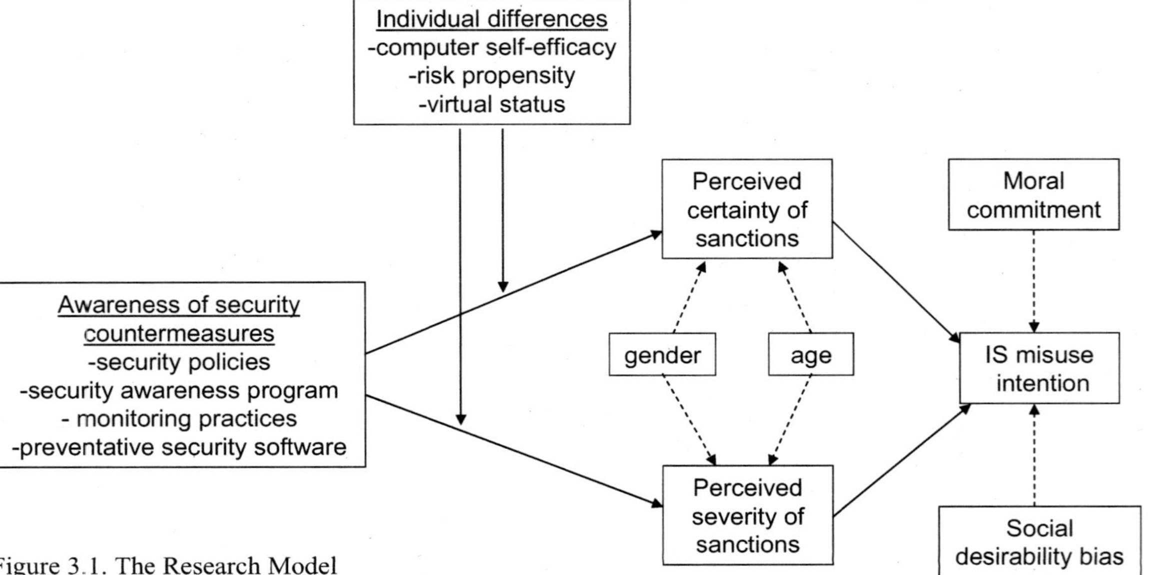

Figure 3.1. The Research Model

The term computer abuse is more closely related to the domain of IS misuse, as it encompasses a wide range of intentional acts that may or may not be specifically prohibited by criminal statutes. Parker (1992) defined computer abuse as "any intentional act involving knowledge of computer use and technology in which one or more perpetrators made or could have made gain and/or one or more victims suffered or could have suffered loss" (p. 439). This definition includes computer crimes (e.g., financial fraud, theft of proprietary information, sabotage) as well as malicious mischief and other innocuous activities in which the perpetrator might be chastised by his/her superior – a chastisement that might result in losing his/her job or embarrassment (Parker 1992). Straub (1986, p. 27) offered an expanded definition of information systems or computer abuse as: unauthorized, deliberate, and internally recognizable misuse of assets of the local organizational information system by individuals, including violations against:

- hardware (and other physical assets associated with computers, such as theft or damage to terminals, CPUs, disk drives, and printers)
- programs (such as theft or modification of programs)
- data (such as embezzlement or modification of data)
- computer service (such as unauthorized use of service or purposeful interruption of service)

Straub's (1986) definition of computer abuse is prevalent throughout most of the research that has examined the improper use of information technology since it encompasses a wide range of misuse behaviors that are illegal, inappropriate, and/or unethical in the context of IT. Therefore, the current study utilizes Straub's (1986) definition of computer abuse to define IS misuse. This definition includes the IS misuse activities of all organizational insiders, or those with legitimate access to organizational information systems and networks, such as full and part-time employees, temporary employees, contractors, and business partners.

IS Misuse Behaviors

The domain of IS misuse is quite varied, ranging from behaviors that are unethical and/or inappropriate (e.g., inappropriate use of e-mail) to those that are illegal (e.g., stealing company information). This study focuses upon five common IS misuse behaviors: distribution of an inappropriate e-mail, use of unlicensed computer software (i.e., software piracy), password sharing, unauthorized access to computer systems, and unauthorized modification of computerized data. Each of these activities have been identified in both the IS security literature and industry surveys as representing a serious threat to organizations (e.g., Furnell 2002; Gattiker and Kelley 1999; Harrington 1996; Whitman 2003). A serious threat is one that can result in operational, financial, or legal damage to the organization.

In terms of e-mail usage, organizations can be held liable for employee distribution of any offensive e-mail messages, including messages containing comments about race, gender, age, sexual orientation, pornography, religious or political beliefs, national origin, or disability (Panko and Beh 2002; White and Pearson 2001). Inappropriate use of e-mail also wastes valuable bandwidth resources, which is an operational concern for organizations. Unlicensed computer software represents a serious threat to organizations since organizations are liable for their employees' use of unlicensed software, whether the organization is aware of such activities or not (Bologna and Shaw 2000). Further, allowing installation of unlicensed computer software on company systems presents an operational threat in the form increased exposure to malicious software such as viruses, worms, and trojan horses that can harm information systems (Sindell 2002). The threat of damage imposed by password sharing is also significant. No matter how well a computer system is protected from unauthorized intrusion using technical countermeasures, all is for naught if authorized users share their passwords with others (Aytes and Connolly 2004). Even if they only share their passwords with other authorized users, audit trails and accountability are compromised. Finally, both unauthorized access to and modifications of computerized data are serious concerns for organizations. Unauthorized access can jeopardize a company's trade secrets and confidential information, which can have negative financial consequences. Campbell et al. (2003) found that public disclosure of a security breach involving unauthorized access to confidential information resulted in a significant drop in affected companies' stock prices. The negative financial consequences of unauthorized modification of computerized data are also significant, as this activity has been reported as one of the most common types of security breaches in organizations (Berinato 2005; Gordon et al. 2006).

THEORETICAL BASE

The theoretical underpinning for the research model utilized in this study comes from criminological research into the effectiveness of deterrents in preventing criminal and deviant behaviors. Within the field of criminology, this is known as general deterrence theory (GDT). GDT focuses on "disincentives" or sanctions against committing an illicit act and the effect of these sanctions on deterring others from committing illicit acts (Nagin 1978; Tittle 1980). The impact of sanctions or sanctioning practices on illicit behavior is thought to work through two constructs: perceived certainty and perceived severity of sanctions (Figure 3.2). The certainty of sanction refers to the probability of being punished, and severity of sanction refers to the degree of punishment (Nagin 1978). The theory predicts that sanctions dissuade potential offenders from illicit behavior and that the greater the certainty and severity of sanction for an illicit act, the more individuals are deterred from that act (Gibbs 1975). GDT is consistent with the economic view of individuals as rational actors that try to maximize their rewards and minimize their costs; if an individual anticipates a penalty that is probable enough and severe enough to outweigh the reward of a contemplated act, then that person will not commit the act.

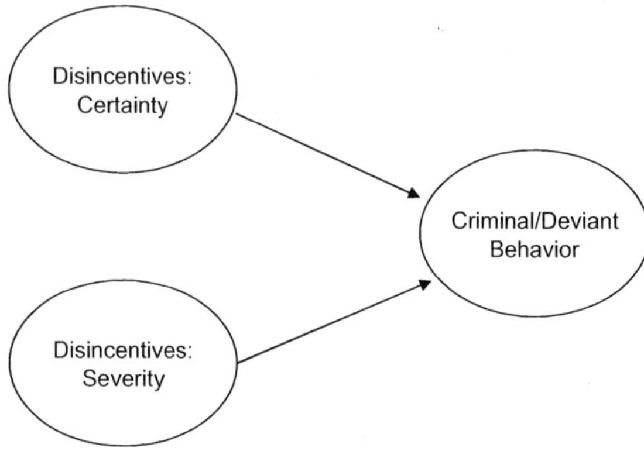

Figure 3.2. General Deterrence Theory

Overall, criminology research has been supportive of GDT, as deterrence has been shown to work across a wide variety of persons, settings, and times (Cook 1982; Nagin and Pogarsky 2001; Straub 1986; Tittle 1980). There is also high consensus among experts on the explanatory power of GDT's two main constructs, perceived certainty and severity of sanctions, in predicting criminal and deviant behaviors (Blumstein, Cohen, and Nagin 1978; Nagin and Pogarsky 2001; Tittle 1980). Straub (1986) asserted that GDT is applicable to computer abuse, since computer abuse is a typical, amateur white-collar crime (i.e., crimes which violate occupational regulations) that takes place in the relatively benign environment of persons who normally abide by rules and regulations. Straub (1990) successfully applied GDT to the IS environment and found that use of deterrent and preventative security countermeasures was associated with lower levels of computer abuse. Hollinger and Clark (1983) applied GDT to the study of deviant behavior against organizations (i.e., taking company property) and concluded that "the theoretical boundaries of deterrence are not necessarily limited to criminal and legal controls but can also apply to the sanctions promulgated by a formal organization" (p. 414). Together, this past research suggests that GDT is an appropriate theoretical lens for examining IS misuse and the impact of security countermeasures.

MODEL DEVELOPMENT AND RESEARCH HYPOTHESES

The model presented in Figure 3.1 posits that (1) security countermeasures influence perceived certainty and severity of sanctions, which in turn, directly impact IS misuse intention and, (2) that the relationship between security countermeasures and perceived certainty and severity of sanctions is moderated by individual differences (i.e., computer self-efficacy, risk propensity, virtual status). To address this study's first research question, "Do security countermeasures increase the perceived threat of punishment associated with IS misuse and therefore decrease IS misuse intentions?", the impact of security countermeasures on perceived certainty and severity of sanctions and the impact of perceived certainty and severity of sanctions on IS misuse intention must be evaluated. To address the second research question, "Do individual differences moderate the impact of security countermeasures on punishment perceptions and therefore impact IS misuse intentions?", the moderating impact of computer self-efficacy, risk propensity, and virtual status on the relationship between security countermeasures and perceived certainty and severity of sanctions must be evaluated. The following sections describe the conceptual model and present specific hypotheses that pertain to the above research questions.

IS Misuse Intention

IS misuse intention is an individual's intention to perform or not to perform the behavior of IS misuse. Intentions are assumed to capture the motivational factors that affect a behavior. They are indicators of how hard a person is willing to try and of how much of an effort he/she is planning to exert to perform a behavior (Ajzen 1988). Intention has repeatedly proven to be a strong predictor of actual future behavior (Ajzen 1991). The use of behavioral intention in this study is in line with much of the research that has explored IS misuse behaviors (e.g., Banerjee, Cronan, and Jones 1998; Foltz 2000; Harrington 1996; Peace, Galletta, and Thong 2003). Further, deterrence researchers have argued for the use of behavioral intention as the dependent variable in deterrence studies (e.g., Bachman, Paternoster, and Ward 1992; Grasmick and Bursik 1990; Klepper and Nagin 1989; Tittle 1980).

Security Countermeasures

Security countermeasures consist of deterrent and preventative controls as defined by Straub (1986, 1990). Deterrents include passive controls such as security policy statements, security awareness programs, and other informational sources designed to deter misuse attempts by providing information regarding correct and incorrect usage of information systems and punishment for incorrect usage (Straub 1990). Deterrents also include active security efforts such as audits on the use of IS assets and monitoring of employee computing activities (Gopal and Sanders 1997; Kankanhalli et al. 2003; Straub 1990). The primary purpose of both active and passive deterrents is to discourage potential offenders by the threat of getting caught and punished for IS misuse.

Preventatives are security measures designed to prevent attempted IS misuse and computer crime by blocking access to the information system or inhibiting use of certain information system functions (Straub 1986). A primary purpose of preventatives is to help enforce policy statements and guidelines by warding off illegitimate activities

(Gopal and Sanders 1997). Examples of preventatives include security software applications that employ access control methods such as passwords and biometric controls (Straub 1990; Ives, Walsh, and Schneider 2004).

Combining both deterrent and preventative controls, this research conceptualizes security countermeasures as security policies, security awareness programs, monitoring practices, and preventative security software. Existing research suggests that individuals are not fully aware of the existence of these security countermeasures within their organizations (Finch, Furnell, and Dowland 2003; Foltz 2000). Therefore, this study focuses on end user awareness of security policies, security awareness programs, monitoring practices, and preventative security software rather than actual measures.

<u>Security Policies:</u>
Information security policies typically include general statements of goals, objectives, beliefs, ethics, controls, and worker responsibilities (Lee, Lee, and Yoo 2004; Whitman, Townsend, Alberts 2001). Procedures and guidelines for acceptable system usage are usually derived from the security policy, and these provide more specific behavioral prescriptions than policy typically does (Stanton et al. 2003; Wood 1999). Lee and Lee (2002) contend that most organizations of at least moderate size now have some type of security policy in place to protect information resources. However, not all organizations have both policies and procedures. Smaller organizations, in particular, tend to have unstated procedures that workers develop through an informal consensus based on policies (Stanton et al. 2003).

Security policies differ greatly between organizations depending on the value and sensitivity of information to be protected, as well as the potential effects of damage, modification, or disclosure of the information to the well-being of the organization (Whitman, Townsend, and Alberts 2001). In general, a security policy should provide detailed guidance for users and managers, allowing secure and responsible use of information systems. A typical security policy includes the following sections (Whitman, Townsend, and Alberts 2001): (1) Statement of Policy – an overview of the scope and applicability of the policy, the technologies addressed in the policy, and details on who is responsible for managing and administering the system(s); (2) Authorized Access and Usage of Equipment – provides an overview of user access requirements and restrictions, and defines acceptable use of the system; (3) Prohibited Usage of Equipment – details uses of the system which are considered abusive, harassing, impermissible, or illegal in nature; (4) Systems Management – places the relevant policy and procedural issues into the context of actual system usage. Includes procedures for management of stored materials, network drive space and file content, employee monitoring, virus protection requirements, etc.; (5) Procedures and Penalties for Policy Violations – specifies procedures for reporting violations and the penalties that can accrue when policy is violated. The final two sections (6 and 7) include the Policy Review and Modification Schedule and Statements of Liability or Disclaimers.

As previously mentioned, a primary purpose of security policies is to deter IS misuse by clearly defining unacceptable or illegal conduct, thereby increasing the perceived threat of punishment (Lee and Lee 2002). Straub (1990) asserted that "a clearly defined set of policies is the precondition to implementing all effective deterrents. The more detailed these policies are, the greater the deterrent impact on unacceptable system use" (p. 272). Foltz (2000) presented empirical evidence that supports the positive relationship between security policies and punishment perceptions, as he found that individuals who were exposed to a computer usage policy had a greater awareness of the negative consequences of IS misuse. This leads to the following hypotheses:

> H1a: Security policies are positively associated with perceived certainty of sanctions.
> H1b: Security policies are positively associated with perceived severity of sanctions.

<u>Security Awareness Program:</u>
Security policies and procedures can only be effective if employees understand and accept the necessary precautions. Therefore, researchers have argued that security awareness education and training programs are also necessary for effectively controlling IS misuse (Dhillon 1999; Furnell, Gennatou, and Dowland 2002; Siponen 2000). Security awareness programs focus on raising employee awareness of their responsibilities regarding the organization's information resources, on the consequences of abusing these resources, and on

providing employees with the necessary skills to fulfill their responsibilities (Wybo and Straub 1989).

Content of security awareness programs can include employee policies, system authorizations, conditionalities for use, penalties for security breaches, password management, workstation security, laptop security, and other topics (e.g., social engineering, identity theft, viruses) that have a bearing on protecting system assets from misuse (Schou and Trimmer 2004; Jensen 2003; Wybo and Straub 1989). Security awareness programs can consist of a single training session that is included during employee orientation programs. However, effective security awareness is a continuous process that requires ongoing effort. For example, reminders for changing passwords, e-mails announcing new virus threats, security awareness newsletters, security/audit compliance checks, and screen savers have all been recommended as security awareness techniques (Hansche 2003; Rasmussen 2003; Siponen 2000).

Similar to security policies, security awareness programs are passive security controls that are designed to deter misuse attempts by providing information regarding correct and incorrect usage of information systems and punishment for incorrect usage (Straub 1990). Straub and Welke (1998) assert that a major reason for such programs is to "convince potential abusers that the company is serious about securing its systems and will not treat intentional breaches of this security lightly" (p. 445), thereby stressing the perceived certainty and severity of sanctions for IS misuse. Hence, the following hypotheses:

> H2a: Security awareness programs are positively associated with perceived certainty of sanctions.
> H2b: Security awareness programs are positively associated with perceived severity of sanctions.

<u>Monitoring Practices:</u>
Deterrent security measures also include active security efforts such as monitoring and surveillance of employee computing activities. While some monitoring of employee computing activities is possible without the assistance of information technology (e.g., physical audits of employee computers to check for installation of unlicensed software), monitoring practices typically involve the use of electronic tools that monitor and record employee computing activities. Electronic monitoring has two basic uses: providing feedback and implementing

control (Urbaczewski and Jessup 2002). Monitoring for feedback is when employees are monitored in order to provide them with performance-related feedback and suggestions for improvement, such as the accuracy of a data entry clerk. Monitoring for control is when employees are monitored in order to gain compliance with rules and regulations, such as using video cameras and badge readers to track employee movement. Within the context of IS security, examples of monitoring for control include monitoring employee use of e-mail and the Internet as well as other network computing activities (Panko and Beh 2002; Urbaczewski and Jessup 2002). This study focuses on monitoring for control as a means of deterring IS misuse.

A common theme within the IS deterrence literature is that active and visible security efforts can reduce IS misuse by increasing the threat of consequences for such behavior (e.g., Kankanhalli et al. 2003; Straub, Carlson, and Jones 1993). Straub (1990) found that people respond to "policing" activities, such as efforts of security administrators to monitor and enforce organizational policies for acceptable systems usage. Straub and Nance (1990) suggested that deterrence is also provided through increased detection activities. Considering that monitoring employee computing activities is an active security measure that increases the organization's ability to detect many forms of IS misuse, it can be expected that such practices will increase potential offenders' perceived threats of getting caught and punished for IS misuse, assuming they are aware that their computing activities are being monitored. Hence, the following hypotheses:

> H3a: Monitoring practices are positively associated with perceived certainty of sanctions.
> H3b: Monitoring practices are positively associated with perceived severity of sanctions.

<u>Preventative Security Software:</u>
Besides focusing on deterrent security efforts such as security policies, security awareness programs, and monitoring of computing activities, researchers have suggested that organizations implement preventative security technologies to assist in managing IS misuse (Dhillon 1999, 2001; Straub and Welke 1998). Preventative security technologies include specialized software that inhibits the misuse of IS resources, such as software that blocks outgoing e-mail messages that contain

inappropriate content. Other preventative security technologies include software programs that protect information systems against authorized access, destruction, and misuse by authenticating the identity of a system user (Irakleous et al. 2002). These programs are designed to keep intruders and masqueraders out, while permitting access to legitimate users. The most common types of preventative security software are access control technologies that utilize a user ID or password mechanism to authenticate IS users (Zviran and Haga 1999). More sophisticated methods of authentication include token-based approaches (e.g., smart cards) and biometric solutions (Irakleous et al. 2002; Ives, Walsh, and Schneider 2004). Biometric authentication techniques rely on physical measurable characteristics that can be automatically checked, such as fingerprint or facial recognition.

Preventative security software directly impacts IS misuse by preventing access to information resources or by preventing unauthorized computing activities. However, Straub and Welke (1998) argued that effective security software also has a deterrent effect on future misuse by convincing potential offenders of the certainty and severity of punishment. Similarly, Lee and Lee (2002) contend that security systems increase computer abusers' fear of detection. Willison (2000) used situational crime prevention theory to predict that decreased opportunity structures such as physical and logical preventatives decrease the incidence of computer misuse by increasing abusers' perceived risk of penalties. Nance and Straub's (1988) empirical results support these arguments, as they found that less serious computer abuse incidents were associated with use of preventative security software. The researchers reasoned that potential offenders were aware of the preventative controls and were therefore deterred from engaging in more serious levels of computer abuse. This leads to the following hypotheses:

> H4a: Preventative security software is positively associated with perceived certainty of sanctions.
> H4b: Preventative security software is positively associated with perceived severity of sanctions.

Individual Differences

Prior research suggests that the relationships between security countermeasures and sanction perceptions are moderated by individual differences (e.g., Harrington 1996; Mann et al. 2003; Shaw, Ruby, and

Post 1998; Tittle 1980). Based on a review of the IS security, criminology, organizational behavior, and social psychology literatures, the following individual factors were identified as variables that should logically moderate the impact of security countermeasures on sanction perceptions.

<u>Computer Self-Efficacy:</u>
Computer self-efficacy is defined as "an individual judgment of one's ability to use a computer" (Compeau and Higgins 1995, p. 192). It has been suggested that computer self-efficacy plays a significant role in a variety of individual behaviors involving information technology (Lewis, Agarwal, and Sambamurthy 2003). Marakas, Yi, and Johnson (1998) distinguish between two levels of computer self-efficacy: task-specific and general. Task-specific computer self-efficacy refers to an individual's perception of the efficacy in performing specific computer-related tasks within the domain of computing. This level of computer self-efficacy considers an individual's assessment of their ability to use a particular application, such as Microsoft Excel. Conversely, general computer self-efficacy refers to an individual's judgment of efficacy across multiple computer application domains. General computer self-efficacy is more a product of lifetime experience and is thought of as a collection of all computer self-efficacies accumulated over time. IS misuse, as defined in this research, encompasses a variety of computing behaviors and therefore can involve a number of different information technologies. For this reason, general computer self-efficacy is used in this study.

Research that has examined risky decision making among various groups suggests that there is a significant relationship between perceptions of self-efficacy and risk-taking behavior. Smith (1974) suggested that individuals who view themselves as potent and efficacious will be more likely to take risks when opportunities arise. Wyatt (1990) studied several risky behaviors among college students and found that self-efficacy was the principle variable influencing risk-taking behavior. Dulebohn (2002) found that self-efficacy was positively related to decisions to invest in risky investment options among employees enrolled in an employer-sponsored retirement plan. Heath and Tversky (1991) conducted a series of experiments that suggested that people take significantly more risks in situations in which they feel competent. Research by Kruegar and Dickinson (1994) suggests that self-efficacy influences risk taking behavior through opportunity recognition. They found that an increase in self-efficacy increases perceptions of opportunity and decreases perceptions of threat and that changing opportunities of threat perceptions changes risk taking behavior. Extending the previous findings to the domain of computer usage suggests that individuals with higher computer self-efficacy have lower perceptions of threats pertaining to IS misuse and therefore are less likely to be threatened by security countermeasures. Hence, the following hypotheses:

> H5a: Computer self-efficacy negatively influences the relationship between security policies and perceived certainty of sanctions.
> H5b: Computer self-efficacy negatively influences the relationship between security awareness program and perceived certainty of sanctions.
> H5c: Computer self-efficacy negatively influences the relationship between monitoring practices and perceived certainty of sanctions.
> H5d: Computer self-efficacy negatively influences the relationship between preventative security software and perceived certainty of sanctions.
> H5e: Computer self-efficacy negatively influences the relationship between security policies and perceived severity of sanctions.
> H5f: Computer self-efficacy negatively influences the relationship between security awareness program and perceived severity of sanctions.
> H5g: Computer self-efficacy negatively influences the relationship between monitoring practices and perceived severity of sanctions.
> H5h: Computer self-efficacy negatively influences the relationship between preventative security software and perceived severity of sanctions.

Risk Propensity:

Risk propensity is defined as an individual's current tendency to take or avoid risks (Sitkin and Weingart 1995). Risk propensity has traditionally been conceptualized as a stable individual trait that is consistent over time and across diverse situations (Fischhoff et al. 1981). However, some researchers now regard risk propensity as a persistent and enduring individual trait but one that can change over time as a result of experience (Sitkin and Weingart 1995). Sitkin and

Weingart (1995) used the analogies of hair color and facial features to illustrate the concept of persistence and change in that hair color responds to exposure to the sun and facial features become altered through aging. Whether risk propensity is viewed as "completely stable" or "stable but changeable," the essential point is that some kind of stable within-person across situation consistency does exist in terms of an individual's tendency to take or avoid risks (Das and Teng 2001).

Zimring and Hawkins (1973) asserted that those who have a high propensity toward risk will be less deterred from deviant behavior than those who avoid risks. This is because risk propensity influences the relative salience of situational threat or opportunity and thus leads to biased risk perceptions. An individual with a high risk-taking propensity is thought to weigh positive opportunities more heavily than negative outcomes, thereby overestimating the probability of a gain relative to the probability of a loss. This overestimation will result in a lowering of risk perceptions (Sitkin and Pablo 1992; Sitkin and Weingart 1995). Conversely, an individual with a low risk-taking propensity will weigh negative outcomes more highly, leading to a heightened perception of risk (Sitkin and Pablo 1992). Sitkin and Weingart (1995) conducted a laboratory experiment that placed student subjects in a situation of risky choice and found that subjects with higher levels of risk propensity also perceived less risk in the situation. Keil et al. (2000) conducted a similar study that placed subjects in a risky choice situation involving a failing software project. Results showed that subjects with higher risk propensity tended to have lower risk perception. Several other studies have reported a positive relationship between risk propensity and risk-taking behavior, which is consistent with the argument that higher risk propensity individuals perceive lower situational risks. For example, Dulebohn (2002) found that individuals who perceived themselves as high general risk takers were more likely to make risky investment decisions in their employee-sponsored retirement plans. Barsky et al. (1997) found that risk propensity was positively related with several risky behaviors, including smoking, drinking, and failing to have insurance. El-Murad and West (2003) found that higher risk propensity marketing professionals were more likely to develop risky advertising campaigns. In terms of IS misuse, the results of these studies suggest that individuals with higher risk propensities perceive less sanction risk for misusing IS resources than those that have lower risk-taking propensities and therefore are less likely to be influenced by security countermeasures. This leads to the following hypotheses:

> H6a: Risk propensity negatively influences the relationship between security policies and perceived certainty of sanctions.
> H6b: Risk propensity negatively influences the relationship between security awareness program and perceived certainty of sanctions.
> H6c: Risk propensity negatively influences the relationship between monitoring practices and perceived certainty of sanctions.
> H6d: Risk propensity negatively influences the relationship between preventative security software and perceived certainty of sanctions.
> H6e: Risk propensity negatively influences the relationship between security policies and perceived severity of sanctions.
> H6f: Risk propensity negatively influences the relationship between security awareness program and perceived severity of sanctions.
> H6g: Risk propensity negatively influences the relationship between monitoring practices and perceived severity of sanctions.
> H6h: Risk propensity negatively influences the relationship between preventative security software and perceived severity of sanctions.

<u>Virtual Status:</u>
Virtual status refers to the degree of work that an employee performs within traditional offices or from dispersed locations via telecommunications equipment (Wiesenfeld, Raghuram, and Garud 1999). Recent estimates indicate that nearly twenty-nine million U.S. workers (approximately 30 percent of the workforce) currently spend at least a portion of their workweek in virtual mode and this number is expected to increase to more than forty million by 2010 (Potter 2003). Fifty-one percent of North American companies now have virtual work programs and almost two-thirds of Fortune 1000 companies offer employees an opportunity to work virtually (Wiesenfeld, Raghuram, and Garud 2001). A common arrangement in which employees work virtually is telecommuting. Telecommuting involves working at home and using the Internet or other forms of telecommunications as the link into business offices (Pearlson and Saunders 2001). Other forms of

dispersed (i.e., virtual) work include mobile or remote working arrangements. Examples of remote work include working "on the road" while traveling and working at a client location (Igbaria and Guimaraes 1999). Martino and Wirth (1990) provide a inclusive definition of telecommuting and remote work as "work carried out in a location where, remote from central offices or production facilities, the worker has no personal contact with co-workers there, but is able to communicate with them using technology" (p. 530).

Organizations cite increased productivity, decreased absenteeism, and cost reductions as just a few of the benefits of virtual work programs (Igbaria and Guimaraes 1999; Potter 2003). However, researchers have pointed out that working away from the office may have potential drawbacks. A common argument is that virtual workers may experience social isolation since they are often separated, both temporally and spatially, from co-workers, supervisors, and other organizational members (Mann, Varey, and Button 2000; Pearlson and Saunders 2001; Wiesenfeld, Raghuram, and Garud 1999, 2001). Studies have reported that virtual workers felt excluded from decision-making and less visible in their organizations (Mann, Varey, and Button 2000; Ramsower 1984; Watad and DiSanzo 2000). The deterrence literature provides evidence that feelings of social isolation lead to perceptions of decreased sanction costs. Williams (1992) studied a specific criminal behavior, marital violence, and found that increased isolation from community resources of social control (i.e., police agencies) was associated with lower perceived costs of arrest for various forms of violence against one's spouse. Williams (1992) concluded that the influence of social isolation was significant since "if people believe their affairs are detached from the jurisdiction of police, then they will perceive themselves as immune to the attention and actions of police agencies" (p. 624). Applying this same argument to the domain of IS misuse suggests that virtual workers, due to the increased temporal and spatial isolation that is associated with their work, will perceive lower sanction costs for misusing IS resources.

Additional evidence that virtual workers perceive lower sanction costs for IS misuse comes from deindividuation theory. Deindividuation is the psychological separation of the individual from others (Zimbardo 1969). According to deindividuation theory, when individuals are not seen or paid attention to, they do not feel scrutinized. The result is reduced inner constraints based on guilt, shame, fear, and commitment and increasing behavior that is uninhibited and antinormative (Postmes and Spears 1998). Deindividuation was originally considered a group phenomenon in which individuals that were immersed in a crowd experienced loss of individuality, leading to decreased self-control (Postmes and Spears 1998). However, Zimbardo (1969) conducted a series of experiments which demonstrated that the situations that cause deindividuation were not limited to groups. Deindividuation has also been used by IS researchers to describe the sense of anonymity that individuals experience when using information technology (Kiesler, Siegel, and McGuire 1984; Loch and Conger 1996). Prior research suggests that virtual workers may experience the psychological state of deindividuation as a result of being temporally and spatially dispersed from supervisors, co-workers, and other organizational members. For example, Watad and DiSanzo (2000) reported that virtual workers expressed concern about "being out of sight, and out of mind" of their employing organizations. In addition, as mentioned above, virtual workers often experience psychological separation from other organizational members through social isolation. Feelings of isolation can contribute to a deindividuated state in which virtual workers feel increasingly anonymous and unaccounted for. According to deindividuation theory, such feelings result in decreased perceptions of fear associated with deviant behavior. The preceding discussion leads to the formulation of the following hypotheses:

H7a: Virtual status negatively influences the relationship between security policies and perceived certainty of sanctions.

H7b: Virtual status negatively influences the relationship between security awareness program and perceived certainty of sanctions.

H7c: Virtual status negatively influences the relationship between monitoring practices and perceived certainty of sanctions.

H7d: Virtual status negatively influences the relationship between preventative security software and perceived certainty of sanctions.

H7e: Virtual status negatively influences the relationship between security policies and perceived severity of sanctions.

H7f: Virtual status negatively influences the relationship between security awareness program and perceived severity of sanctions.

H7g: Virtual status negatively influences the relationship between monitoring practices and perceived severity of sanctions.
H7h: Virtual status negatively influences the relationship between preventative security software and perceived severity of sanctions.

Perceived Certainty and Severity of Sanctions

GDT posits that the impact of formal sanctions or sanctioning practices on deviant behavior works through two main constructs: certainty of sanctions and severity of sanctions. Certainty of sanctions refers to the probability of being punished, and severity of sanctions refers to the degree of punishment (Nagin 1978). Within the current study, these two constructs refer to perceptions of the probability and degree of punishment associated with committing IS misuse.

Deterrence studies have shown that sanction fear can predict various criminal and deviant behaviors (Hollinger and Clark 1983; Nagin and Pogarsky 2001; Silberman 1976; Tittle 1980). Silberman (1976) found a negative correlation between the perceived certainty and severity of punishment and several criminal behaviors including assault, vandalism, and being drunk and disorderly. Similarly, Tittle (1980) found that sanction fear was negatively associated with intention to engage in several socially deviant behaviors as well as deviant behavior in the workplace. Grasmick and Bryjak (1980) studied several of the same behaviors as Tittle (1980) and found similar results. Specifically, the perceived certainty and severity of arrest were inversely related to involvement in illegal activities including theft of something worth $20 or more, gambling illegally, physically hurting someone on purpose, and cheating on tax returns. Klepper and Nagin (1989) also studied illegal behavior involving tax returns. They found that both perceived probability of detection and severity of prosecution were negatively related to the likelihood of various tax non-compliance gambles. Cole (1989) reported that perceived probability of being caught and severity of penalty were significant predictors of individuals' intentions to steal from retail stores. Hollinger and Clark (1983) examined theft within organizations and found that employees who perceived lower certainty and severity of organizational sanctions were more likely to steal from their employers. Within the domain of IS, Skinner and Fream (1997) found that perceived severity of punishment was negatively associated with college students' intentions to illegally access other students' computer accounts. Hollinger (1993) studied software piracy among college students and found that as perceived estimates of getting caught increased, self-reported levels of software piracy decreased. Overall, prior research provides strong evidence that an increase in perceived certainty and severity of punishment has a negative impact on criminal and deviant behaviors. IS misuse is typically characterized as an amateur, white-collar crime or deviant behavior that violates organizational rules and regulations (Straub 1990; Parker 1981). Therefore, both perceived certainty and severity of sanctions should be inversely related to IS misuse behavior intentions:

> H8a: Perceived certainty of sanctions is negatively associated with IS misuse intention.
> H8b: Perceived severity of sanctions is negatively associated with IS misuse intention.

Control Variables

Prior research that has examined IS misuse and the general area of criminal and deviant behavior suggests additional factors that should be included because of their potential influence on perceived certainty and severity of sanctions and IS misuse intention:

1. The deterrence literature indicates that gender is an important predictor of sanction perceptions, as research has shown that the impact of sanctions is weaker on men than on women (e.g., Dulebohn 2002; Grasmick and Bursik 1990; Hollinger and Clark 1983; Richards and Tittle 1981; Tittle 1980; Tittle and Rowe 1974). Several IS studies also suggest that men perceive less sanction risk for misusing IS resources. Empirical results have shown males more likely to commit software piracy (Kreie and Cronan 1998; Hollinger 1993; Sims, Cheng, and Teegen 1996), gain unauthorized access to others' computer accounts (Hollinger 1993), and engage in numerous unethical and criminal behaviors involving the use of computers (Cronan, Leonard, and Kreie 2005; Gattiker and Kelley 1999; Leonard and Cronan 2001; Loch and Conger 1996). For this reason, gender is included as a control variable on the relationships between (i) security countermeasures and perceived certainty of sanctions and (ii) security countermeasures and perceived severity of sanctions.

2. Age has also been shown to predict sanction perceptions. Hollinger and Clark (1983) found that perceived certainty and severity of sanctions for stealing from an employer were much lower among younger employees. Additional studies that have examined deviant behavior within organizations have reported similar results (e.g., Robin 1969; Tittle 1980). The IS literature also suggests that age influences sanction perceptions, as younger employees have been shown more likely to pirate software and engage in other unethical computing behaviors (Gattiker and Kelley 1999; Leonard, Cronan, and Kreie 2004; Sims, Cheng, and Teegen 1996). Therefore, age is included as a control variable on the relationships between (i) security countermeasures and perceived certainty of sanctions and (ii) security countermeasures and perceived severity of sanctions.

3. Both the criminology and IS literature lends support to the role of morality in predicting IS misuse. Bachman, Paternoster, and Ward (1992) found that males' projected sexual assault intentions were influenced by whether or not they thought the behavior was morally wrong. Silberman (1976) found a negative correlation between moral propensity and several criminal and deviant behaviors. Within the IS literature, Sacco and Zureik (1990) found that beliefs about ethics had a significant impact on computer misuse. Other IS studies have also shown a relationship between moral judgments and IS misuse intentions (Kreie and Cronan 1998; Leonard and Cronan 2001; Leonard, Cronan, and Kreie 2004; Lee, Lee, and Yoo 2004). As such, a measure of moral commitment is included as a control variable in order to better assess the effect of perceived certainty and severity of sanctions on IS misuse intention.

Hypotheses 1, 2, 3, 4, and 8 follow directly from GDT's theoretical prediction that security countermeasures increase individuals' perceptions of the likelihood and severity of punishment and therefore dissuade them from engaging in illegal, inappropriate, and/or unethical computing behaviors. Hypotheses 5, 6, and 7 are a test of the differential deterrence hypothesis, which posits that the impact of security countermeasures does not occur consistently across all persons but rather is dependent upon individual factors. Figure 3.3 summarizes the hypotheses tested in this study.

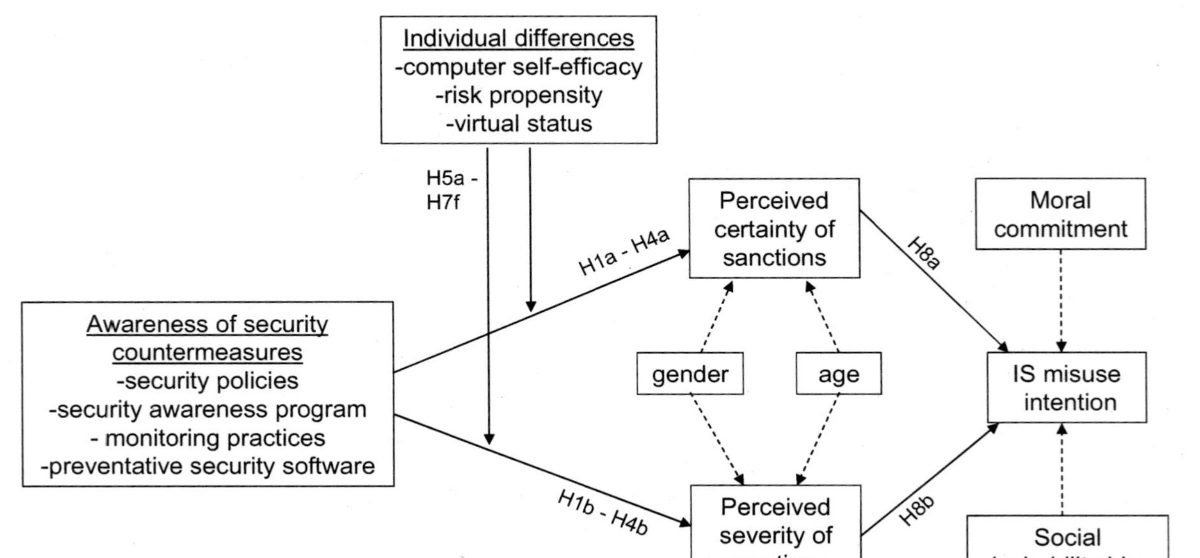

Figure 3.3. Summary of Hypothesized Relationships

CHAPTER 4

IS Misuse in the Workplace

RESEARCH DESIGN

The goal of the current study is to assess the effectiveness of IS security countermeasures within their naturally occurring contexts of organizations. Therefore, a field study approach was used to test the research model rather than a controlled experimental design. Kerlinger (1973) defined field studies as "any scientific studies, large or small, that systematically pursue relations and test hypotheses, that are ex post facto, and that are done in life situations like communities, schools, factories, organizations, and institutions" (p. 405). Field studies are strong in realism, significance, and heuristic quality (Kerlinger 1973). However, unlike in controlled designs such as field or laboratory experiments, researchers using field studies cannot manipulate independent variables or control the influence of confounding variables (Boudreau, Gefen, and Straub 2001).

As is common in field studies, this study utilized a survey methodology for data collection (Boudreau, Gefen, and Straub 2001). The strength of surveys is that responses can be generalized to other members of the population studied and often to other similar populations (Newsted et al. 1996). Further, specific theoretical propositions can be tested in an objective fashion. Pinsonneault and Kraemer (1993) suggested that surveys are appropriate when the researcher has very clearly defined independent and dependent variables and a specific model of the expected relationships among these variables. The research model depicted in Figure 3.1 contains strong a priori theoretical relationships as specified by general deterrence theory (GDT). Hence, the survey methodology was deemed appropriate for the current study.

Overall, the design of this study can be classified as a non-experimental, cross-sectional survey design in which all data are collected at once. Using the notation of Campbell and Stanley (1963), the research design appears as:

$$X \quad O$$

where O is an observation and X a "treatment." In terms of the current study, the treatment is the use of security countermeasures within organizations.

SURVEY INSTRUMENT

A survey instrument was designed to capture respondents' intentions and perceived certainty and severity of organizational sanctions regarding different IS misuse scenarios and to measure the other variables included in the research model. The instrument is divided into three sections. The first section contains five scenarios, each depicting an individual engaging in a particular IS misuse behavior. Following each scenario, respondents are presented with a series of questions intended to measure their perceptions of the risk of organizational sanctions and the estimated likelihood that they would behave as the scenario character did. The second section consists of questions that measure existence of security policies, security awareness programs, monitoring practices, and preventative security software within the organization. The final section of the instrument contains measures for computer self-efficacy, risk propensity, virtual status, moral commitment, social desirability bias, along with basic demographic questions. All variables are either measured with standard instruments or with specific scales designed for the study. With the exception of the demographic questions, all survey items are anchored on appropriately labeled seven-point Likert-type scales. Seven-point scales were chosen over five-point scales since they allow for finer distinctions in the measurement of the variables (Sommer and Sommer 2002). Further, increasing scale end points from five to seven tends to reach the upper limits of reliability (Nunnally 1978). Details of the content of the survey instrument are presented in the following sections.

Scenarios

The scenario-based instrument was selected for the following reasons:

1. Scenarios are useful for obtaining standardized responses across subjects and providing a nearly real-life decision-making situation (Finch 1987; Harrington 1996). Kerlinger (1986) suggests that if scenarios are properly constructed, they will hold participants' interest while approximating realistic psychological and social situations. Further, by presenting respondents with concrete and detailed scenarios, the survey researcher gains a degree of control over the stimulus situation approximating that achieved by researchers using experimental designs (Alexander and Becker 1978).

2. Scenarios are a less intimidating method for respondents who are confronted with sensitive issues (Barter and Renold 1999; Kerlinger 1986). Scenarios allow respondents to express their own perceptions on hypothetical situations, but remain detached from them and safe from personal threat. Since scenarios are less personally threatening, respondents are not as likely to consciously bias their responses and give socially approved answers (Alexander and Becker 1978; Harrington 1996). The result is improved internal validity (Gattiker and Kelley 1999).

3. Scenarios have been suggested for studies involving behavioral intentions (Carifio and Lanza 1992).

The use of scenarios in this study is consistent with prior IS misuse studies (e.g., Banerjee, Cronan, and Jones 1998; Eining and Lee 1997; Harrington 1996; Leonard, Cronan, and Kreie 2004) as well as much of the deterrence research that has examined the impact of formal sanctions on individual behavior (e.g., Bachman, Paternoster, and Ward 1992; Grasmick and Bursik 1990; Klepper and Nagin 1989; Nagin and Pogarsky 2001). Researchers have argued for the continued use of scenarios in deterrence studies (Bachman, Paternoster, and Ward 1992; Klepper and Nagin 1989).

The scenarios used in the survey instrument consist of modified versions of scenarios used in prior IS misuse research as well as scenarios that were developed specifically for this study. The scenarios contain representative IS misuse issues faced by computer-using professionals, including privacy, accuracy, property, and accessibility (Mason 1986), as well as security issues.

The five scenarios included in the survey are: (1) distribution of an inappropriate e-mail message – developed for this study; (2) use of unlicensed computer software – modified from Christensen and Eining (1994) and Pierce and Henry (2000); (3) password sharing – developed for this study; (4) unauthorized access to computer systems – modified from Paradice (1990) and Pierce and Henry (2000); and (5) unauthorized modification of computerized data – modified from Parker (1981) and Paradice (1990).

Guidelines from the literature (e.g., Barter and Renold 1999; Finch 1987; Poulou 2001) were utilized in creating/modifying the scenarios and for incorporating the scenarios into the survey instrument. Specifically, the stories in the scenarios were written to appear plausible and real to respondents and avoided descriptions of disastrous IS misuse events. Finch (1987) suggested that scenarios should focus on mundane occurrences in order to improve respondents' ability to project themselves into the scenarios. In addition, names were given to the hypothetical characters in the scenarios in order to make the situations seem more concrete (Finch 1987).

The scenarios appear at the beginning of the survey instrument to eliminate respondent bias. It is likely that reading the security countermeasure questions (discussed in the next section) prior to reading the scenarios would influence respondents' reactions to the scenarios and their answers to the questions that pertain to the scenarios. The five scenarios included in the survey instrument are presented in Appendix A.

Measures

A review of the IS, organizational behavior, and social psychology literatures identified previously validated scales that measure computer self-efficacy, risk propensity, perceived certainty of sanctions, perceived severity of sanctions, moral commitment, and social desirability bias. In addition, previously used measures of virtual status and behavioral intention were found. These same scales, or modified versions of these scales, are utilized in the current study. The IS security literature was examined for validated measures of security countermeasures, but the literature showed that existing measures were not adequate for the current study. The few existing scales that measure various security countermeasures (e.g., Lee, Lee, and Yoo 2004; Straub 1990) are either operationalized at the organizational level or are written from the perspective of IS security administrators. The current study differs from previous work by collecting perceived security countermeasures from the end user rather than asking security administrators to indicate actual security measures. It is not assumed that the individual is aware of all security countermeasures. Hence, original scales that measure end users' awareness of security policies, security awareness programs, monitoring practices, and preventative security software were developed for this study. These scales were developed based on a review of extant IS security literature (e.g., Lee, Lee and Yoo 2004; Stanton et al. 2005; Straub 1986), IS security practitioner surveys (e.g., Dinnie 1999; Furnell 2002; Thompson 1998), and IS security assessment tools (e.g., Swanson 2001; Thiagarajan and Comp 2003). A pretest and pilot test (discussed later in the chapter) were conducted to ensure the conceptual clarity and face validity of the security countermeasure scales. The survey measures are presented in Appendix B.

<u>Security Policies:</u>
Security policies is measured with seven original items that assess awareness of the organization's security policies and guidelines toward the use of computer resources. Five of the items measure the extent of security policies pertaining to the specific IS misuse behaviors depicted in the scenarios. For example, "My organization has specific guidelines that describe acceptable use of e-mail." In addition, two global items assess the overall level of security policies and guidelines within the organization (e.g., "My organization has specific guidelines that govern what employees are allowed to do with their computers"). Respondents are asked to rate their level of agreement or disagreement with each of the items, with response options anchored on a seven-point scale ranging from 1 (strongly disagree) to 7 (strongly agree).

<u>Security Awareness Program:</u>
Security awareness program is measured with eight items that assess awareness of the organization's IS security education and training efforts. Five items were developed to measure the extent of security awareness efforts pertaining to the specific IS misuse behaviors

depicted in the scenarios. For example, "My organization provides employees with education on computer software copyright laws." In addition, two global items were developed to assess the overall level security awareness efforts (e.g., "My organization educates employees on their computer security responsibilities"). A third global item that measures the level of security awareness training was taken from Stanton et al. (2005). Respondents are asked to rate their level of agreement or disagreement with each of the items, with response options anchored on a seven-point scale ranging from 1 (strongly disagree) to 7 (strongly agree).

<u>Monitoring Practices:</u>
Monitoring practices is measured with seven original items that assess awareness of the organization's computer monitoring activities. Five of the items measure that extent of monitoring practices pertaining to the specific IS misuse behaviors depicted in the scenarios. For example, "I believe that my organization monitors any modification or altering of computerized data by employees." In addition, two global items assess overall monitoring practices within the organization (e.g., "I believe that my organization reviews logs of employees' computing activities on a regular basis"). Respondents are asked to rate their level of agreement or disagreement with each of the items, with response options anchored on a seven-point scale ranging from 1 (strongly disagree) to 7 (strongly agree).

<u>Preventative Security Software:</u>
Preventative security software is measured with seven original items that assess awareness of the availability and use of preventative security software by the organization. Four of the items measure the extent of security software that is in place to prevent the specific IS misuse behaviors depicted in the scenarios. For example, "Computers in my organization are configured with security controls that prevent employees from installing their own software." The other three items assess the extent of preventative security software that blocks access to computer systems (e.g., "A password is required to gain access to any computer system in my organization"). These items deal with the overall level of access control within the organization. Respondents are asked to rate their level of agreement or disagreement with each of the

items, with response options anchored on a seven-point scale ranging from 1 (strongly disagree) to 7 (strongly agree).

<u>Computer Self-Efficacy</u>:
Computer self-efficacy is measured using six items adapted from Compeau and Higgins (1995). The items assess respondents' confidence in their ability to use an unfamiliar computer package under a variety of conditions. Chau (2001) reported a reliability of .93 for this six-item scale. Response options for the items are measured on a seven-point scale ranging from 1 (strongly disagree) to 7 (strongly agree). This modification to Compeau and Higgins' (1995) original ten-point response scale was made to achieve consistency with the other measures on the survey instrument.

<u>Risk Propensity</u>:
Risk propensity is measured with a six-item scale that incorporates both general risk propensity and work-related risk propensity. Two items are modified from Dahlback (1990) and one item is adapted from Gomez-Mejia and Balkin's (1989) "willingness to take risks" scale, which is based on original research by Slovic (1972) and later adaptations by Gupta and Govindarajan (1984). These three items assess the extent to which an individual is willing to take risks within the context of his/her job (e.g., "I always try to avoid situations involving a risk of getting into trouble with my boss/supervisor"). The remaining three items are adapted from Dulebohn (2002) and measure respondents' perceptions of their general willingness to take risks (e.g., "I am a cautious person who generally avoids risks"). Dulebohn (2002) reported a Cronbach alpha of .73 for this three-item general risk propensity scale. Response options for all six items are measured on a seven-point scale ranging from 1 (strongly disagree) to 7 (strongly agree) and items were recoded so that higher scores indicated greater risk propensity.

It should be noted that other measures of risk propensity were considered for this study. Within the IS literature, Keil et al. (2000) utilized a single-item risk propensity measure in their study of escalation of commitment within software development projects. However, MacCrimmon and Wehrung (1990) presented evidence that risk propensity is too complex to be captured by a single measure and therefore Keil et al.'s (2000) measure was not selected. Other measures within the psychology literature focus solely on risk propensity as a general personality trait (e.g., Dahlback 1990; El-Murad and West 2003). However, there is some argument that the general personality trait of risk propensity may differ from risk propensity within the context of one's job (Gupta and Govindarajan 1984). To account for both dimensions of risk propensity, a combined scale that measures both general and work-related risk propensity is utilized in this study.

Virtual Status:
Virtual status is measured using three open-ended questions that ask respondents to indicate how many days per week they spend in the office, home, and mobile work modes, respectively (Wiesenfeld, Raghuram, and Garud 1999). From the data, a virtual status variable that captures the number of days that an employee spends working outside the office was generated. Higher scores on this measure indicate a greater number of working days outside the office and thus a higher virtual status, while lower numbers indicate fewer days outside the office and thus a lower virtual status (Wiesenfeld, Raghuram, and Garud 1999).

Perceived Certainty of Sanctions:
Perceived certainty of sanctions is measured using a two-item scale consisting of one item adapted from Peace, Galletta, and Thong (2003) and one item created for this study. The two items are posed on all five IS misuse scenarios with slight modifications to reference the specific IS misuse behavior depicted in each scenario. The items assess the respondent's perception of the likelihood of the scenario character getting caught for performing the same IS misuse behavior within the respondent's place of work. This indirect questioning approach was chosen due to concerns about potential socially desirable responses. Compared with more direct approaches (i.e., asking the respondent the probability that he/she would be caught), indirect questioning has been found to reduce social desirability bias (Fisher 1993) and provide a better representation of respondents' true scores (Fisher and Tellis 1998). Moreover, indirect questions have been used successfully in previous assessments of perceived certainty of sanctions within the deterrence literature (Bachman, Paternoster, and Ward 1992; Nagin and Pogarsky 1989; Silberman 1976). For the current study, respondents' judgments of the probability of the scenario characters

getting caught are considered a projection of their own perceived probability of getting caught (Fisher 1993). Response options for the two items are anchored on seven-point scales ranging from 1 ('very low' or 'strongly disagree') to 7 ('very high' or 'strongly agree'). A composite score was constructed for each item by summing responses across the five scenarios[1]. Thus, the scoring for each item ranged from 5 to 35.

<u>Perceived Severity of Sanctions:</u>
Perceived severity of sanctions is measured using a two-item scale consisting of one item adapted from Peace, Galletta, and Thong (2003) and one item created for this study. The two items are posed on all five IS misuse scenarios with slight modifications to reference the specific IS misuse behavior depicted in each scenario. The items assess the respondent's perception of the severity of punishment that the scenario character would incur if caught performing the same IS misuse behavior within the respondent's place of work. Respondents' judgments of the severity of sanctions for the scenario characters are considered a projection of their own perceived severity of sanctions if caught performing the IS misuse behaviors (Fisher 1993). Response options are anchored on seven-point scales ranging from 1 ('not severe at all' to 'strongly disagree') to 7 ('very severe' or 'strongly agree').

---

[1] Instead of measuring perceived certainty of sanctions for engaging in a specific IS misuse behavior, this composite score measures the perception of getting caught over a range of IS misuse behaviors (i.e., the five IS misuse scenarios). Composite scales created by summing a respondent's answers to a particular item over a range of offense categories have been used in prior deterrence studies (e.g., Grasmick and Bryjak 1980; Grasmick, Jacobs, and McCollom 1983; Hollinger and Clark 1983) as well as in studies of IS misuse (Banerjee, Cronan, and Jones 1998; Skinner and Fream 1997). In this study, composite scores were constructed for each of perceived certainty of sanctions, perceived severity of sanctions, and IS misuse intention items. Silberman (1976) provides a theoretical rationale for this approach by suggesting that we may be able to predict generalized patterns of deviance better than specific deviant acts.

As with the perceived certainty of sanction items, a composite score was constructed for each item by summing responses across the five scenarios, resulting in a scoring range of 5 to 35 for each item.

<u>IS Misuse Intention:</u>
IS misuse intention is measured using a two-item scale consisting of one item adapted from Leonard and Cronan (2001) and one item created for this study. The items ask respondents to indicate the likelihood that they would engage in the same IS misuse behavior as the character in each scenario. This direct approach of asking respondents to project their own behavior if in the scenario character's position has been used to measure behavioral intention in previous criminological and IS misuse studies (e.g., Bachman, Paternoster, and Ward 1992; Harrington 1996; Klepper and Nagin 1989; Leonard and Cronan 2001; Leonard, Cronan, and Kreie 2004). Both IS misuse intention items are posed on all five scenarios with response options anchored on a seven-point scale ranging from 1 ('very unlikely' or 'strongly disagree') to 7 ('very likely' or 'strongly disagree'). As with the perceived certainty and severity of sanction items, a composite score was constructed for each item by summing responses across the five scenarios, resulting in a scoring range of 5 to 35 for each item.

<u>Control Variables:</u>
Gender is measured with a single demographic item, male or female. Age is measured with a single item that asks respondents to report their age group. The age groups consist of five levels: (1) 18-24; (2) 25-34; (3) 35-44; (4) 45-54; (5) 55 and over (Seyal et al. 2002). Moral commitment is measured using eight items from Tooke and Ickes' (1988) adherence to conventional morality scale. This measure reflects a general orientation to morality based on traditional, Western ethical rules of conduct (Tooke and Ickes 1988). Response options are anchored on a seven-point scale ranging from 1 ('strongly disagree') to 7 ('strongly agree').

In addition to these three theoretically based control variables, this study attempts to control for the possibility that the measure of IS misuse intention is confounded by social desirability bias (SDB). As recommended by Nancarrow, Brace, and Wright (2001), the survey includes a measure of SDB for use as a covariate in the statistical analysis. SDB is measured using a short-form version (i.e., five-item measure) of the Marlowe-Crowne SDB response scale developed by Hays, Hayashi, and Stewart (1989). The scale measures an individual's tendency to respond in a culturally appropriate and acceptable manner. Response options are anchored on a seven-point scale ranging from 1 ('strongly disagree') to 7 ('strongly agree'). Following Hays, Hayashi, and Stewart (1989), only the most extreme SDB response option (i.e., either a 1 or 7, depending on the directionality of the question) was considered indicative of socially desirable responding, resulting in a 1 or 0 coding for each item. Dichotomizing the responses was done to minimize incorrect classifications of borderline responses as socially desirable.

PRETEST

Boudreau, Gefen, and Straub (2001) contend that every instrument should be pretested as a preliminary step to ensure that there are no unanticipated difficulties. Therefore, a pretest of the initial version of the survey instrument was conducted with a panel of "experts" consisting of six MIS faculty members, two MIS doctoral students, and two IS practitioners. Each of these individuals received a copy of the drafted instrument along with sections titled "General Instructions" and "Purpose of the Study." They were asked to respond to the survey in three ways: (1) to indicate whether they felt that the individual items and the scenarios serve to answer the larger research-guiding questions, (2) to recommend other items that they felt would be useful for the survey, and (3) to comment on the content and structure of the instrument as whole. The MIS faculty members were specifically asked to assess the security countermeasure items in terms of content validity, since these measures were developed specifically for the current study and had not yet been validated.

Following survey completion, debriefing sessions were conducted with each of the panel members. The feedback focused primarily on revising the wording of some of the security countermeasure questions to eliminate ambiguities. Minor wording changes to some of the scenarios and additional demographic questions were also suggested. These suggestions were used to modify and refine the instrument. There was general agreement among the panel on the importance of the IS misuse scenarios included in the survey and on the dimensionality of the security countermeasure questions. Thus, the results of the pretest suggest that the instrument possessed adequate content validity.

PILOT TEST

After the pretest, the survey was pilot tested on a convenience sample of fifty-four participants consisting of the researcher's personal contacts (eighteen respondents), graduate students from the part-time MBA program of a large Northeastern U.S. university (ten respondents), and upper-level undergraduate business students from the same university (twenty-six respondents). The pilot test served two purposes: (1) the time for filling out the survey was determined to insure that the instrument length was reasonable, and (2) an additional test of the clarity and validity of the scenarios and the questionnaire in general could be performed and revisions made if necessary.

Based on the pilot data, minor changes to the wording of one of the perceived certainty of sanctions items were made (e.g., "Taylor would probably be caught sending the e-mail" was changed to "Taylor would probably be caught, eventually, after the sending the e-mail") to improve scale reliability. In addition, two of the risk propensity items were modified.

Some of the respondents commented that organizational factors, such as industry type and company size, might influence the study's results. Therefore, two items that ask respondents to indicate their organization/company's industry and number of employees were added. Items that measure computer experience were also added (i.e., number of applications used and hours per day spent using a computer).

SAMPLE AND DATA COLLECTION

Much of the previous literature on IS misuse has focused solely on IS employees (e.g., Banerjee, Cronan, and Jones 1998; Harrington 1996; Pierce and Henry 1996). This research does not reflect the larger community of computer-using professionals that are confronted with opportunities to engage in IS misuse. The population of interest for the current study is all individuals that use computers in their everyday workplace. The target sample was a large mix of computer users drawn from various user departments and diverse work arrangements (i.e., traditional, telecommuters, consultants, and part-time employees) within their respective organizations. Data were collected from two groups of participants: part-time MBA students and employees working in eight organizations across the U.S.

MBA Sample

The survey questionnaire was distributed to a sample of working adults taking evening classes in two large Northeastern U.S. universities during the Fall 2004 and Spring 2005 semesters. These individuals were employed in a variety of organizations and held professional and managerial positions in a wide range of functional areas. Instructors for several courses (i.e., accounting, finance, healthcare management, human resource management, international business, information technology, risk management) were contacted via e-mail and asked if they would encourage their students to participate in the research. Out of the eleven instructors initially contacted, six responded and agreed to ask their students to complete the survey on a voluntary basis. Five instructors did not reply. A second e-mail was sent to these five instructors again asking for their assistance. All five instructors responded to this e-mail and agreed to ask their students to complete the survey. In addition, instructors in three elective courses in the MIS specialization also asked their students to complete the survey. In summary, the sampling frame consisted of students in eleven core MBA courses and three MBA elective courses in the MIS specialization.

The survey was completely anonymous (although the respondents were informed that group totals may be released) and was administered to the students in one of three ways, depending on the preference of the instructor: (1) the instructor distributed the questionnaires and invited the students to take some time to complete them before starting class; (2) the instructor distributed the questionnaires and invited the students to complete them on their own time (to be handed in prior to the next class); (3) the instructor introduced the researcher to make some brief comments about the study, and the researcher invited the students to take some time to complete the questionnaires before starting class. No rewards were given for participation and no penalties were incurred for not participating. Out of 356 questionnaires distributed, 252 were completed and returned, representing a response rate of 71 percent. The high response rate can be attributed to the willingness of the students to participate, given the requests of the professors and the convenient nature in which the questionnaire was administered. The exclusion of nine questionnaires due to missing data and five questionnaires from respondents who indicated that they did not use a computer as part of their job resulted in 238 usable questionnaires, yielding a response rate of 67 percent.

The MBA student sample includes a diverse group of computer-using professionals that is similar to the population of interest for this study and therefore appears to be highly appropriate (for a summary of demographic characteristics of MBA respondents see Table 5.1 in the next chapter). However, the use of student samples has been criticized in the business literature due to problems of generalizability (e.g., Gordon, Slade, and Schmitt 1986; Randall and Gibson 1990). Igbaria, Guimaraes, and Davis (1995) pointed out that part-time MBA students may differ from the general population in terms of age level, education, and experience. Therefore, it is possible that the MBA sample is not an accurate representation of the general population of computer users within organizations. To address this concern, a second sample consisting of industry participants was obtained by contacting several companies and asking that they encourage their employees to participate in the research.

Industry Sample

A list of twelve potential companies located across the U.S. was developed based on the researcher's personal contacts and through various research institute contacts at a large Northeastern U.S. university. An executive/manager (either the chief executive officer (CEO) or the chief information officer (CIO)) within each company received a letter that described the benefits and costs involved in participating in the research study. Approximately one week after receiving the letter, each executive/manager was contacted by the researcher and the willingness to participate in the research was solicited. Eight companies agreed to participate, three companies declined due to time constraints, and one company did not respond. The executives/managers from the eight participating companies were asked to provide the name of a contact person who would serve as a liaison with the researcher and facilitate the administration of the survey. Each nominated contact person was given a brief description of the purpose of the study, along with instructions for survey distribution. Specifically, the contact persons were instructed on the concept of random sampling and asked to select a sample of employees from various user departments and work arrangements to receive the questionnaire.

A web-based survey was chosen as the medium for collecting data because it was the fastest and easiest way to deliver the instrument to the respondents who were located across different geographic locations and time zones. Also, the participating companies preferred the online survey to a paper-based survey. In early 2005 (January - March), the researcher provided the contact persons with the survey URL, which was subsequently forwarded to the selected employees as a link embedded in an e-mail message. The text of the message contained the cover letter explaining the research and offering participation in a lottery to win a $100 gift certificate for completing the survey. This incentive was used to help overcome the difficulties of obtaining organizational and subject participation (Kotulic and Clark 2003). The cover letter stressed the anonymous nature of the survey and explained that management would only receive high-level summaries of the results. Approximately two weeks after the initial e-mail, the contact persons within each company sent a reminder e-mail which again invited employees to complete the online survey.

Eight hundred and five employees received the invitation to complete the online survey, of which 304 filled it out, for an initial response rate of 38 percent. Incomplete or otherwise unusable entries were discarded from the dataset, leaving 269 usable questionnaires for a response rate of 33 percent. Information on participating companies and the response rates by company are presented in Table 4.1.

Table 4.1. Company Information and Response Rates

Company/ Industry	Total Employees	Possible Subjects	Usable Responses	Response Rate
1. Software	1,074	290	73	25%
2. Aerospace	20,000	250	61	24%
3. Manuf.	1,300	74	51	69%
4. Financial	21,700	45	32	71%
5. Financial	83	83	25	30%
6. Marketing	38	38	14	37%
7. Real Estate	33	20	9	45%
8. Marketing	750	5	4	80%
Total		**805**	**269**	**33%**

CHAPTER 5

Security Countermeasures as Deterrents to IS Misuse

DEMOGRAPHIC INFORMATION AND DESCRIPTIVE STATISTICS

The population of interest for this study is individuals that use computers in their everyday workplace. Data were collected from two groups of participants: part-time MBA students and employees working in eight organizations across the U.S. Table 5.1 contains the demographic information of the survey participants.

As shown in Table 5.1, both the MBA and industry sample groups were diverse in terms of respondents' position within the organization. Both groups contained a large percentage of male respondents and the MBA sample contained a large percentage of respondents in the 25-34 age group. In addition, the MBA sample covered a wider spectrum of industry types and company sizes than the industry sample, which was limited to eight organizations. Due to these differences, all analyses were conducted separately on the MBA and industry samples throughout the study. Results of the instrument validation and hypotheses tests were largely consistent across the two sample groups. Therefore, the data were pooled into a combined sample to increase power and facilitate brevity of results reporting. This chapter presents the analysis and results for the combined sample. Details of the separate analyses for the MBA and industry samples are provided in Appendices C and D.

Table 5.2 contains descriptive statistics for all constructs used in the research model. As these statistics show, there is enough variability in each construct so there are no restrictions of range issues.

Table 5.1. Demographic Characteristics of Respondents

		Combined Sample (n=507)		MBA Sample (n=238)		Industry Sample (n=269)	
Gender	Male	329	64.9%	162	68.1%	167	62.1%
	Female	178	35.1%	76	31.9%	102	37.9%
Age	18 – 24	43	8.5%	27	11.3%	16	5.9%
	25 – 34	267	52.3%	175	73.5%	92	34.2%
	35 – 44	116	22.9%	28	11.8%	88	32.7%
	45 – 54	64	12.6%	7	2.9%	57	21.2%
	55 and over	17	3.4%	1	0.4%	16	5.9%
Work Status	Full-time	448	88.4%	203	85.3%	245	91.1%
	Part-time	32	6.3%	25	10.5%	7	2.6%
	Temporary	3	0.6%	2	0.8%	1	0.4%
	Contract	24	4.7%	8	3.4%	16	5.9%
Position	Managerial	124	24.5%	63	26.5%	61	22.7%
	Technical	159	31.4%	54	22.7%	105	39.0%
	Professional staff	196	38.7%	108	45.4%	88	32.7%
	Administrative	28	5.5%	13	5.5%	15	5.6%

Table 5.1 (continued). Demographic Characteristics of Respondents

		Combined Sample (n=507)		MBA Sample (n=238)		Industry Sample (n=269)	
Industry	Academic/Education	27	5.3%	27	11.3%	0	0.0%
	Advertising/Marketing	22	4.3%	8	3.4%	14	5.2%
	Aerospace	68	13.4%	7	2.9%	61	22.7%
	Financial Services	120	23.7%	63	26.5%	57	21.2%
	Healthcare	39	7.7%	39	16.4%	0	0.0%
	Info. Technology	94	18.5%	21	8.8%	73	27.1%
	Manufacturing	91	17.8%	39	16.4%	51	19.0%
	Other	47	9.4%	34	14.3%	13	4.8%
Company Size (# of employees)	Less than 100	81	16.0%	33	13.9%	48	17.8%
	100 – 499	22	4.3%	22	9.2%	0	0.0%
	500 – 999	20	3.9%	16	6.7%	4	1.5%
	1000 – 2499	89	17.6%	16	6.7%	73	27.1%
	2500 – 9999	29	5.7%	29	12.2%	0	0.0%
	More than 9999	213	42.0%	69	29.0%	144	53.5%
	Missing	53	10.5%	53	22.3%	0	0.0%
Computer Use at Work (hrs/day)	Range	1 – 12		1 – 12		3 – 12	
	Mean	7.24		6.99		7.47	
	Std. Deviation (SD)	1.84		2.07		1.57	

Table 5.2. Descriptive Statistics

Study Variable	Min	Max	Mean	SD
IS misuse intention (INT)	5.0	30.0	12.47	5.50
Perceived certainty (PC)	6.0	35.0	19.64	5.64
Perceived severity (PS)	9.0	35.0	23.14	5.06
Security policies (P)	1.0	7.0	5.12	1.40
Awareness program (SA)	1.0	7.0	4.42	1.42
Monitoring practices (M)	1.0	7.0	4.42	1.32
Preventative software (PR)	1.4	7.0	4.77	.95
Risk propensity (RP)	1.2	6.8	3.99	.93
Computer self-efficacy (CSE)	1.8	7.0	5.70	.99
Social desirability bias (SDB)	0.0	0.1	.12	.20
Moral commitment (MC)	2.9	6.9	4.68	.64
Virtual status (VS)	0.0	8.0	.91	1.59

INITIAL ASSESSMENT OF VALIDITY AND RELIABILITY

Before proceeding with the evaluation of the research hypotheses, the validity and reliability of each construct was assessed. In order to claim the validity of a construct it is necessary to have both convergent and discriminant validity (Trochim 2002). Convergent validity refers to the state when items measure their intended construct and no other construct, whereas discriminant validity is confirmed when the construct as a whole differs from other constructs (Straub 1989). Reliability measures the internal consistency of a construct, or the degree to which several measurement items that reflect it are inter-correlated (Gefen 2003).

Because several new or modified scales are utilized in this study, analysis of the validity and reliability of the construct measures included both an exploratory and confirmatory validation phase. Details of the exploratory phase are discussed next. Details of the confirmatory phase are discussed later in the chapter in the PLS analyses section.

Exploratory Factor Analysis

Heck (1998) suggested that exploratory factor analysis (EFA) is an important first step in data analysis when relationships among observed indicators and underlying factors are not well known. Several questions for measuring the constructs were developed for this study, so EFA was used for an initial assessment of the convergent and discriminant validity of the measures. The technique employed was EFA (using SPSS 13.0) with principal components analysis and promax rotation. As stated by Hair et al. (1998), the choice of an orthogonal or oblique rotation should be made on the basis of the particular needs of a given research problem. If the goal of the factor analysis is to reduce the number of original variables, regardless of how meaningful the resulting factors may be, orthogonal rotation methods are appropriate. However, if the purpose is to obtain several theoretically meaningful factors or constructs, an oblique solution is the appropriate approach. When factors are intercorrelated, which is usually the case with real-world data, using oblique rotation generally simplifies interpretation of the factor pattern matrix (Heck 1998). In this study, promax rotation, an oblique rotation method, was chosen over orthogonal rotation since the independent variables were not assumed to be completely unrelated.

Because of the large number of constructs and measures employed in the study, and because there was a specific interest in determining the factor structure of the newly created security countermeasure items independent of the other measures in the model, two separate EFA's were conducted: (1) one with the endogenous, moderator, and control variables (perceived certainty of sanctions (PC), perceived severity of sanctions (PS), IS misuse intention (INT), moral commitment (MC), social desirability bias (SDB), computer self-efficacy (CSE), and risk propensity (RP)); and (2) one with the security countermeasure variables (security policies (P), security awareness program (SA), monitoring practices (M), and preventative security software (PR)). The practice of conducting separate factor analyses based on groups of related sets of measures is well established in management research (e.g., Menon et al. 1999; Moorman and Miner 1997) and has been recommended by IS researchers (Straub, Boudreau, and Gefen 2004) to simplify analysis of complex research models. Table 5.3 presents the results of the EFA for the first group of variables.

As shown in Table 5.3, the EFA produced nine factors with eigenvalues greater than or equal to 1.0. The nine factor solution accounted for 63.4 percent of the total variance, which is above the generally accepted 60 percent level in social science research (Hair et al. 1998). Guidelines from Comrey (1973) and Hair et al. (1998) were used to assess the factor loadings – loadings of 0.40 to 0.54 are considered fair; 0.55 to 0.62 are considered good; 0.63 to 0.70 are considered very good; and above 0.71 are considered excellent. Items which either did not load strongly on any factor (<.40), or that loaded highly (>.40) or relatively equally on more than one factor were eliminated. The first constructs analyzed were perceived certainty and perceived severity of sanctions. As shown in Table 5.3, the two perceived certainty items (PC1, PC2) and the two perceived severity items (PS1, PS2) loaded together on a single factor. This was not expected and therefore additional analysis was conducted. The PC and PS items are composite scores, obtained by summing the responses to these items across the five IS misuse intention scenarios. To help determine why the items did not load as expected (i.e., as separate factors), the PC and PS items for each of the five scenarios were analyzed separately. Examination of the individual scenarios revealed that the PC and PS items loaded most strongly on a single factor for the password sharing scenario. Further, the intercorrelations between the PC and PS items were highest for the password sharing scenario (ranging from .61 to .68), significantly higher than any of the other four scenarios. Due to the difficulties in discriminating the PC and PS constructs caused by the password sharing scenario, this scenario was dropped from further analysis. All subsequent analyses in the study are based on the remaining four IS misuse scenarios and all composite items (PC1, PC2, PS1, PS2, INT1, INT2) are summed responses to the items over these four scenarios[1].

Following removal of the password sharing scenario, another EFA was conducted using the revised PC (PC1, PC2) and PS (PS1, PS2) items. Again, the four items loaded on a single factor. However, the loadings for the PS items were not as strong and showed evidence of crossloading. As an additional step, the correlation between the PC and PS constructs was calculated (using the averages of the PC and PS items). The correlation was .54, well below the .70 threshold commonly used to assess discriminant validity (Hair et al. 2003; Ping 2004). This suggests that PC and PS are distinct constructs. Further evidence of the distinctness of the PC and PS constructs was provided

---

[1] Eliminating the password sharing scenario changed the scoring range for each of these items from [5 to 35] to [4 to 28].

Table 5.3. EFA for Endogenous, Moderator, and Control Variables

Item				Factor					
	1	2	3	4	5	6	7	8	9
CSE3	.854								
CSE4	.834								
CSE5	.830								
CSE6	.801								
CSE2	.795								
CSE1	.760								
PS1		.881							
PS2		.874							
PC1		.861							
PC2		.837							
RP3			.810						
RP2			.747						
RP5			.692						
RP1			.605						
RP4*			.510			.480			
RP6			.486						
SDB3				.733					
SDB4				.664					
SDB2				.651					
SDB1				.563					

Table 5.3 (continued). EFA for Endogenous, Moderator, and Control Variables

Item	Factor								
	1	2	3	4	5	6	7	8	9
SDB5				.541					
INT2					.957				
INT1					.944				
MC8*						.757			
MC5*						.687			
MC3*									
MC6*							.701		
MC7*							.670		
MC1*								.838	
MC2*								.748	
MC4*									.857
Eigenvalue	4.17	3.56	2.75	2.71	2.69	2.16	1.77	1.43	1.19
Variance explained (%)	14.08	13.65	8.31	6.93	4.64	4.49	4.47	3.48	3.37
Cumulative variance (%)	14.08	27.72	36.03	42.95	47.60	52.09	56.56	60.03	63.41

Note: Loadings less than .40 not shown; * Marked for deletion

Through a confirmatory factor analysis (discussed later in the chapter). Using a more stringent test of discriminant validity called average variance extracted (AVE), the confirmatory factor analysis showed that the amount of unique variance captured by each of the PC and PS constructs was greater than the amount of variance shared between the constructs. Finally, there is strong a priori theoretical justification for the distinctness of the PC and PS constructs, as specified by general deterrence theory. Heck (1998) contends that theory should always be used as a guide in analyzing an EFA to avoid solutions that do not make practical sense. For these reasons, perceived certainty of sanctions (PC) and perceived severity of sanctions (PS) remained as separate constructs throughout the study.

Several of the remaining constructs emerged fairly "cleanly" as factors, while others did not emerge as expected. Specifically, the IS misuse intention (INT), computer self-efficacy (CSE), and social desirability bias (SDB) items all loaded strongly on their intended factors. The risk propensity (RP) items loaded strongly on a single factor, with the exception of RP4. This item cross-loaded on factors three and six and therefore was dropped from further analysis. RP4 was the only reverse-scaled item in the risk propensity scale, which may explain why its loading was not consistent with the other RP items (Ping 2004). Contrary to expectations, the moral commitment (MC) items did not load strongly on a single factor. The factor pattern of the MC items displayed no discernable structure, as the items loaded on four separate factors. Additional analysis of potential subconstructs (i.e., MC1 and MC2; MC5 and MC8; MC6 and MC7) produced reliabilities well below .50 for each of the item subsets, eliminating the possibility that moral commitment could be respecified as a second-order factor. A confirmatory factor analysis (in which the MC items were forced to load on a single factor) explained a very small percentage of variance and again suggested that the items were not measuring a single, underlying construct. Due to these difficulties, the eight-item moral commitment scale was dropped from further analysis. The inadequate convergent validity of the moral commitment scale is somewhat of a mystery. Tooke and Ickes (1988) empirically validated these same items and reported a unidimensional construct with acceptable validity and reliability. Determining why similar results were not obtained in the current study is a subject for future research.

Moral commitment was included as a control variable in the research model based on theoretical considerations and findings from earlier research. Hence, it was necessary to find a replacement moral commitment measure for the study. While not discussed previously, the survey instrument contained an additional item that assessed respondents' moral judgment of each IS misuse scenario (e.g., "It was morally acceptable for Alex to access the computer system.") The item was posed on all five scenarios with slight modifications to reference the specific IS misuse behavior depicted in each scenario. The item was anchored on a seven-point response scale ranging from 1 ('strongly agree') to 7 ('strongly disagree'). As with the perceived certainty of sanction, perceived severity of sanction, and IS misuse intention items, a composite score was constructed for this item by summing responses across the four remaining scenarios (reverse coded prior to summation so that higher scores indicate higher moral commitment), resulting in a scoring range of 4 to 28. This single-item composite scale served as the new measure of moral commitment. While single-item measures may pose measurement difficulties (Churchill 1979), they do not render the results of structural equation modeling analysis (Hair et al.1998; Ping 2004). Moreover, single-item composite scales have been used to measure moral commitment in prior deterrence research (e.g., Silberman 1976). Finally, the single-item moral commitment scale was considered a better alternative to having no measure of this construct in the study.

Referring to Table 5.3, the factor solution (after eliminating the items marked for deletion) demonstrated satisfactory convergent and discriminant validity. Convergent validity was satisfactory because all items loaded strongly (>.40) on their respective constructs (Hair et al. 1998; Straub, Boudreau, and Gefen 2004). Discriminant validity was satisfactory because all items loaded stronger on their respective constructs than on any other constructs (Straub, Boudreau, and Gefen 2004). In addition, factor patterns consistent with that of Table 5.3 emerged in separate EFAs of the MBA and industry samples (Appendix C). The consistent factor pattern across the combined, MBA, and industry samples provide additional evidence of the construct validity of the measures (Heck 1998).

The second EFA was conducted on the security countermeasure variables. As shown in Table 5.4, this EFA produced five factors with eigenvalues greater than or equal to 1.0. The five factor solution accounted for 65.7 percent of the total variance, which is above the generally accepted level of 60 percent (Hair et al. 1998). Most items loaded relatively "cleanly" on their expected factors (i.e., the four security countermeasure constructs), with the exception of factor four. Factor four consisted of three items that pertain specifically to the use of unauthorized software. Considering that this study focused on more generalized patterns of IS misuse (as measured by a composite scale of IS misuse intention), incorporating an act-specific security countermeasure variable into the analysis would not have been appropriate. Hence, the items from factor four (i.e., PR7, P4, and M5) were not used in further analyses. The emergence of a specific "unauthorized software countermeasures" construct is, however, an interesting finding that can be explored in future research.

As with the previous EFA, guidelines from Comrey (1973) and Hair et al. (1998) were used in assessing the factor loadings for the remaining items. Items which either did not load strongly on any factor (<.40), or that loaded highly (>.40) or relatively equally on more than one factor were eliminated. An exception is item P3, which assessed awareness of a policy against unauthorized access to computer systems. This item had a relatively low loading (.31) and therefore was considered for deletion. However, after checking the domain coverage of the security policies (P) construct (Moore and Benbasat 1991), it was decided that eliminating this item would weaken the content validity of this construct. Hair et al. (1998) provide some justification for keeping P3, as they consider .30 to be the minimal level for significance. The confirmatory factor analysis (discussed later in the chapter) showed that retaining this item was not problematic.

In accordance with the above procedure, item SA7 was dropped because it cross-loaded on factors one and two. This item pertained to education on appropriate use of e-mail in the workplace. It appears that either this item did not clearly discriminate between the security awareness program and security policies constructs, or that respondents viewed policies and awareness efforts regarding the use of e-mail as a single concept. Item SA1 (which was not dropped) measured the same concept from a more general IT perspective (i.e., "Employees in my organization are instructed on the appropriate use of information technologies"), and therefore removing SA7 did not appear problematic in terms of content validity. Next, items PR1, PR2, PR3, SA2, and P7 were dropped because they did not load on their intended constructs.

Table 5.4. EFA for Security Countermeasure Variables

	Factor				
Item	**1**	**2**	**3**	**4**	**5**
SA4	**.937**				
SA3	**.807**				
SA6	**.729**				
SA8	**.692**				
SA5	**.665**				
PR2*	.633				
SA1	**.565**				
P7*	.507				
P1		**.948**			
P2		**.869**			
PR1*		.710			
SA2*		.602			
P6		**.542**			
SA7*	.404	.527			
P5		**.407**			
P3					
M7			.834		
M4			.828		
M3			.803		
M2			.730		
PR3*			.601		
M1			**.461**		
M6			**.404**		
PR7				.914	
P4				.831	
M5				.600	
PR4					**.779**
PR5					**.763**
PR6					**.761**
Eigenvalue	10.06	9.42	7.84	7.56	6.93
Variance explained (%)	15.81	14.80	12.32	11.87	10.89
Cumulative variance (%)	15.81	30.61	42.93	54.80	65.69

Note: Loadings less than .40 not shown; * Marked for deletion

Items PR1 and SA2 pertained to password management practices in the organization. Recall that the password sharing scenario was removed from the analysis since it did not seem to fit the domain of IS misuse. Therefore, removal of these two items that assessed countermeasures against password sharing was justified. Item P7 assessed awareness of a policy against unauthorized modification of computerized data. Considering that item P6 (which was not dropped) assessed awareness of guidelines that govern "what employees are allowed to do with their computers," removing item P7 did not appear to weaken the content validity of the security policies (P) scale. Items PR2 and PR3 measured the organization's use of biometric controls and e-mail content filters, respectively. Item PR2 loaded on the security awareness program (SA) construct, which is puzzling. The mean for this item was very low compared to the other PR items, suggesting that either most organizations do not use biometric controls, or that respondents were not aware of their existence. Alternatively, the ambiguous loading could be due to item complexity (i.e., respondents may not have understood the term 'biometric controls'). Item PR3 loaded on the monitoring practices (M) construct. This suggests that respondents viewed e-mail content filters as monitoring devices and not preventative technologies. This item should be modified in future research to clearly distinguish between the two forms of countermeasures. Overall, the EFA results for the PR items show that only items PR4, PR5, and PR6 loaded together as a single factor. These three items pertained to basic access control technologies. The remaining PR items all loaded rather sporadically, suggesting that more sophisticated preventative security technologies are conceptually distinct from basic access controls. Items PR4, PR5, and PR6 are used as the final measure of preventative security software (PR) in this study, and therefore the domain coverage of this construct is limited to basic access control technologies. Following the modifications discussed above, the security countermeasures constructs emerged as follows (item loadings in bold in Table 5.4): (SA) – items SA1, SA3, SA4, SA5, SA6, SA8; (P) – items P1, P2, P3, P5, P7; (M) items M1, M2, M3, M4, M6, M7; (PR) – items PR4, PR5, PR6.

Referring to Table 5.4, the factor solution (after eliminating the items marked for deletion) demonstrated satisfactory convergent and discriminant validity. Convergent validity was satisfactory because all (except for P3, discussed previously) items loaded strongly (>.40) on their respective constructs (Hair et al. 1998; Straub, Boudreau, and Gefen 2004). Discriminant validity was satisfactory because all items loaded stronger on their respective constructs than on any other constructs (Straub, Boudreau, and Gefen 2004). In addition, with a few exceptions, factor patterns consistent with that of Table 5.4 emerged in separate EFAs of the MBA and industry samples (Appendix C). The largely consistent factor pattern across the combined, MBA, and industry samples provide additional evidence of the construct validity of the measures (Heck 1998).

Assessment of Reliability

Following purification and elimination of items in the EFAs, the reliability of the revised construct measures was assessed. Reliability is an important step in instrument validation to ensure measurement accuracy (Straub 1989). Cronbach's alphas, which are calculated based on average inter-item correlations, were used for the reliability testing. High Cronbach's alphas are usually signs that the measures are reliable (Straub 1989). Table 5.5 shows the results of the reliability analysis.

There is no standard cut-off point for the alpha coefficient, but the generally agreed upon lower limit for Cronbach's alpha is .70, although it may decrease to .60 (Hair et al. 1998) or even .50 (Nunnally 1978) in exploratory research. As summarized in Table 5.5, with the exception of social desirability bias, all construct reliabilities exhibited alpha values greater than 0.70. The social desirability bias scale showed a reliability of 0.63, which is still considered satisfactory in exploratory investigations.

Testing for Common Method Bias

When dependent and independent variable data are collected from a single informant (such as the self-report method in the current study), common method bias can be a potential problem (Straub, Boudreau, and Gefen 2004). Following Podaskoff and Organ (1986), Harmon's one-factor test was performed to examine the extent of common method bias. The one-factor test involves subjecting items presumably measuring a variety of different constructs to a single factor analysis and analyzing the unrotated factor solution. The dominance of one factor would suggest that the items are related because of a common method. The factor analysis for the combined sample produced thirteen factors with eigenvalues greater than one that together accounted for

63.1 percent of the total variance. The first factor accounted for 23 percent of the variance. Since a single factor did not emerge and one general factor did not account for the majority of the variance, a substantial amount of common method variance was not evident.

Table 5.5. Reliability of Constructs

Construct	Number of Items	Cronbach's Alpha
IS misuse intention (INT)	2	0.97
Perceived certainty (PC)	2	0.93
Perceived severity (PS)	2	0.91
Security policies (P)	5	0.89
Awareness program (SA)	6	0.88
Monitoring practices (M)	6	0.87
Preventative software (PR)	3	0.72
Risk propensity (RP)	5	0.72
Computer self-efficacy (CSE)	6	0.90
Social desirability bias (SDB)	5	0.63
Moral commitment (MC)	1	-
Virtual status (VS)	1	-

PARTIAL LEAST SQUARES (PLS) ANALYSES

The partial least squares (PLS) structural modeling technique was used for the confirmatory instrument validation phase (i.e., confirmatory factor analysis) and to evaluate the relationships in the research model. PLS is superior to traditional statistical methods (e.g., factor analysis, regression, and path analysis) because it allows the measurement model (relationships between constructs and measures) and structural model (theoretical relationships among constructs) to be tested simultaneously (Gefen, Straub, and Boudreau 2000). To do so, PLS first estimates loadings of indicators on constructs and then estimates causal relationships among constructs iteratively (Fornell and Larcker 1981).

PLS was selected for two main reasons. First, PLS does not impose normality requirements on the data (Chin 1998). An inspection of histograms and scatter-plots indicated that item responses were not normally distributed in this study, as is often the case in survey-based research (Ping 2004). Formal tests revealed significant departures from normal distributions in the data (see Table 5.6). Thus, a statistical technique robust to non-normality was needed. Second, PLS is useful in situations where the theoretical model or measures are in the early stages of development (Chin 1998). Compared to covariance-based SEM techniques (e.g., LISREL, AMOS), PLS is more prediction-oriented and seeks to maximize the variance explained in constructs, thus making it "closer to data, more exploratory, and more data analytic" (Barclay, Higgins, and Thompson 1995, p. 290). Given the prediction-oriented nature of this study, the emphasis on expanding the theoretical framework of general deterrence theory, and the use of newly developed scales, PLS was well-suited for the data analysis. The software used to perform the analysis was PLS-Graph Version 3.00.

The PLS analysis typically consists of two stages (Barclay, Higgins, and Thompson 1995). First, the reliability and validity of the measurement model is assessed. Second, the structural model is assessed. This ensures that the constructs' measures are valid and reliable before assessing the nature of the relations between the constructs (Anderson and Gerbing 1988).

Table 5.6. Revised Descriptive Statistics and Tests for Normality

Construct	Mean	SD	Skewedness		Kurtosis	
			Stat	z-score	Stat	z-score
INT	9.38	4.36	0.80	**7.38**	0.34	1.57
PC	16.71	4.67	0.19	1.81	-0.29	-1.32
PS	19.57	3.99	-0.09	-0.90	-0.31	-1.43
P	5.24	1.44	-1.08	**-9.87**	0.89	**4.12**
SA	4.27	1.44	-0.12	-1.08	-0.65	**-2.99**
M	4.44	1.33	-0.31	-2.87	-0.29	-1.31
PR	5.71	1.19	-1.08	**-9.95**	0.87	**3.99**
RP	4.00	1.01	-0.01	-0.12	-0.38	-1.76
CSE	5.70	0.99	-0.78	**-7.13**	0.37	1.71
SDB	0.12	0.20	1.98	**18.20**	3.78	**17.43**
MC	23.07	3.95	-0.78	**-7.18**	0.45	**2.05**
VS	0.91	1.60	2.22	**20.39**	4.86	**22.38**

Note: Bolded z-scores indicate a significant ($p<0.025$) departure from normality.

Measurement Model

The assessment of the measurement model served as the confirmatory phase of instrument validation (Gefen, Straub, and Boudreau 2000). The results obtained from the exploratory factor analyses (EFA) using SPSS were submitted to PLS-Graph and tests of convergent validity, discriminant validity, and reliability of constructs were carried out.

Two different assessments were made for convergent validity: (1) items loading on constructs; and (2) average variance extracted (AVE). A generally accepted rule of thumb is to accept items with loadings of .70 or above, which suggests that there exists more shared variance between the construct and its measures than error variance (Barclay, Thompson, and Higgins 1995). However, loadings of 0.50 or 0.60 may still be acceptable for an item if other indicators within the same block of measures have high loadings (Chin 1998). AVE measures the amount of variance in a construct captured by its indicators relative to measurement error (Fornell and Larcker 1981). The guideline threshold for AVE is 0.50, meaning that 50 percent or more variance of the indicators is accounted for (Chin 1998).

As can be seen in Table 5.7, nearly all of the item loadings exceeded the .70 recommended level and AVEs for most of the constructs exceeded 0.50. The only exceptions involved the security awareness program (SA), risk propensity (RP), and social desirability bias (SDB) constructs. SA1 was below .70. Since this loading was not below the .50 minimum, and the SA construct had five other items with very high loadings (>.74), the item was retained. Risk propensity (RP) had three item loadings below .70 and an AVE slightly below .50. Fornell and Larcker (1981) pointed out that AVE is a conservative test of convergent validity so it is possible that an AVE below .50 is still satisfactory. Moreover, the risk propensity measure had two other indicators with high loadings and none of the loadings were below 0.50, all loadings were very significant, and the composite reliability was high (.82; see Table 5.8). For these reasons, all RP items were retained.   The social desirability bias (SDB) construct had three weak item loadings and a low AVE. Items SDB2 and SDB4 appeared especially problematic, and therefore were considered for deletion. However, a check was made to determine whether the domain coverage (i.e., content validity) of the construct would suffer as a result of dropping the items (Moore and Benbasat 1991). The five-item SDB scale (Hays, Hayashi, and Stewart 1989) used in this study is a subset of the original thirty-three item Marlowe-Crowne SDB response set scale (Crowne and Marlowe 1960). Given that the scale had already been reduced from thirty-three to five items, it was deemed that eliminating additional items would weaken its content validity. Ping (2004) suggested that in situations where eliminating items from a previously validated measure to improve its consistency undermines the face or content validity of the measure, items can instead be summed and averaged to form a single indicator of the construct for structural equation modeling analysis. The criterion for using this approach is that the measure should be unidimensional in an exploratory factor analysis (EFA). As seen in Table 5.3, the five SDB items loaded on a single factor in the EFA, suggesting unidimensionality. Therefore, Ping's (2004) methodology was considered appropriate. The five SDB items were summed and averaged to form a single indicator for analysis in the structural model.

Discriminant validity between constructs was examined using Fornell and Larcker's (1981) recommendation that the square root of AVE for each construct should exceed the correlations between that and all other constructs (i.e., the average variance shared between the construct and its indicators should be larger than the variance shared between the construct and other constructs). As shown in Table 5.8, the square root of the AVE for each construct (diagonal elements) was greater than the correlation between that construct and other constructs, without exception. Hence, the discriminant validity criterion was met.

As an additional assessment of discriminant validity, tests for multicollinearity were performed due to the relatively high correlations among some of the constructs (especially the security countermeasure constructs.). All constructs had variance inflation factor (VIF) values less than 3.0, which is well below the usual cutoff level of 10.0 and within the more conservative cutoff level of 5.0 (Hair et al. 2003). Multicollinearity typically is considered a serious problem if the correlation between two variables is greater than 0.8 or 0.9 (Bagozzi, Yi, and Phillips 1991). As can be seen in Table 5.8, the highest correlation between any pair of constructs was .72 (between security awareness program and security policies), which is below this standard. Thus, while several of the constructs are likely to be related, the tests of discriminant validity revealed that they were all empirically distinct.

Table 5.7. Loadings and AVEs for Multi-Item Constructs (All loadings significant at p<.001)

Item	Loading	T-value	AVE	Item	Loading	T-value	AVE
INT1	.9796	208.34	0.96	M6	.7771	37.73	
INT2	.9820	220.33		M7	.7615	29.70	
PC1	.9659	258.33	0.93	PR4	.7969	29.19	0.64
PC2	.9672	268.70		PR5	.8587	46.67	
PS1	.9586	205.29	0.92	PR6	.7342	16.29	
PS2	.9613	247.92		RP1	.6085	16.42	0.48
P1	.8366	47.31	0.69	RP2	.7712	34.44	
P2	.8694	50.95		RP3	.8065	46.08	
P3	.7900	37.51		RP5	.6554	18.63	
P5	.8052	39.28		RP6	.5776	12.21	
P6	.8559	51.01		CSE1	.7590	30.26	0.66
SA1	.6785	22.85	0.62	CSE2	.7883	31.56	
SA3	.7419	29.62		CSE3	.8581	49.88	
SA4	.7576	29.39		CSE4	.8363	42.59	
SA5	.8424	59.43		CSE5	.8377	44.46	
SA6	.8708	69.19		CSE6	.8033	33.10	
SA8	.8329	56.14		SDB1	.5918	8.34	0.40
M1	.7604	39.64	0.61	SDB2	.5239	5.15	
M2	.8157	44.12		SDB3	.7077	13.36	
M3	.7644	30.68		SDB4	.4611	4.71	
M4	.7855	30.65		SDB5	.7655	16.60	

Table 5.8. Reliability and Inter-Construct Correlations

Construct	CR	Inter-Construct Correlations											
		1	2	3	4	5	7	7	8	9	10	11	12
(1) INT	.98	.98											
(2) PC	.97	-.30	.96										
(3) PS	.96	-.35	.54	.96									
(4) SA	.91	-.32	.45	.43	.79								
(5) P	.92	-.37	.38	.47	.72	.83							
(7) M	.90	-.21	.55	.37	.61	.64	.78						
(7) PR	.84	-.27	.33	.36	.53	.62	.49	.80					
(8) RP	.82	-.04	-.04	.00	.02	-.01	-.05	-.03	.69				
(9) CSE	.92	-.03	-.15	-.02	-.03	.05	-.08	.11	-.14	.81			
(10) SDB	.77	-.21	.21	.16	.08	.06	.09	.14	-.01	.04	.64		
(11) MC	-	-.59	.27	.30	.30	.32	.21	.27	-.02	.06	.25	-	
(12) VS	-	.11	.04	.05	.00	-.08	-.05	-.14	.02	-.09	.07	.05	-

CR = Composite reliability
Note: Shaded items are the square root of the average variance extracted (AVE). Off-diagonal elements are the correlations among constructs.

The final test of the measurement model was reliability analysis. Reliability was assessed using composite reliability, a measure of internal consistency included in the PLS output. Interpreted like a Cronbach's alpha, a composite reliability of .70 or greater is considered acceptable (Fornell and Larcker 1981). As shown in the second column of Table 5.8, the composite reliabilities of the constructs ranged from .77 to .98. Thus, the reliabilities of the measures were acceptable.

Structural Model

With an adequate measurement model in place, the hypotheses were tested by examining the structural model. In PLS analysis, the test of the structural model includes estimating the path coefficients, which indicate the strength of the relationships between the independent and dependent variables, and the R^2 value, which represents the amount of variance explained by the independent variables (Chin 1998). Together, the R^2 and path coefficients (loadings and significance) indicate how well the model is performing. R^2 indicates the predictive power of the model, and the values should be interpreted in the same manner as R^2 in a regression analysis (Barclay, Thomson, and Higgins 1995). The path coefficients should be significant and directionally consistent with expectations. Significance tests for the path coefficients are not directly provided by the PLS method. In order to estimate the significance of paths in the structural model, the bootstrapping resampling procedure (500 samples) was used. Considering the investigative nature of this research, and in order to increase the power of the statistical tests, the 10 percent significance level ($\alpha = .10$) was used.

Hypotheses testing proceeded in two phases. The first phase examined the main effects specified in hypotheses H1 – H4 and H8. The second phase examined the interaction effects stated in hypotheses H5 – H7. The analysis described below was conducted on the combined sample. The hypotheses were also tested on the MBA and industry samples (see Appendix D). The results of the main effects hypotheses tests are depicted in Figure 5.1 and summarized in Table 5.9.

As shown in Figure 5.1, the structural model explained 33 percent of the variance for perceived certainty of sanctions, 26 percent of the variance for perceived severity of sanctions, and 39 percent of the variance for IS misuse intention. All of these figures exceeded Falk and

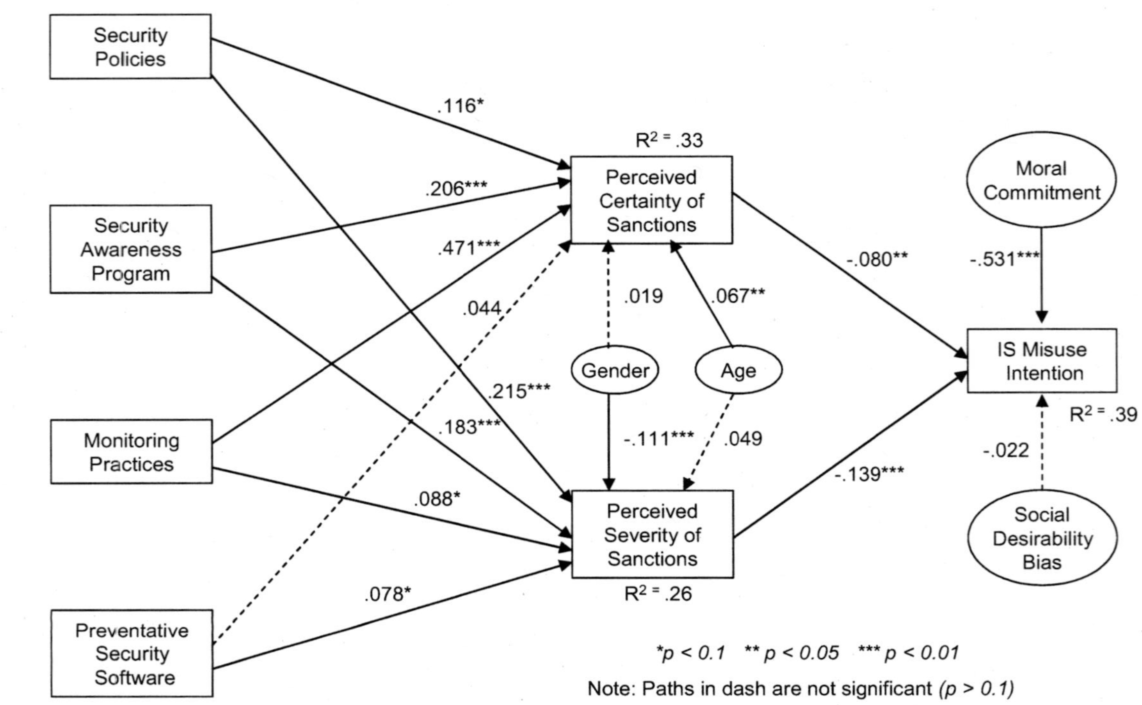

Figure 5.1. PLS Analysis of Main Effects

Table 5.9. Main Effect Path Coefficients

H#	Hypothesis (Direction)	Path Coefficient	T-value	Significance (one-tailed)	Supported?
H1a	P → PC (+)	0.116	1.589	$p < 0.10$	Yes
H1b	P → PS (+)	0.215	3.024	$p < 0.01$	Yes
H2a	SA → PC (+)	0.206	3.508	$p < 0.01$	Yes
H2b	SA → PS (+)	0.183	2.460	$p < 0.01$	Yes
H3a	M → PC (+)	0.471	8.608	$p < 0.01$	Yes
H3b	M → PS (+)	0.088	1.581	$p < 0.10$	Yes
H4a	PR → PC (+)	0.044	0.977	n.s.	No
H4b	PR → PS (+)	0.078	1.528	$p < 0.10$	Yes
H8a	PC → INT (-)	-0.080	2.198	$p < 0.05$	Yes
H8b	PS → INT (-)	-0.139	3.400	$p < 0.01$	Yes
INT = IS misuse intention; PC = Perceived certainty of sanctions; PS = Perceived severity of sanctions; P = Security policies; SA = Security awareness program; M = Monitoring practices; PR = Preventative security software					

Miller's (1992) 10 percent criterion for substantive explanatory power, making interpretation of path coefficients meaningful.

Consistent with hypotheses H1a – H3a, security policies, security awareness program, and monitoring practices each had significant direct effects on perceived certainty of sanctions, after controlling for age and gender. Monitoring practices and security awareness program had the strongest effects (β = .471 and .206, p<0.01, respectively), while the influence of security policies was moderate (β = .116, p<0.10). The relationship between preventative security software and perceived certainty of sanctions was not significant, and therefore H4a was not supported.

Consistent with hypotheses H1b – H4b, security policies, security awareness program, monitoring practices, and preventative security software each had significant direct effects on perceived severity of sanctions, after controlling for age and gender. Security policies and security awareness program had the strongest effects (β = .215 and .183, p<0.01, respectively), while the influences of monitoring practices and preventative security software were modest (β = .089 and .078, p<0.10, respectively). Chin (1998) suggested that the substantive significance (or effect magnitudes) of the relationships must also be considered in the assessment of the structural model. The path coefficients in the PLS model represent standardized regression coefficients. The suggested lower limit of substantive significance for regression coefficients is 0.05 (Pedhazur 1982). As a more conservative position, path coefficients of 0.10 or above are preferable (Compeau and Higgins 1995). Thus, the paths from monitoring practices and preventative security software to perceived severity of sanctions, while statistically significant, were both fairly weak in terms of substantive significance.

Hypotheses H8a and H8b, which predicted that perceived certainty and severity of sanctions would be negatively related to IS misuse intention (after controlling for moral commitment and social desirability bias), were both supported. The influence of perceived severity of sanctions was stronger (β = -.139, p<0.01) than that of perceived certainty of sanctions (β = -.080, p<0.05). As noted above, path coefficients of at least 0.10 are preferable to demonstrate substantive significance. Therefore, the substantive significance of the relationship between perceived certainty of sanctions and IS misuse intention could be considered weak. A post hoc analysis examined the relationship between perceived certainty and severity of sanctions by adding an additional path between these two constructs in the structural model. The purpose of this analysis was to determine whether perceived certainty of sanctions had an indirect effect on IS misuse intention through perceived severity of sanctions. The post hoc results showed a highly significant relationship (β = .460, p<0.001) between perceived certainty and severity of sanctions, in addition to significant relationships between perceived certainty of sanctions and IS misuse intention (β = -.079, p<0.05) and perceived severity of sanctions and IS misuse intention (β = -.139, p<0.01). Thus, perceived certainty of sanctions had significant direct and indirect (through perceived severity of sanctions) effects on IS misuse intention. It should be noted that the significance of the path between security awareness program and perceived severity of sanctions dipped just below significance when the path between perceived certainty and severity of sanctions was added to the model. However, the path between security awareness program and perceived certainty of sanctions remained significant, which indicated that security awareness program still had a positive effect on overall punishment perceptions. The significance levels of all other paths in the structural model were unchanged in the post hoc analysis.

In terms of the control variables, age was a significant correlate of perceived certainty of sanctions and gender was a significant correlate of perceived severity of sanctions. Moral commitment had a very strong negative association with IS misuse intention (this relationship is discussed further in the next chapter). Finally, social desirability bias was not significantly associated with IS misuse intention. This suggests that respondents' self-reported IS misuse intentions were not contaminated by impression management concerns.

Hypotheses H5 – H7 predicted that the relationships between each of the security countermeasure variables and perceived certainty and severity of sanctions would be moderated by risk propensity, computer self-efficacy, and virtual status. To test for these moderating effects, the PLS product-indicator approach was employed (Chin, Marcolin, and Newsted 2003). For this analytic technique, product indicators reflecting latent interaction variables are created by multiplying the indicators from the predictor and the moderator variables. The new latent interaction variables, composed of the product-indicator items, are then added to the main effects model to test for interaction effects.

Guidelines from Chin, Marcolin, and Newsted (2003) were used to create the interaction term measures. First, all indicators reflecting the predictor (i.e., security policies (P), security awareness program (SA), monitoring practices (M), preventative security software (PR)) and moderator (i.e., computer self-efficacy (CSE), risk propensity (RP), virtual status (VS)) constructs were standardized. This step was necessary for interpretation of the interaction construct scores. The standardizations were calculated using SPSS 13.0. Once the standardized indicators were calculated, product indicators were developed by creating all possible products from the two sets of indicators for each predictor-moderator combination. These product indicators were used to represent the latent interaction variables. For example, the six measures reflecting the SA construct (a predictor variable) and the six measures reflecting the CSE construct (a moderator variable) were cross-multiplied to create thirty-six items that represented the interaction construct SA*CSE. This same procedure was followed for each combination of the security countermeasure and moderator variables, resulting in the following interaction constructs: CSE*P (thirty items), CSE*SA (thirty-six items), CSE*M (thirty-six items), CSE*PR (eighteen items), RP*P (twenty-five items), RP*SA (thirty items), RP*M (thirty items), RP*PR (eighteen items), VS*P (five items), VS*SA (six items), VS*M (six items), and VS*PR (three items). The interaction testing consisted of three separate PLS runs: (1) one with the CSE interaction constructs added to the main effects; (2) one with the RP interaction constructs added to the main effects; and (3) one with the VS interaction constructs added to the main effects. This is similar to the procedure followed in moderated multiple regression in which separate analyses are run for each moderator variable to overcome the possibility that they would cancel one another out. In terms of interpretation, the path coefficient between the interaction construct CSE*P and perceived certainty of sanctions, for example, would indicate how a change in the level of CSE would change the influence of security policies on perceived certainty of sanctions. This same interpretation applies to the rest of the path coefficients between the interaction constructs and perceived certainty and severity of sanctions. The results of the interaction tests are provided in Table 5.10.

Table 5.10. Interaction Effect Path Coefficients

H#	Hypothesis (Direction)	PLS Model Description	Path Coefficient	T-value	Sig.	Supported?
H5a	CSE moderates P → PC (-)	CSE*P → PC (-)	-0.086	0.910	n.s.	No
H5b	CSE moderates SA → PC (-)	CSE*SA → PC (-)	0.074	0.895	n.s.	No
H5c	CSE moderates M → PC (-)	CSE*M → PC (-)	0.116	0.878	n.s.	No
H5d	CSE moderates PR → PC (-)	CSE*PR → PC (-)	0.013	0.723	n.s.	No
H5e	CSE moderates P → PS (-)	CSE*P → PS (-)	-0.114	1.261	n.s.	No
H5f	CSE moderates SA → PS (-)	CSE*SA → PS (-)	0.060	0.424	n.s.	No
H5g	CSE moderates M → PS (-)	CSE*M → PS (-)	-0.174	1.518	$p < 0.10$	**Yes**
H5h	CSE moderates PR → PS (-)	CSE*PR → PS (-)	-0.093	1.482	$p < 0.10$	**Yes**
H6a	RP moderates P → PC (-)	RP*P → PC (-)	0.085	1.105	n.s.	No
H6b	RP moderates SA → PC (-)	RP*SA → PC (-)	0.032	0.540	n.s.	No
H6c	RP moderates M → PC (-)	RP*M → PC (-)	0.025	0.417	n.s.	No
H6d	RP moderates PR → PC (-)	RP*PR → PC (-)	-0.035	0.541	n.s.	No

Table 5.10 (continued). Interaction Effect Path Coefficients

H#	Hypothesis (Direction)	PLS Model Description	Path Coefficient	T-value	Sig.	Supported?
H6e	RP moderates P → PS (-)	RP*P → PS (-)	0.013	0.181	n.s.	No
H6f	RP moderates SA → PS (-)	RP*SA → PS (-)	0.051	0.544	n.s.	No
H6g	RP moderates M → PS (-)	RP*M → PS (-)	0.030	0.483	n.s.	No
H6h	RP moderates PR → PS (-)	RP*PR → PS (-)	-0.032	0.509	n.s.	No
H7a	VS moderates P → PC (-)	VS*P → PC (-)	-0.126	1.528	$p < 0.10$	**Yes**
H7b	VS moderates SA → PC (-)	VS*SA → PC (-)	0.071	1.136	n.s.	No
H7c	VS moderates M → PC (-)	VS*M → PC (-)	0.033	0.403	n.s.	No
H7d	VS moderates PR → PC (-)	VS*PR → PC (-)	-0.067	1.129	n.s.	No
H7e	VS moderates P → PS (-)	VS*P → PS (-)	-0.111	1.153	n.s.	No
H7f	VS moderates SA → PS (-)	VS*SA → PS (-)	0.147	1.533	$p < 0.10$	No*
H7g	VS moderates M → PS (-)	VS*M → PS (-)	0.065	1.010	n.s.	No
H7h	VS moderates PR → PS (-)	VS*PR → PS (-)	-0.045	0.707	n.s.	No

* Significant but in opposite direction than hypothesized.

Computer self-efficacy had a moderately significant negative effect on both the relationship between monitoring practices and perceived severity of sanctions and the relationship between preventative security software and perceived severity of sanctions (β = -.174 and -.093, p<0.10, respectively), thus providing marginal support for hypotheses H5g and H5h. Virtual status had a moderately significant negative effect on the relationship between security policies and perceived certainty of sanctions (β = -.126, p<0.10), providing marginal support for H7a.

Unexpectedly, virtual status had a significant positive effect on the association between security awareness program and perceived severity of sanctions (β = .147, p<0.10), opposite to the direction predicted by H7f. None of the other moderating effects were significant. Overall, these results suggest that the impacts of the security countermeasure variables on perceived certainty and severity of sanctions are uniform regardless of one's risk propensity; however, computer self-efficacy and virtual status have some moderating effects. The lack of significant moderating effects in the PLS product-indicator analysis was unexpected. As an additional test of hypotheses H5 – H7, the combined sample was split into subsamples based on the medians of the moderator variables. That is, separate high and low subsamples (based on whether or not the overall computer self-efficacy, risk propensity, and virtual status score was above or below its median) were created for three moderator variables. Separate PLS runs were conducted for each subsample and the differences between the high-low subsamples for each moderator variable were evaluated. A significant difference in path coefficients between the high and low subsamples is indicative of a moderating effect on the particular relationship examined (Chin 2000). This same procedure has been used in prior IS studies that have tested for moderation using PLS (e.g., Armstrong and Sambamurthy 1999; Keil et al. 2000; Venkatesh and Morris 2000).

The moderating influence of computer self-efficacy was assessed first. Results showed that the path coefficients from security policies and preventative security software to perceived severity of sanctions in the high computer self-efficacy subsample were significantly weaker than the corresponding path coefficients in the low computer self-efficacy subsample (t = 2.01, p<0.05 and t = 11.18, p<0.001, respectively). Thus, hypotheses H5e and H5h were supported. For comparison purposes, hypothesis H5h was also supported in the PLS product-indicator analysis, but hypothesis H5e was not (although it approached significance). In addition to these hypothesized interaction effects, the results also showed that the path coefficients from security awareness program to perceived certainty and severity of sanctions in the high computer self-efficacy subsample were significantly stronger than the corresponding path coefficients in the low computer self-efficacy subsample (t = 31.31 and 16.50, p<0.001, respectively). These differences are opposite to what was predicted by hypotheses H5b and H5f. The PLS product-indicator analysis also found results opposite to the posited direction for hypotheses H5b and H5f, although the moderating effects were not significant in that analysis.

The risk propensity analysis showed no significant differences in path coefficients between the high and low subsamples for the relationships in hypotheses H6a – H6h. Consistent with the PLS product-indicator analysis, these results indicated that risk propensity did not have a moderating influence on the relationships between the security countermeasure variables and perceived certainty and severity of sanctions. To further investigate these non-significant results, additional follow-up analysis was conducted based on a review of the deterrence literature. As stated in Mendes (2004), early conceptualizations of general deterrence theory posited that the influences of certainty and severity of punishment are conditional upon individuals' attitude toward risk. Specifically, risk averse individuals are more influenced by the threat of punishment than risk acceptant individuals (Becker 1968). This argument is supported by empirical research that found that risk attitudes moderate the impact of punishment perceptions on deviant behavior (e.g., Nagin and Pogarsky 2001; Rindfleisch and Crockett 1999). In terms of the current study, this suggests that risk propensity does influence the effectiveness of security countermeasures, but not as conceptualized in the research model. Instead of moderating the relationships between the security countermeasures and perceived certainty and severity of sanctions, risk propensity moderates the relationships between perceived certainty and severity of sanctions and IS misuse intention. To empirically examine the plausibility of this assertion, the path coefficients from perceived certainty and severity of sanctions to IS misuse intention in the low risk propensity subsample were compared to their corresponding path coefficients in the high risk propensity subsample. Inconsistent with the preceding argument, the results showed no significant differences in the path coefficients between the subsamples for the specified relationships. Thus, risk propensity did not moderate the impacts of perceived certainty and severity of punishment on IS misuse intention. Taken together, the results of the interaction tests showed that risk propensity had no moderating effect in the research model.

Finally, the moderating influence of virtual status was assessed. The median for virtual status was zero, so the subsamples were formed by splitting those who worked at least one day per week outside the office from those who performed all of their work within the office. Results showed that the path coefficients from security policies to perceived certainty and severity of sanctions in the "virtual worker" subsample were significantly weaker than the corresponding paths in the "non-virtual worker" subsample (t = 26.51 and 22.08, p<0.001, respectively). Thus, hypotheses H7a and H7e were supported. Hypotheses H7a was also supported in the PLS product-indicator analysis, but H7e was not (although it approached significance). Interestingly, the results also showed that the path coefficient from security awareness program to perceived severity of sanctions in the "virtual worker" subsample was significantly stronger than the corresponding path in the "non-virtual worker" subsample (t = 22.75, p<0.001). This result is opposite to what was predicted by H7f. However, the same result was found in the PLS product-indicator analysis.

Aside from those discussed above, none of the other hypothesized moderating effects were significant in the subsample analyses. Thus, the additional interaction tests largely confirmed the results of the PLS product-indicator analysis, while providing some evidence of additional moderating effects. Overall, there is marginal support for hypotheses H5 and H7 in this study.

Summary of Hypotheses Tests

Table 5.11 presents a summary of the hypotheses tests. The results of the separate MBA and industry sample analyses are provided for comparison purposes. Note that tests of the interaction effects using subsample analyses were not conducted on the MBA and industry datasets because in some cases the size of the subsamples would have dropped below the required limit for PLS model testing.

Table 5.11. Summary of Hypotheses Tests

H#	Hypothesis (Direction)	Combined Sample	MBA Sample	Industry Sample
H1a	Security policies → Perceived certainty (+)	X		X
H1b	Security policies → Perceived severity (+)	X	X	X
H2a	Awareness program → Perceived certainty (+)	X	X	X
H2b	Awareness program → Perceived severity (+)	X	X	X
H3a	Monitoring → Perceived certainty (+)	X	X	X
H3b	Monitoring → Perceived severity (+)	X		X
H4a	Security software → Perceived certainty (+)			
H4b	Security software → Perceived severity (+)	X	X	
H8a	Perceived certainty → IS misuse intention (-)	X	indirectly	indirectly
H8b	Perceived severity → IS misuse intention (-)	X	X	X

X = Hypothesis was supported; * = Significant but in opposite direction than hypothesized

Table 5.11(continued). Summary of Hypotheses Tests

H#	Hypothesis (Direction)	Combined Sample	MBA Sample	Industry Sample
H5a	Computer self-efficacy moderates Policies → Perceived certainty (-)		X	
b	Computer self-efficacy moderates Awareness program → Perceived certainty (-)	*		
c	Computer self-efficacy moderates Monitoring → Perceived certainty (-)			X
d	Computer self-efficacy moderates Security software → Perceived certainty (-)		*	
e	Computer self-efficacy moderates Policies → Perceived severity (-)	X		
f	Computer self-efficacy moderates Awareness program → Perceived severity (-)	*		
g	Computer self-efficacy moderates Monitoring → Perceived severity (-)	X		
h	Computer self-efficacy moderates Security software → Perceived severity (-)	X		

X = Hypothesis was supported ; * = Significant but in opposite direction than hypothesized

Table 5.11(continued). Summary of Hypotheses Tests

H#	Hypothesis (Direction)	Combined Sample	MBA Sample	Industry Sample
H6a	Risk propensity moderates Policies → Perceived certainty (-)			
b	Risk propensity moderates Awareness program → Perceived certainty (-)			
c	Risk propensity moderates Monitoring → Perceived certainty (-)			
d	Risk propensity moderates Security software → Perceived certainty (-)			
e	Risk propensity moderates Policies → Perceived severity (-)			
f	Risk propensity moderates Awareness program → Perceived severity (-)			
g	Risk propensity moderates Monitoring → Perceived severity (-)			
h	Risk propensity moderates Security software → Perceived severity (-)			
X = Hypothesis was supported ; * = Significant but in opposite direction than hypothesized				

Table 5.11(continued). Summary of Hypotheses Tests

H#	Hypothesis (Direction)	Combined Sample	MBA Sample	Industry Sample
H7a	Virtual status moderates Policies → Perceived certainty (-)	X		X
b	Virtual status moderates Awareness program → Perceived certainty (-)		*	
c	Virtual status moderates Monitoring → Perceived certainty (-)			
d	Virtual status moderates Security software → Perceived certainty (-)			
e	Virtual status moderates Policies → Perceived severity (-)	X		
f	Virtual status moderates Awareness program → Perceived severity (-)	*		*
G	Virtual status moderates Monitoring → Perceived severity (-)			
H	Virtual status moderates Security software → Perceived severity (-)			

X = Hypothesis was supported ; * = Significant but in opposite direction than hypothesized

CHAPTER 6

Discussion, Implications, and Conclusions

MAIN FINDINGS

Overall, the results suggest that security countermeasures are effective in deterring IS misuse. Respondents who reported greater awareness of security policies, security awareness programs, monitoring practices, and preventative security software within their organizations perceived a greater threat of punishment for committing IS misuse, which in turn was associated with lower IS misuse intentions. The results also suggest that computer self-efficacy and virtual status have some impact on the effectiveness of security countermeasures, but risk propensity does not. There are also some interesting findings regarding the impacts of the security countermeasures on perceived certainty and severity of sanctions, and the impact of punishment perceptions on IS misuse. The following paragraphs discuss the research findings, starting with the GDT constructs, and then the antecedent and moderator variables.

Consistent with the predictions of GDT, perceived certainty and severity of sanctions both had significant negative influences on IS misuse intention. These findings reiterate the key role that perceived certainty and severity of sanctions play in predicting IS misuse. The importance of perceived certainty of sanctions was further illustrated by its significant indirect effect on IS misuse intention through perceived severity of sanctions. From a substantive perspective, perceived severity of sanctions had a stronger impact on IS misuse intention than perceived certainty of sanctions. These results suggest that while perceptions of getting caught are influential in predicting IS misuse, the impact of punishment severity is greater. This is inconsistent with a number of prior deterrence studies in the fields of sociology and criminology, which generally reported that the impact of perceived certainty of sanctions was much greater than that of perceived severity (e.g., Grasmick and Bryjak 1980; Hollinger and Clark 1983; Nagin and Pogarsky 2001; Silberman 1976). However, the finding with respect to the impact of perceived severity of sanctions is consistent with prior IS deterrence studies. Skinner and Fream (1997) found that severity of punishment, but not certainty of punishment, was negatively associated with various illegal computing activities. Straub (1990) reported that deterrent severity had almost twice the explanatory power of deterrent certainty in predicting computer abuse. Thus, it appears that within the IS domain, severity of punishment has a stronger influence on misuse behaviors than certainty of punishment. This could be because, up until recently, convicted computer abusers were rarely punished severely (Lee and Lee 2002; Skinner and Fream 1997). Consequently, users may feel that even if they get caught for IS misuse, they will receive very little punishment.

In terms of the research model, the above findings demonstrate that perceived certainty and severity of sanctions are key intervening variables linking security countermeasures to IS misuse intention. Thus, the effects of the security countermeasures on IS misuse, as discussed below, are indirect through perceived certainty and severity of sanctions.

Security policies had a positive impact on both perceived certainty and severity of sanctions, although the impact on perceived severity of sanctions was much stronger. These results suggest that security policies deter IS misuse, and this deterrent effect is largely achieved by increasing perceptions of punishment severity. In general, these findings are consistent with prior research that found that clearly defined security policies increase the perceived threat of punishment by making users aware of the negative consequences of IS misuse (Foltz 2000; Straub 1990). The results therefore challenge earlier findings (Doherty and Fulford 2005; Harrington 1996; Wiant 2003) that security policies have little or no impact on IS misuse. A possible explanation for the conflicting results is the way in which security policies were measured in the studies. Doherty and Fulford (2005), Harrington (1996), and Wiant (2003) each measured security policies by asking IS department managers whether or not their organizations had stated policies or guidelines on appropriate use of IS resources.

Thus, it is possible that the employees who participated in these studies were not fully aware of the existence of security policies within their organizations. Finch, Furnell, and Dowland (2003) presented evidence that supports this line of thinking. In contrast, the current study assessed security policies from the user perspective. The results suggest that when users are aware of policy statements and guidelines regarding correct and incorrect usage of information systems, their perceptions of punishment for IS misuse are increased, which in turn reduces IS misuse intentions.

Security awareness program had a significant positive effect on both perceived certainty and severity of sanctions. This suggests that efforts to inform and educate users on security policies, and the penalties that can accrue when policies are violated, increase perceptions of getting caught and punished severely for IS misuse. This is a significant finding. Researchers have extolled the benefits of security awareness programs (e.g., Hansche 2001; Schultz 2004; Straub and Welke 1998; von Solms and von Solms 2004), but little empirical work has attempted to substantiate these claims. This study provides empirical evidence that security awareness programs help deter IS misuse through their impact on punishment perceptions. The observed effects of security awareness program on perceived certainty and severity of sanctions are consistent with Straub and Welke's (1998) proposition that security awareness programs have a deterrent effect by convincing users (and potential abusers) that the company is serious about IS security and will not treat intentional breaches of this security lightly. It appears that ongoing efforts to communicate security policies are indeed effective in convincing users that the company is serious about IS security, and this translates into a greater perceived likelihood of getting caught and punished for IS misuse.

Monitoring practices had a positive impact on both perceived certainty and severity of sanctions, although the impact on perceived certainty of sanctions was much stronger. This suggests that making users aware that their computing activities are being monitored deters IS misuse by increasing users' perceptions of getting caught, and to a lesser extent by increasing their perceptions of punishment severity. These findings provide empirical support for the argument in the IS security literature that people respond to "policing" activities, such as efforts from security administrators to monitor their computing activities and audits on the use of IS assets (Kankanhalli et al. 2003;

Parker 1998; Straub and Nance 1990). It should be pointed out that the influence of monitoring practices on perceived certainty of sanctions was stronger than for any of the other security countermeasures, suggesting that computer monitoring is perhaps the most effective means of deterring IS misuse.

Preventative security software had a moderate positive impact on perceived severity of sanctions and no impact on perceived certainty of sanctions. These results suggest that having preventative software in place somewhat increases individuals' perceptions of punishment severity for IS misuse, but does not influence whether or not they think they will be caught. Hence, preventative security software does not appear particularly effective in deterring IS misuse. The relatively weak support for the impact of preventative security software on punishment perceptions is contrary to expectations and inconsistent with prior research by Straub (1990). This could be due to measurement differences. The preventative security software measure in this study consisted of basic access control technologies (e.g., password protection), while Straub (1990) measured preventative software as a combination of access controls and specialized security packages. It is possible that more specialized security technologies have a greater effect on users' punishment perceptions than basic access controls, and this accounted for the significance of preventative security software in Straub's (1990) study. This reasoning is supported by Ives, Walsh, and Schneider's (2004) proposition that alternative authentication methods such as smart cards and biometrics are more effective than password security. Additional indirect support comes from the factor analysis results presented in the previous chapter. These results showed that advanced security technologies emerged as conceptually distinct from basic access controls, which is consistent with the notion that users view more advanced security technologies differently than basic access controls. Another possibility is that the timing of this study in comparison to Straub's (1990) explains the inconsistent results. Straub's (1990) security research was conducted almost two decades ago, at time when computer security in general and preventative security software in particular were relatively new, at least from the end user perspective. In fact, as reported in Hoffer and Straub (1989), 27 percent of companies in Straub's (1990) sample did not even have password protection on user workstations. Contrast those findings with more recent research that found that almost all companies use password-protection mechanisms as well as other types of access control technologies (Finch, Funell, and Dowland 2003; InformationWeek 2005). It is possible that the preventative security technologies measured in this study have become so commonplace that users no longer view them as serious deterrents. Ives, Walsh, and Scheider (2004) presented several cases where password protection technologies failed to deter both employees and external hackers from unauthorized access to organizational computing systems. The researchers concluded that password protection is a weak form of security that leaves organizations vulnerable to security breaches. The results of this study support these assertions by showing that basic access control technologies have a weak deterrent effect on IS misuse intention. Then again, the results indicate that preventative security software influences perceptions of punishment severity and therefore has some deterrent effect, even though the effect is not very strong ($p<0.10$). At this point, it is impossible to come to a definitive conclusion as to why preventative security software had a relatively weak influence on IS misuse intention. It is an issue only additional research can address. Nevertheless, the data suggests that preventative security software has some deterrent effect on IS misuse and this effect is largely due to increased punishment severity.

To sum it up, the results suggest that each of the security countermeasures increase the perceived threat of punishment for IS misuse, which in turn reduces IS misuse intentions. Computer monitoring appears to be the most effective in deterring IS misuse, followed by security policies and a security awareness program; preventative security technologies deter IS misuse to a lesser extent than the other three countermeasures.

The second research question addressed whether the impact of security countermeasures is moderated by individual differences, as predicted by the differential deterrence hypothesis (DDH). Based on theoretical considerations, the specific individual characteristics examined in this study were computer self-efficacy, risk propensity, and virtual status. The results of two interaction analyses (using the PLS product-indicator procedure and comparison of subsamples) showed partial support for the moderating influence of these individual differences. However, several of the moderating effects that were detected were only moderately significant ($p<0.10$) and were not consistent in separate analyses of the MBA and industry datasets

(Appendix D). Therefore, the findings should be interpreted with caution.

As predicted, computer self-efficacy had a negative influence on effectiveness of security policies, monitoring practices, and preventative security software. Thus, it appears that these three countermeasures are less effective in deterring IS misuse for "computer savvy" employees. Contrary to expectations, the results also provide evidence that security awareness programs are more effective in deterring IS misuse for computer savvy employees. A possible explanation for this unexpected finding is that individuals who feel more comfortable using computers can better comprehend the messages conveyed in a security awareness program and therefore become more convinced of the organization's seriousness toward IT security. This explanation is consistent with Munro and Cohen's (2004) findings that IS codes of ethics are more effective in deterring unethical computing behaviors when they are better understood. Considered together, the above findings suggest that computer savvy employees are less impacted by security policies, computer monitoring, and preventative security software. However, efforts to inform and educate computer savvy employees on the consequences of IS misuse do have a deterrent effect.

There is no evidence that risk propensity moderates the impact of security countermeasures on punishment perceptions. A subsequent analysis also showed that risk propensity did not moderate the impact of punishment perceptions on IS misuse intention. Thus, the results suggest that the deterrent effects of security countermeasures are the same regardless of individuals' risk propensities. These findings are inconsistent with hypothesized predictions and with prior deterrence research (e.g., Rindfleisch and Crockett). A speculative explanation is that risk propensity in the context of IT is distinct from the more general characteristic of risk propensity. This reasoning is consistent with Slovic's (1972) findings that risk propensity can vary across dissimilar decision contexts. If individuals' risk attitudes toward IT-related behaviors are unique, then the more general risk propensity measure used in this study would have lacked explanatory power. On the other hand, the risk propensity measure included a work-related dimension, which would seemingly account for the use of computers in the workplace. Only future research can assess whether the non-significance of risk propensity is unique to this study, or if indeed risk propensity does not impact the effectiveness of security countermeasures. It should be pointed out that Mendes (2004) recently questioned the usefulness of incorporating risk attitudes into general deterrence theory, suggesting that variations in risk attitudes largely cancel each other out from a policy perspective. The results of this study support this view.

Finally, there is some evidence that virtual status impacts the effectiveness of security countermeasures. Virtual status negatively influenced the impact of security policies on punishment perceptions, suggesting that employees who spend more time working outside the office are less deterred by policies and guidelines regarding appropriate use of IS resources. Inconsistent with expectations, virtual status also positively influenced the impact of security awareness programs on punishment perceptions. Thus, it appears that security awareness programs have a greater deterrent effect on workers that spend more time working outside the office. A possible explanation for this unexpected finding is that efforts to inform users of the consequences of illegitimate use of information systems, and ultimately the company's seriousness about IS security, are more convincing to virtual workers due to their increased physical separation from company resources. Such efforts may have less incremental deterrent effect, over and above that of security policies, for non-virtual workers (i.e., those who perform all of their work within the office) to whom the company's IS security resources are more visible. Taken together, the above findings suggest that security policies are less effective in deterring virtual workers, but this shortfall can be offset by increased security awareness efforts. In addition, the non-significance of the other virtual status moderating effects suggests that monitoring practices and preventative security software are just as effective in deterring virtual workers as they are for non-virtual workers.

In retrospect, the failure to find consistent evidence of the hypothesized moderating effects is not entirely surprising considering the history of detecting moderating influences in IS research. Chin, Marcolin, and Newsted (2003) performed an extensive analysis of 8,110 published IS studies over a fifteen-year period (1982-1995), and reviewed seventy-four articles that employed moderator variables. They found that of the 290 interaction effects tested, only sixty-six were significant at the 0.05 level or better. Considering that the analysis included only top-level IS journals (e.g., MIS Quarterly,

Information Systems Research, Journal of Management Information Systems) which generally only publish studies with significant results, it is likely that the findings are overestimates of the true level of interaction effects discovered by IS researchers. Thus, the interaction effects detected in the current study are significant findings and offer avenues for future research.

CONTRIBUTIONS TO RESEARCH

This study contributes to existing research that has successfully applied GDT to the IS security domain. Perceived certainty and severity of sanctions were both shown to predict IS misuse intention, after accounting for the effects of moral commitment and social desirability bias. The results are consistent with prior IS deterrence studies in that perceived severity of sanctions had a greater influence on IS misuse than perceived certainty of sanctions. The research also extends the framework of GDT by (1) modeling security countermeasures as antecedents to perceived certainty and severity of sanctions, and (2) introducing computer self-efficacy, risk propensity, and virtual status as moderators between security countermeasures and perceived certainty and severity of sanctions. The antecedent and moderator variables were chosen based on theoretical considerations and past research. By integrating the security countermeasure, moderator, and GDT constructs into a single theoretical model, and subsequently providing an empirical test of the proposed model, this study offers significant advances over previous work.

First, this is the only known study that assessed the impact of security countermeasures on GDT's two main constructs – perceived certainty and severity of sanctions – and therefore provides an explicit test of GDT based on its original specification (e.g., Gibbs 1975). The results challenge the assumption of previous IS deterrence studies that objective measures of security countermeasures can be used as surrogates for perceived certainty and severity of sanctions. Preventative security software, for example, had a weak impact on sanction perceptions. This suggests that perceptions of security countermeasures can differ from their objective characteristics. The implication for research is that future studies that employ GDT to assess the impact of security countermeasures on IS misuse should account for sanction perceptions. Failure to do so may produce results that are conceptually flawed.

This research also represents one of the few attempts to assess the impact of a combination of procedural and technical security countermeasures within a single study. The results help sift out and provide insights into the relative effects of each of the countermeasures. Further, by including perceived certainty and severity of sanctions as mediator variables in the theoretical model, this research expands our understanding of the underlying process through which security countermeasures impact IS misuse. For example, the results suggest that security policies deter IS misuse primarily by increasing users' perceptions of punishment severity, while computer monitoring deters IS misuse by increasing users' perceptions of getting caught.

By assessing the moderating influences of computer self-efficacy, risk propensity, and virtual status on the effectiveness of security countermeasures, this study provides one of the few tests of the differential deterrence hypothesis in the IS literature. Prior IS deterrence studies have largely assumed that the impact of security countermeasures is uniform for all individuals. However, the differential deterrence hypothesis suggests that individual and situational factors may moderate the impact of security countermeasures. Failure to account for such factors may explain the inconsistent findings of prior IS deterrence studies. IS researchers have called for further research to better understand what factors influence the effectiveness of IS security countermeasures (Banerjee, Cronan, and Jones 1998; Gattiker and Kelley 1999; Harrington 1996; Ives, Walsh, and Schneider 2004). This study is an initial attempt to address this issue. The results provide evidence that computer self-efficacy and virtual status impact the effectiveness of security countermeasures. However, additional research is needed to further validate these findings.

From the perspective of theoretical advancement, this study contributes to a better understanding of the factors that predict IS misuse. The proposed model explains 39 percent of the variance in IS misuse intention, which is higher than that obtained in several previous IS misuse studies (Galletta and Polak 2003; Gopal and Sanders 1997; Lee, Lee, and Yoo 2004; Loch and Conger 1996; Munro and Cohen 2004; Straub 1990). Further, the antecedent variables (i.e., security countermeasures) explain a substantial amount of variance in both perceived certainty and severity of sanctions (33 percent and 26 percent, respectively).

This study also makes methodological contributions. The development and validation of measures of security policies, security awareness program, monitoring practices, and preventative security software are an important step in the development of behavioral IS security research. As previously mentioned, the few existing scales that measure various security countermeasures are either operationalized at the organizational level or are written from the perspective of IS security administrators. The security countermeasures scales developed in this study will permit future researchers to use common definitions and assumptions for assessing existence of security countermeasures from the user perspective. Researchers are encouraged to refine the measurement scales developed here, especially since some of the scales had weak item loadings and items that cross loaded. Researchers are also encouraged to assess the measurement properties of these scales over a variety of studies in similar and different contexts to further test their validity.

This study also provides support for the usefulness of scenarios in IS security research. Results showed that social desirability bias was not significantly associated with IS misuse intention, which suggests that respondents felt comfortable with the IS misuse scenarios and did not consciously bias their answers in the direction of social approval. Considering that industry professionals are very reluctant to discuss IS security-related issues with researchers, and that it is nearly impossible to gain access to actual data on security breaches without having a major supporter (Kotulic and Clark 2004), scenarios offer a useful methodological approach for studying IS security in organizations.

Finally, the combined sample consisting of both part-time MBA students and industry participants presented a unique opportunity to compare and contrast findings across the two sample groups. Researchers have criticized the use of MBA samples in organizational research due to concerns about generalizability (e.g., Igbaria, Guimaraes, and Davis 1995; Randall and Gibson 1990). However, generalizability issues were not apparent in this study. Results of the instrument validation and hypotheses tests were largely consistent across the MBA and industry groups. Thus, it appears that the MBA sample was representative of the general population of computer users within organizations. This is a powerful finding because it lends support for the use of part-time MBA students in IS research, and organizational research in general. MBA student samples can be obtained relatively easy in most business schools. In contrast, obtaining industry participants may require major personal, financial, and professional commitments.

IMPLICATIONS FOR PRACTICE

This research has several implications for practice. Overall, the results provide evidence that security policies, security awareness programs, computer monitoring, and preventative security software are each effective in deterring IS misuse. As such, each of these countermeasures should be included as part of the organization's security management program. These findings are significant because prior research found that managers were not convinced that security efforts could deter IS misuse (Hoffer and Straub 1989; Straub and Welke 1998). Instead, they considered IS security a preventative function – procedures designed to restrict abusive activities. The results of this study suggest, to the contrary, that organizations can help deter IS misuse by doing the following: (1) developing policy statements and guidelines for appropriate use of IS resources, (2) informing and educating users on what constitutes legitimate use of IS resources and what are the consequences of illegitimate use, (3) conducting ongoing surveillance of employees' computing activities and carrying out periodic audits on the use of IS assets, and (4) implementing preventative security technologies that control access to IS resources. These countermeasures should be considered as a group in order to be effective. Security awareness programs, for example, build upon a clear set of security policies and procedures that have been put in place; preventative security software, at least in the form of basic access control technologies, is not particularly effective in deterring IS misuse on its own. Employees must also be made aware of security countermeasures for them to be effective. Security policies can be introduced during employee orientation sessions and employees should be required to sign an acknowledgement indicating that they have read and understand the policy. The security policy should also be prominently displayed on the company website. In terms of monitoring practices, the security policy should specifically state that the organization reserves the right to monitor employee computing activities. Other techniques for increasing awareness of monitoring practices include reminders on screen savers, announcements of upcoming audits on the use of IS assets, and footer messages on company e-mails.

In addition, while this study considered the existence of security policies and security awareness programs, the results have implications for their content. Security policies should include language that makes it clear to employees that all behavior violating the acceptable use guidelines might lead to stern penalties up to and including termination. Security awareness programs should reinforce this message through a well defined process of education, reminders, and refresher courses (von Solms and von Solms 2004). Periodic security briefings that emphasize the penalties that can accrue when policy is violated can be used as awareness tactics. The strength of moral commitment in the research model also points to the need to incorporate an ethical component within security policies and security awareness programs. IS researchers have advocated ethics training as an effective means of influencing employee moral development – the goal being a reduction in computer abuse (Banerjee, Cronan and Jones 1998; Harrington 1996; Leonard, Cronan, and Kreie 2004). Hence, security awareness programs could include a module on IT ethical issues and instructions on how individuals are expected to behave when faced with ethical dilemmas. The security policy and security awareness program should also stress the negative effects of IS misuse on fellow workers, the organization, and society as a whole.

This study also provides insights into the impacts of virtual status, computer self-efficacy, and risk propensity on the effectiveness of security countermeasures. First, the results suggest that organizations can use the same monitoring techniques and preventative security software for virtual workers as they do for non-virtual workers. However, considering the dispersed nature of virtual work, organizations may consider more frequent reminders informing virtual workers that their computing activities are still being monitored while working outside the office. Results also showed that security policies were less effective in deterring IS misuse for virtual workers, while security awareness programs were more effective for these employees. In practical terms, this suggests that organizations can offset the lesser deterrent effect that security policies have on virtual workers through increased security awareness education and training. One recommendation is to make attending a security awareness training session a prerequisite for approval to telecommute or work from any other dispersed location. Security policies should also explicitly state that guidelines for appropriate use of IS resources, and subsequent penalties that can accrue for inappropriate usage, are applicable to work conducted from dispersed locations. The findings with respect to computer self-efficacy suggest that organizations need to focus their deterrent efforts on security awareness education and training for computer savvy employees. All internal computer training should include a security module relevant to the particular training. In addition, the organization may want to consider more sophisticated security awareness training for employees with more computer experience. Finally, the non-significance of risk propensity is a positive finding for managers since it suggests that security countermeasures deter IS misuse regardless of the risk propensity of the user. In terms of practice, this suggests that organizations should feel comfortable implementing the same security countermeasures across functional areas that have traditionally differed in their "risk cultures," such as accounting and marketing (Mills and Tsamenyi 2000).

The observed effects of security policies and security awareness program on IS misuse have implications for the allocation of IS security budgets. Straub and Welke (1998) found that managers were generally unaware of the benefits of acceptable use policies and security awareness programs and instead relied on a combination of technical preventatives (e.g., access controls) and remedial actions (e.g., fines, prosecution, suspensions) to combat IS misuse. Recent industry statistics are consistent with these findings, as 82 percent of organizations have reported using some sort of advanced access control technology while only 28 percent reported that they have security awareness programs in place (InformationWeek 2005). Moreover, research suggests that firms are shifting resources away from procedural security measures to security technologies (CIO Magazine 2006). The results of this study suggest that organizations should consider allocating a greater portion of their IS security budgets to the development of security policies and ongoing security education and training efforts.

This research also has potential implications for how IS security investments are "sold" to upper management. Management will often view the acquisition of IS security as one of several competing alternatives for capital investment (Baskerville 1991). Therefore, IS managers must produce evidence of the benefits of security countermeasures to justify their investment. The results of this study provide empirical evidence of the deterrent value of security countermeasures, and therefore can further substantiate certain IS security investments. Consider monitoring technologies and preventative security software as two examples. From a practical perspective, the primary purpose of computer monitoring is to *detect* unauthorized activity, while the primary purpose of preventative security software is to *prevent* unauthorized activity (Venter and Eloff 2003; Straub and Welke 1998). Thus, the apparent deterrent effect that is achieved by implementing these security countermeasures is over and above their core functionality. Considered in this light, the relatively weak deterrent effect that preventative security software had on IS misuse is still a significant finding for managers, because it was probably not even expected. Thus, IS managers should highlight the value of deterrence, in addition to core functionality, when proposing investments in monitoring technologies (e.g., keystroke monitoring tools) and preventative security software (e.g., smart cards, biometric controls) to upper management. Similarly, investments in security awareness programs can be promoted based on a combination of their deterrent value and their ability to advance "positive" security behaviors (e.g., selecting strong passwords, not sharing passwords, scanning unknown e-mail attachments for viruses). Determining the benefits of security awareness programs is particularly important because these programs have traditionally achieved low priority in comparison to other security areas such as risk assessment and intrusion detection (Schultz 2004). Hence, they usually need more justification during the budget planning process. A caveat in regards to the preceding discussion is that the deterrent value of security countermeasures is difficult, if not impossible, to quantify in monetary terms. Such intangible benefits often fare poorly in capital budget decisions where quantification is desirable. Nevertheless, IS managers should still point to the value of deterrence when attempting to gain upper management support for security investments.

Finally, this research has implications for the burgeoning cyber-insurance field. Cyber-insurers can include assessments of security policies, security awareness programs, monitoring practices, and preventative security software as part of their information security audits and offer premium reductions based on whether or not such countermeasures are sufficiently in place.

LIMITATIONS AND FUTURE RESEARCH

Like most empirical research, this study has limitations that should be taken into account. Several of these limitations point to important issues for further research. The main limitation is the single source for both dependent and independent variables, which could introduce common method bias. Although unlikely due to the sequence of questions in the research instrument, it could be that respondents were primed as to the purpose of the study. A test for common method variance across all responses revealed thirteen factors that explained 63 percent of variance in the dataset, with no single factor accounting for a majority of the variance. Hence, common method bias did not appear to be a substantial problem in this study. Nevertheless, the research would be strengthened by a longitudinal design with a lag (e.g., two weeks, one month, six months, etc.) between collection of the dependent and independent variables. Such designs can help overcome common method effects (Woszczynksi and Whitman 2004).

A related limitation is the absence of an actual measure of IS misuse. As is customary in scenario-based studies, self-reported behavioral intentions were measured instead of actual behaviors. There is a significant body of research in IS (Taylor and Todd 1995; Venkatesh and Morris 2000), organizational behavior (Morris and Venkatesh 2000; Venkatesh and Spier 1999), and psychology (see Sheppard, Hartwick, and Warsaw 1988 for a meta-analysis) supporting intention as a predictor of actual behavior. Moreover, respondents in the current study appeared to provide honest assessments of their IS misuse intentions, as evidenced by the non-significance of social desirability bias. However, there is no guarantee that individuals would behave as they have indicated. It is possible that their reactions to the scenarios may differ from on-the-job reactions. Future research should examine the findings of the current work in a context where IS misuse can be measured in order to add additional credibility to the model.

Third, there are some limitations related to measurement that should be noted. While the newly developed security countermeasure scales exhibited sufficient psychometric properties, additional work is certainly needed to further validate the scales. Some of the items had weak loadings or cross loaded, and therefore had to be eliminated. In addition, the correlations between the constructs were relatively high which causes some concerns about discriminant validity. Another measurement issue involves the moral commitment measure. The original eight-item moral commitment scale (which is a subset of Tooke and Ickes's (1988) adherence to morality scale) had poor convergent validity and therefore had to be replaced by a single-item composite scale. Although such single-item measures do not render the results of structural equation modeling invalid (Hair et al. 1998), they do weaken the measurement model and can pose theoretical difficulties. Hence, multi-item scales are preferred. Future research should further assess the validity of the eight-item moral commitment scale to determine whether its poor psychometric properties are idiosyncratic to this study or are common across IS research.

Fourth, the scenarios used in this research represent an over-simplified view of IS misuse in the workplace. Hence, it is possible that the IS misuse behaviors depicted are not indicative of actual misuse situations encountered within organizations. It does not appear, however, that this was the case in this research. Results of the pilot study and informal communication with MBA student participants indicated that respondents viewed the scenarios as realistic and had little difficulty placing themselves in the hypothetical position of the scenario characters.

Fifth, this study is limited to the measurement of IS misuse under the specific hypothetical scenarios chosen. While the scenarios covered a wide range of security issues, including privacy, accuracy, and property, as well as access and security issues, they do not include every type of IS misuse. Other scenarios may produce different results. Future research should test the explanatory power of the proposed model on a larger number of IS misuse behaviors.

Sixth, it is possible that the organizations in the industry sample are not representative of all organizations, and likewise, those who participated might not be representative of all users. Firms that decided to participate in the research may have been supportive of the research, or simply participated because of personal contact with the researcher. The same may be true for the respondents that filled out the online questionnaire. Replications with different samples are necessary for validation of the results reported here.

Seventh, not all possible significant variables were included in the research model, as evidenced by the fact that 61 percent of the variance in IS misuse intention was unexplained. Deterrence studies in criminology and sociology have shown that GDT can be expanded and improved through the inclusion of additional factors such as moral considerations, social stigma (e.g., embarrassment), and peer involvement (e.g. Bachman, Paternoster, and Ward 1992; Grasmick and Bursik 1990; Klepper and Nagin 1989; Nagin and Pogarsky 2001). A handful of studies have also integrated GDT constructs with other factors to predict IS misuse (Lee and Lee 2002; Lee, Lee, and Yoo 2004; Peace, Galletta, and Thong 2003; Skinner and Fream 1997). Future research should continue the trend toward theoretical integration in IS deterrence research by examining additional factors that predict IS misuse. Additional theoretical perspectives that could potentially improve the proposed model include social learning theory (Akers 1985), social bond theory (Hirschi 1969), Kolhberg's theory of moral development (Kohlberg 1983), and the theory of planned behavior (Ajzen 1991). Future studies should also assess the impact of additional security countermeasures (e.g., biometric controls) on IS misuse.

Finally, because this study is cross-sectional, the posited causal relationships (although firmly based on generally accepted theory) can only be inferred. A longitudinal research design is needed to validate the causal structure of the model.

In addition to those already mentioned, additional areas for future research remain. First, while there is evidence that security countermeasures deter various forms of IS misuse, it is not known whether this impact is sustained over time. Moreover, there is no research on the long term "side effects" associated with security countermeasures. Siponen (2000a) argued that the long term negative consequences associated with the use of security countermeasures may include loss of trust, productivity, and loyalty, increased dissatisfaction and stress, aggression, fear, and withdrawal behavior. Researchers have also discussed some of the negative long term effects of computer monitoring on workers (George 1996; Stanton and Weiss 2000). Future research should employ longitudinal designs to examine the impact of security countermeasures over extended periods, and also consider the impacts of security countermeasures beyond deterrence factors.

Future research can also continue testing the differential deterrence hypothesis by exploring additional individual and situational factors that impact the effectiveness of security countermeasures. The current study provides evidence that computer self-efficacy and virtual status influence the effectiveness of security countermeasures. However, additional validation of these findings is needed. A potentially fruitful area of research would be to examine the impact of security countermeasures on various organizational stakeholders such as vendors, clients, contractors, and third-party business partners. For example, are contract workers, who likely have a lower stake in the organization, less deterred by security countermeasures than other types of workers?

Another topic for future research is the effectiveness of specific versus general IS security countermeasures. Deterrence research has shown the precise effects of formal sanctions – one where a sanction or sanction threat is attached to particular offense – have no advantage over generalized sanctions (Silberman 1976; Tittle 1980). From an IS security perspective, this suggests that general security countermeasures (e.g., guidelines on appropriate use of IS resources) are just as effective as system-specific countermeasures (e.g., guidelines on appropriate use of e-mail) in deterring certain IS misuse behaviors. Future research should attempt to verify this prediction and examine whether general security countermeasures are just as effective as specific countermeasures in deterring certain IS misuse behaviors.

Future research could also compare the organizational (i.e., IS management) perceptions of security to those of the users. Finch, Furnell, and Dowland (2003) conducted a preliminary study of small businesses in the United Kingdom and found that users were unaware of the existence of several security countermeasures within their organizations. Hence, the IS departments were overvaluing their security efforts. This research could be expanded to include a more diverse sample of organizations within the U.S.

The results of this study confirmed that moral commitment has a strong influence on IS misuse intention. Hence, future research could examine various predictors of moral commitment as an additional approach for understanding IS misuse and ultimately managing IS misuse within the workplace. Potential factors that could be examined for their impact on moral commitment include trust in the organization, job satisfaction, organizational commitment, and perceived job benefits.   Finally, the current study focuses on the existence of security countermeasures without consideration of their characteristics.

Now that the significance of having security countermeasures in place has been established, future research should explore the salient characteristics that contribute to the effectiveness of security countermeasures. For example, future research could examine the specific content of security policies, how such policies are enforced, different security awareness techniques, levels of password protection, etc., and determine whether such characteristics impact the deterrent capabilities of the security countermeasures.

CONCLUSIONS

This research uses the framework of general deterrence theory to (1) investigate the impact of security policies, security awareness programs, monitoring practices, and preventative security software on IS misuse, and (2) examine the moderating influences of computer self-efficacy, risk propensity, and virtual status on the impact of these security countermeasures. Based on analyses of three different datasets (i.e., combined, MBA, and industry), strong support was found for the effectiveness of security policies, security awareness programs, and computer monitoring in deterring IS misuse. Preventative security software, at least in the form of basic access control technologies, appears only moderately effective in deterring IS misuse.

The results also suggest that risk propensity does not impact the effectiveness of security countermeasures, but computer self-efficacy and virtual status do. Specifically, security policies, computer monitoring, and preventative security software are less effective in deterring IS misuse for individuals with greater computer self-efficacy, while security awareness programs are more effective for these individuals. Security awareness programs also have a greater deterrent effect on virtual workers, but security policies are less effective for these individuals.

Overall, this study presents significant progress toward explaining the relationships between security countermeasures and IS misuse, while reaffirming the applicability of general deterrence theory to the IS security domain. The study also represents one of the few empirical tests of the differential deterrence hypothesis. The results shed light on the equivocal findings of prior IS deterrence studies, which largely assumed that the impact of security countermeasures is uniform across all persons.

From a practical perspective, the results have strong implications for IS security management programs. Specifically, the results suggest that a combined proactive and preventative approach to security can deter users from IS misuse: This includes the following:

- Develop policy statements and guidelines for appropriate use of IS resources.
- Inform and educate users on what constitutes legitimate use of IS resources and what are the consequences of illegitimate use.
- Alert users that all computing activities are logged and monitored and that any use of IS resources is subject to audit.
- Implement preventative security technologies that control access to IS resources.

Finally, the results suggest that a "one size fits all" approach to IS security may not be effective for managing IS misuse. Specifically, organizations may need to tailor their security management strategies to effectively deter IS misuse among computer savvy employees and those that spend a portion or all of their working days outside the office.

References

Ajzen, I. 1988. *Attitudes, personality, and behavior*. Chicago: Dorsey Press.

Ajzen, I. 1991. The theory of planned behavior. *Organizational Behavior and Human Decision Processes* 50 (2):179-211.

Ajzen, I., and M. Fishbein. 1969. The prediction of behavioral intentions in a choice situation. *Journal of Experimental Psychology* 5:400-416.

Akers, R. L. 1985. *Deviant behavior: A social learning approach*. Belmont, CA: Wadsworth.

Alavi, M., and I. R. Weiss. 1985. Managing the risks associated with end-user computing. *Journal of Management Information Systems* 2 (3):5-20.

Alexander, C. S., and H. J. Becker. 1978. The use of vignettes in survey research. *Public Opinion Quarterly* 42 (1):93-104.

Allen, B. 1968. Danger ahead! Safeguard your computer. *Harvard Business Review* 46 (6):97-101.

American Bar Association. 1984. *Report on computer crime*. Pamphlet prepared by the Task Force on Computer Crime, Section on Criminal Justice. Washington, D.C: American Bar Association.

Anderson, J. C., and D. W. Gerbing. 1988. Structural equation modeling in practice: A review and recommended two-step approach. *Psychological Bulletin* 103 (3):411-423.

Anderson, L. S. 1979. The deterrent effect of criminal sanctions: Reviewing the evidence. In *Structure, law, and review*, edited by P. J. Brentingham and J. M. Kress. Beverly Hills, CA: Sage Publications.

Anderson, R. 2001. Why information security is hard - an economic perspective. In *Proceedings of the Seventeenth Annual Computer Security Applications Conference*, December 10-14, New Orleans, LA.

Anthes, G. H. 1996. Hack attack: Cyberthieves siphon millions from U.S. Firms. *Computerworld* 30 (17):81.

Armstrong, C. P., and V. Sambamurthy. 1999. Information technology assimilation in firms: The influence of senior leadership and IT infrastructures. *Information Systems Research* 10 (4):304-327.

Axelsson, S. 2000. The base-rate fallacy and the difficulty of intrusion detection. *ACM Transactions on Information and System Security* 3 (3):186-205.

Aytes, K., and T. Connolly. 2004. Computer security and risky computing practices: A rational choice perspective. *Journal of Organizational and End User Computing* 16 (3):22-40.

Bachman, R., R. Paternoster, and S. Ward. 1992. The rationality of sexual offending: Testing a deterrence/rational choice conception of sexual assault. *Law and Society Review* 26 (2):343-372.

Bagchi, K., and G. Udo. 2003. An analysis of the growth of computer and internet security breaches. *Communications of the AIS* 12 (46):684-700.

Bagozzi, R. P., Y. Yi, and L. W. Phillips. 1991. Assessing construct validity in organizational research. *Administrative Science Quarterly* 36 (3):421-458.

Ball, L., and R. Harris. 1982. SMIS members: A membership analysis. *MIS Quarterly* 6 (1):19-38.

Banerjee, D., T. P. Cronan, and T. W. Jones. 1998. Modeling IT ethics: A study in situational ethics. *MIS Quarterly* 22 (1):31-60.

Barclay, D. C., C. Higgins, and R. Thompson. 1995. The partial least squares approach to causal modeling: Personal computer adoption and use as an illustration. *Technology Studies* 2 (2):285-308.

Barsky, R. B., T. F. Juster, M. S. Kimball, and M. D. Shapiro. 1997. Preference parameters and behavioral heterogeneity: An experimental approach in the health and retirement study. *Quarterly Journal of Economics* 112 (2):536-579.

Barter, C., and E. Renold. 1999. The use of vignettes in qualitative research. *Social Research Update* 25.

Baskerville, R. 1988. *Designing information systems security*. Chichester, U.K.: John Wiley & Sons.

Baskerville, R. 1991. Risk analysis: An interpretive feasibility tool in justifying information systems security. *European Journal of Information Systems* 1 (2):121-130.

Baskerville, R. 1993. Information systems security design methods: Implications for information systems development. *ACM Computing Surveys* 25 (4):375-414.

Becker, G. S. 1968. Crime and punishment: An economic approach. *Journal of Political Economy* 78:169-217.

Benson, D. H. 1983. A field study of end user computing: Findings and issues. *MIS Quarterly* 7 (4):35-45.

Berghel, H. 2001. The code red worm. *Communications of the ACM* 44 (12):15-19.

Berinato, S. 2005. The global state of information security. *CIO Magazine*, September 15.

Birch, D. G. W., and N. A. McEvoy. 1992. Risk analysis for information systems. *Journal of Information Technology* 7 (1):44-53.

Blumstein, A., J. Cohen, and D. S. Nagin. 1978. *Deterrence and incapacitation: Estimating the effects of criminal sanctions on crime rates*. Edited by A. Blumstein, J. Cohen and D. S. Nagin. Washington, D.C.: National Academy of Sciences.

Bologna, G. J., and P. Shaw. 2000. *Avoiding cyberfraud in small businesses*. New York: John Wiley & Sons.

Boockholdt, J. L. 1989. Implementing security and integrity in micro-mainframe networks. *MIS Quarterly* 13 (2):135-144.

Bostrom, R. P., L. Olfman, and M. K. Sein. 1988. End-user computing: A research framework for investigating the training/learning process. In *Human factors in management information systems*, edited by J. M. Carey. Norwood, NJ: ABLEX.

Boudreau, M. C., D. Gefen, and D. W. Straub. 2001. Validation in information systems research: A state-of-the-art assessment. *MIS Quarterly* 25 (1):1-16.

Brancheau, J. C., and J. C. Wetherbe. 1987. Key issues in information systems management. *MIS Quarterly* 11 (1):23-36.

Campbell, D. T., and J. C. Stanley. 1963. Experimental and quasi-experimental designs for research on teaching. In *Handbook of research on teaching*, edited by N. L. Gage. Chicago: Rand McNally.

Campbell, K., L. A. Gordon, M. P. Loeb, and L. Zhou. 2003. The economic cost of publicly announced information security breaches: Empirical evidence from the stock market. *Journal of Computer Security* 11 (3):431-448.

Carifio, J., and M. Lanza. 1992. The need to use controlled vignettes in social science research. *Work* 2:28-38.

Cavusoglu, H., H. Cavusoglu, and S. Raghunathan. 2004. Economics of IT security management: Four improvements to current security practices. *Communications of the AIS* 14 (3):65-75.

Cavusoglu, H., B. Mishra, and S. Raghunathan. 2004. A model for evaluating IT security investments. *Communications of the ACM* 47 (7):87-92.

Cavusoglu, H., B. Mishra, and S. Raghunathan. 2004a. The effect of internet security breach announcements on shareholder wealth: Capital market reactions for breached firms and internet security developers. *International Journal of Electronic Commerce* 8 (4).

Cavusoglu, H., B. Mishra, and S. Raghunathan. 2005. The value of intrusion detection systems in information technology security architecture. *Information Systems Research* 16 (1): 28-46.

Chau, P. Y. K. 2001. Influence of computer attitude and self-efficacy on it usage behavior. *Journal of End User Computing* 13 (1):26-33.

Chen, T. M. 2003. Trends in viruses and worms. *The Internet Protocol Journal* 6 (3):23-33.

Chin, W. 1998. The partial least squares approach to structural equation modeling. In *Modern methods for business research*, edited by G. A. Marcoulides. Mahwah, NJ: Lawrence Erlbaum Associates.

Chin, W. 2000. *Frequently asked questions – partial least squares & pls-graph*: [homepage], http://disc-nt.cba.uh.edu/chin/plsfaq.htm.

Chin, W., B. L. Marcolin, and P. R. Newsted. 2003. A partial least squares latent variable modeling approach for measuring interaction effects: Results from a monte carlo simulation study and an electronic-mail emotion/adoption study. *Information Systems Research* 14 (2):189-217.

Christensen, A., and M. M. Eining. 1994. Instructional case: Software piracy - who does it impact? *Issues in Accounting Education* 9 (1):151-159.

Churchill, G. A. 1979. A paradigm for developing better measures of marketing constructs. *Journal of Marketing Research* 16 (1):64-73.

CIO Magazine. 2006. The global state of information security. *CIO Magazine*, September 16.

Cohen, F. 1984. Computer viruses: Theory and experiments. In *Computer security: A global challenge*, edited by J. H. Finch and E. G. Dougall. Elsevier: North-Holland.

Cole, C. A. 1989. Deterrence and consumer fraud. *Journal of Retailing* 65 (1):107-120.

Compeau, D. R., and C. A. Higgins. 1995. Computer self-efficacy: Development of a measure and initial test. *MIS Quarterly* 19 (2):189-211.

Comrey, A. L. 1973. *A first course in factor analysis*. New York, NY: Academic Press.

CompTIA Research. 2002. *Committing to security: A CompTIA analysis of IT security and the workforce*. Oakbrook Terrace, IL: CompTIA Research.

Conway, R. W., W. L. Maxwell, and H. L. Morgan. 1972. On the implementation of security measures in information systems. *Communications of the ACM* 15 (4):211-220.

Cook, P. J. 1982. Research in criminal deterrence: Laying the groundwork for the second decade. In *Crime and justice: An annual review of research, vol. 2*, edited by N. Morris and M. Tonry. Chicago: The University of Chicago Press.

Coursen, S. 1997. The financial impact of viruses. *Information Systems Security* 6 (1):74-70.

Cronin, D. J. 1986. *Microcomputer data security: Issues and strategies for business*. New York: Prentice-Hall.

Cronan, T.P., L.N.K. Leonard, and J. Kreie. 2005. An empirical validation of perceived importance and behavior intention in IT ethics. *Journal of Business Ethics* 56 (231-238).

Cronan, T.P., and D. Douglas. 2006. Toward a comprehensive ethical behavior model for information technology. *Journal of Organizational and End User Computing* 18 (1): i-x.

Crowne, D. P., and D. Marlowe. 1960. A new scale of social desirability independent of psychopathology. *Journal of Consulting Psychology* 24 (349-354).

CSO Magazine. 2006. *2006 E-Crime watch survey*.

D'Arcy, J., and A. Hovav. 2007. Towards a best fit between organizational security countermeasures and information systems misuse behaviors. *Journal of Information System Security* 3 (2): 1-31.

Dahlback, O. 1990. Personality and risk-taking. *Personality and Individual Differences* 11 (12):1235-1242.

Das, T. K., and B.S. Teng. 2001. Strategic risk behaviour and its temporalities: Between risk propensity and decision context. *Journal of Management Studies* 38 (4):515-534.

Deloitte and Touche. 2005. *2005 Global security survey*. London, U.K: Deloitte Global Financial Services Industry Group.

Denning, D. E., and D. K. Branstad. 1996. A taxonomy for key escrow encryption systems. *Communications of the ACM* 39 (3):32-40.

Denning, P. J., D. B. Parker, S. H. Nycum, and W. H. Ware. 1984. Computers, crime and privacy - a national dilemma, congressional testimony from the industry. *Communications of the ACM* 27 (4):312-321.

Dhillon, G. 1999. Managing and controlling computer misuse. *Information Management & Computer Security* 7 (4):171-175.

Dhillon, G. 2001. *Information security management: Global challenges in the new millennium*. Hershey, PA: Idea Group Publishing.

Dhillon, G., and J. Backhouse. 2001. Current directions in IS security research: Towards socio-organizational perspectives. *Information Systems Journal* 11 (2):127-153.

Dinnie, G. 1999. The second annual global information security survey. *Information Management & Computer Security* 7 (3):112-120.

Doherty, N., and H. Fulford. 2005. Do information security policies reduce the incidence of security breaches: An exploratory analysis. *Information Resources Management Journal* 18 (4):21-39.

Dulebohn, J. H. 2002. An investigation of the determinants of investment risk behavior in employer-sponsored retirement plans. *Journal of Management* 28 (1):3-26.

Dutta, A., and R. Roy. 2003. The dynamics of organizational information security. In *Proceedings of the Twenty-Fourth International Conference on Information Systems*, December 14-17, Seattle, WA.

Eining, M. M., and A. L. Christensen. 1991. A psycho-social model of software piracy: The development and test of a model. In *Ethical issues in information systems*, edited by R. Dejoie, G. Fowler and D. Paradice. Boston: Boyd & Fraser.

Eining, M. M., and G. M. Lee. 1997. Information ethics: An exploratory study from an international perspective. *Journal of Information Systems* 11 (1):1-17.

Ekenberg, L., S. Oberoi, and I. Orci. 1995. A cost model for managing information security hazards. *Computers & Security* 14:707-717.

El-Murad, J., and D. C. West. 2003. Risk and creativity in advertising. *Journal of Marketing Management* 19 (5/6):667-673.

Ernst and Young. 2004. *Global Information Security Survey 2004*.

Falk, R. F., and N. B. Miller. 1992. *A primer for soft modeling*. Akron, OH: University of Akron Press.

Ettredge, M. L., and V. J. Richardson. 2003. Information transfer among internet firms: The case of hacker attacks. *Journal of Information Systems* 17 (2):71-82.

Finch, J. 1987. The vignette technique in survey research. *Sociology* 21 (1):105-114.

Finch, J. H., S. M. Furnell, and P. S. Dowland. 2003. Assessing IT security culture: System administrator and end-user. In *Proceedings of the ISOneWorld Conference 2003*, April 23-25, Las Vegas, NV.

Fischhoff, B., S. Lichtenstein, P. Slovic, S. L. Derby, and R. L. Keeney. 1981. *Acceptable risk*. Cambridge, UK: Cambridge University Press.

Fisher, R. 1984. *Information systems security*. Englewood Cliffs, CA: Prentice Hall.

Fisher, R. J. 1993. Social desirability bias and the validity of indirect questioning. *Journal of Consumer Research* 20 (September):303-315.

Fisher, R. J., and G. J. Tellis. 1998. Removing social desirability bias with indirect questioning: Is the cure worse than the disease? *Advances in Consumer Research* 25 (1):563-567.

Foltz, C. B. 2000. The impact of deterrent countermeasures upon individual intent to commit misuse: A behavioral approach. PhD diss., University of Arkansas.

Foltz, C. B., T. P. Cronan, and T. W. Jones. 2002. Human behavior as a factor in the control of information systems misuse and computer crime. In *Proceedings of the Thirty-Third Annual Meeting of the Decision Sciences Institute*, November 23-26, San Diego, CA.

Fornell, C., and D. F. Larcker. 1981. Evaluating structural equation models with unobservable variables and measurement error. *Journal of Marketing Research* 18 (1):39-50.

Freeman, E. 2003. Biometrics, evidence, and personal privacy. *Information Systems Security* 12 (3):4-8.

Frincke, D. 2000. Balancing cooperation and risk in intrusion detection. *ACM Transactions on Information and System Security* 3 (1):1-29.

Frolick, M. N. 2003. A new webmaster's guide to firewalls and security. *Information Systems Management* 20 (1):29-35.

Furnell, S. M. 2002. *Cybercrime: Vandalizing the information society*. London: Addison-Wesley.

Furnell, S. M., M. Gennatou, and P. S. Dowland. 2002. A prototype tool for information security awareness and training. *Logistics Information Management* 15 (5/6):352-357.

Garg, A., J. Curtis, and H. Halper. 2003. Quantifying the financial impact of IT security breaches. *Information Management & Computer Security* 11 (2):74-83.

Galletta, D. F., and P. Polak. 2003. An empirical investigation of antecedents of internet abuse in the workplace. In *Proceedings of the Second Annual Workshop on HCI Research in MIS*, December 12-13, Seattle, WA.

Gattiker, U. E., and H. Kelley. 1999. Morality and computers: Attitudes and differences in moral judgments. *Information Systems Research* 10 (3):233-254.

Gefen, D. 2003. Unidimensional validity: An explanation and example. *Communications of the AIS* 12 (2):23-47.

Gefen, D., D. W. Straub, and M. C. Boudreau. 2000. Structural equation modeling techniques and regression: Guidelines for research practice. *Communications of the AIS* 7 (7):1-78.

George, J. F. 1996. Computer-based monitoring: Common perceptions and empirical results. *MIS Quarterly* 20 (4):459-480.

Giampaolo, B. 2003. Inductive verification of smart card protocols. *Journal of Computer Security* 11 (1):87-132.

Gibbs, J. P. 1975. *Crime, punishment, and deterrence.* New York: Elsevier.

Glover, S., S. Liddle, and D. Prawitt. 2001. *Electronic commerce: Security, risk management, and control.* Upper Saddle River, NJ: Prentice Hall.

Gomez-Mejia, L. R., and D. B. Balkin. 1989. Effective of individual and aggregate compensation strategies. *Industrial Relations* 28 (3):431-445.

Gopal, R. D., and G. L. Sanders. 1997. Preventative and deterrent controls for software piracy. *Journal of Management Information Systems* 13 (4):29-47.

Gordon, L. A., and M. P. Loeb. 2002. The economics of information security investment. *ACM Transactions on Information and System Security* 5 (4):438-457.

Gordon, L. A., M. P. Loeb, W. Lucyshyn, and R. Richardson. 2006. *2006 CSI/FBI Computer crime and security survey.* San Francisco, CA: Computer Security Institute.

Gordon, L. A., M. P. Loeb, and T. Sohail. 2003. A framework for using insurance for cyber-risk management. *Communications of the ACM* 46 (3):81-85.

Gordon, M. E., L. A. Slade, and N. Schmitt. 1986. The "science of sophomore" revisited: From conjecture to empiricism. *Academy of Management Review* 11 (1):191-207.

Grasmick, H. G., and G. J. Bryjak. 1980. The deterrent effect of perceived severity of punishment. *Social Forces* 59 (2):471-491.

Grasmick, H. G., and R. Bursik. 1990. Conscience, significant others, and rational choice: Extending the deterrence model. *Law and Society Review* 24 (3):837-861.

Grasmick, H. G., D. Jacobs, and C. B. McCollom. 1983. Social class and social control: An application of deterrence theory. *Social Forces* 62 (2):359-374.

Gupta, A., Y. A. Tung, and J. R. Marsden. 2004. Digital signature: Use and modification to achieve success in next generational e-business processes. *Information & Management* 41 (5):561-575.

Gupta, A. K., and V. Govindarajan. 1984. Business unit strategy, managerial characteristics, and business unit effectiveness at strategy implementation. *Academy of Management Journal* 27 (1):25-41.

Hair, J. F., R. E. Anderson, R. L. Tatham, and W. C. Black. 1998. *Multivariate data analysis.* Englewood Cliffs, NJ: Prentice Hall.

Hair, J. F., B. Babin, A. M. Money, and P. Samouel. 2003. *Essentials of business research methods.* Hoboken, NJ: John Wiley & Sons.

Hansche, S. 2001. Designing a security awareness program: Part 1. *Information Systems Security* 9 (6):14-22.

Harrington, S. J. 1996. The effect of codes of ethics and personal denial of responsibility on computer abuse judgments and intentions. *MIS Quarterly* 20 (3):257-278.

Hartog, C., and M. Herbert. 1986. 1985 opinion survey of MIS key issues. *MIS Quarterly* 10 (4):351-371.

Hays, R. D., T. Hayashi, and A. L. Stewart. 1989. A five-item measure of socially desirable response set. *Educational and Psychological Measurement* 49:629-637.

Heath, C., and A. Tversky. 1991. Preference and belief: Ambiguity and competence in choice under uncertainty. *Journal of Risk and Uncertainty* 4:5-28.

Heck, R. H. 1998. Factor analysis: Exploratory and confirmatory approaches. In *Modern methods for business research*, edited by G. A. Marcoulides. Mahwah, NJ: Lawrence Erlbaum Associates.

Hill, L. B., and M. Pemberton. 1995. Information security: An overview and resource guide for information managers. *Records Management Quarterly* 29 (1):14-24.

Hinde, S. 2000. Love conquers all? *Computers & Security* 19 (5):409-420.

Hirschi, T. 1969. *Causes of delinquency*. Berkeley, CA: University of California Press.

Hoffer, J. A., and D. W. Straub. 1989. The 9 to 5 underground: Are you policing computer crimes? *Sloan Management Review* 30 (4):35-43.

Hollinger, R. C. 1993. Crime by computer: Correlates of software piracy and unauthorized account access. *Security Journal* 4 (1):2-12.

Hollinger, R. C., and J. P. Clark. 1983. Deterrence in the workplace: Perceived certainty, perceived severity, and employee theft. *Social Forces* 62 (2):398-418.

Hovav, A., and J. D'Arcy. 2003. The impact of denial-of-service attack announcements on the market value of firms. *Risk Management and Insurance Review* 6 (2):97-121.

Hovav, A., and J. D'Arcy. 2004. The impact of virus attack announcements on the market value of firms. *Information Systems Security* 13 (3):32-40.

Hovav, A., and J. D'Arcy. 2005. Capital market reaction to defective IT product: The case of computer viruses. *Computers & Security* 24 (5):409-424.

Igbaria, M., and T. Guimaraes. 1999. Exploring differences in employee turnover intentions and its determinants among telecommuters and non-telecommuters. *Journal of Management Information Systems* 16 (1):147-164.

Igbaria, M., T. Guimaraes, and G. B. Davis. 1995. Testing the determinants of microcomputer usage via a structural equation model. *Journal of Management Information Systems* 11 (4):87-114.

Im, G.P., and R. Baskerville. 2005. A longitudinal study of information system threat categories: The enduring problem of human error. *The DATA BASE for Advances in Information Systems* 36 (4): 68-79.

InformationWeek. 2005. *U.S. information security research report 2005.* United Business Media.

Irakleous, I., S. M. Furnell, P. S. Dowland, and M. Papadaki. 2002. An experimental comparison of secret-based user authentication technologies. *Information Management & Computer Security* 10 (3):100-108.

Ives, B., K. R. Walsh, and H. Schneider. 2004. The domino effect of password reuse. *Communications of the ACM* 47 (4):75-78.

Jain, A. K., and H. Lin. 2000. Biometric identification. *Communications of the ACM* 43 (2):90-98.

Jain, A. K., and A. Ross. 2004. Mulitbiometric systems. *Communications of the ACM* 47 (1):34-40.

Jensen, B. 2003. *The Importance of Security Awareness Training.* Bethesda, MD: SANS Institute.

Johnston, J., J. H. P. Eloff, and L. Labuschagne. 2003. Security and human computer interfaces. *Computers & Security* 22 (8):675-684.

Kamara, S., S. Fahmy, E. E. Schultz, F. Kerschbaum, and M. Frantzen. 2003. Analysis of vulnerabilities in internet firewalls. *Computers & Security* 22 (3):214-232.

Kankanhalli, A., H.H. Teo, B. C. Y. Tan, and K.K. Wei. 2003. An integrative study of information systems security effectiveness. *International Journal of Information Management* 23 (2):139-154.

Keil, M., B. C. Y. Tan, K.K. Wei, T. Saarinen, V. Tuunainen, and A. Wassenaar. 2000. A cross-cultural study on escalation of commitment in software projects. *MIS Quarterly* 24 (2):299-325.

Kerlinger, F. N. 1973. *Foundations of behavioral research, second edition.* New York: Holt, Rinehart & Winston.

Kerlinger, F. N. 1986. *Foundations of behavioral research, third edition.* New York: Holt, Rinehart & Winston.

Kiesler, S., J. Siegel, and T. W. McGuire. 1984. Social psychological aspects of computer-mediated communication. *American Psychologist* 39 (10):1123-1134.

Klepper, S., and D. S. Nagin. 1989. The deterrent effect of perceived certainty and severity of punishment revisited. *Criminology* 27 (4):721-746.

Kohlberg, L. 1983. *Moral stages: A current formulation and response to critics*. Basil, U.K.: Karger.

Kotulic, A. G., and J. G. Clark. 2004. Why there aren't more information security research studies. *Information & Management* 41 (5):597-607.

Kreie, J., and T. P. Cronan. 1998. How men and women view ethics. *Communications of the ACM* 41 (9):70-76.

Kreie, J., and T. P. Cronan. 2000. Making ethical decisions. *Communications of the ACM* 43 (12):66-71.

Kruegar, N. J., and P. R. Dickson. 1994. How believing in ourselves increases risk taking: Perceived self-efficacy and opportunity recognition. *Decision Sciences* 25 (3):385-400.

Landwehr, C. E. 2001. Computer security. *International Journal of Information Security* 1 (1):3-13.

Lee, C.L. 1995. A study of financial institutions' information security: Factors that influence employees' willingness to adhere to information security procedures. PhD diss., Golden Gate University.

Lee, J., and Y. Lee. 2002. A holistic model of computer abuse within organizations. *Information Management & Computer Security* 10 (2):57-63.

Lee, S. M., S.G. Lee, and S. Yoo. 2004. An integrative model of computer abuse based on social control and general deterrence theories. *Information & Management* 41 (6):707-718.

Leonard, L. N. K., and T. P. Cronan. 2001. Illegal, inappropriate, and unethical behavior in an information technology context: A study to explain influences. *Journal of the AIS* 1 (12): 1-31.

Leonard, L. N. K., T. P. Cronan, and J. Kreie. 2004. What influences IT ethical behavior intentions - planned behavior, reasoned action, perceived importance, individual characteristics? *Information & Management* 42 (1):143-158.

Lewis, W., R. Agarwal, and V. Sambamurthy. 2003. Sources of influence on beliefs about information technology use: An empirical study of knowledge workers. *MIS Quarterly* 27 (4):657-678.

Liao, L., and R. Vemuri. 2002. Use of k-nearest neighbor classify for intrusion detection. *Computers & Security* 21 (5):439-448.

Loch, K. D., H. H. Carr, and M. E. Warkentin. 1992. Threats to information systems: Today's reality, yesterday's understanding. *MIS Quarterly* 16 (2):173-186.

Loch, K. D., and S. Conger. 1996. Evaluating ethical decision making and computer use. *Communications of the ACM* 39 (7):74-83.

Lou, D., and J. Liu. 2002. Stenographic method for secure communications. *Computers & Security* 21 (5):449-460.

Luftman, J., R. Kempaiah, and E. Nash. 2006. Key issues for IT executives 2005. *MIS Quarterly Executive* 5 (2):27-44.

MacCrimmon, K. R., and D. A. Wehrung. 1990. Characteristics of risk taking executives. *Management Science* 36 (4):422-435.

Magklaras, G. B., and S. M. Furnell. 2002. Insider threat prediction tool: Evaluating the probability of IT misuse. *Computers & Security* 21 (1):62-73.

Magklaras, G. B., and S. M. Furnell. 2005. A preliminary model of end user sophistication for insider threat prediction in IT systems. *Computers & Security* 24 (5):371-380.

Mann, R. E., R. G. Smart, G. Stoduto, E. M. Adlaf, E. Vingilis, D. Beirness, R. Lamble, and M. Ashbridge. 2003. The effects of drinking-driving laws: A test of the differential deterrence hypothesis. *Addiction* 98 (11):1531-1536.

Mann, S., R. Varey, and W. Button. 2000. An exploration of the emotional impact of tele-working via computer-mediated communication. *Journal of Managerial Psychology* 15 (7):668-690.

Manski, C. F. 1978. Prospects for inference on deterrence through empirical analysis of individual criminal behavior. In *Deterrence and incapacitation: Estimating the effects of criminal sanctions on crime rates*, edited by A. Blumstein, J. Cohen and D. S. Nagin. Washington, D.C.: National Academy of Sciences.

Marakas, G. M., M. Y. Yi, and R. D. Johnson. 1998. The multilevel and multifaceted character of computer self-efficacy: Toward clarification of the construct and an integrative framework for research. *Information Systems Research* 9 (2):126-163.

Martino, V., and L. Wirth. 1990. Telework: A new way of working and living. *International Labour Review* 129 (5):529-540.

Mason, R. 1986. Four ethical issues of the information age. *MIS Quarterly* 10 (1):4-12.

McAfee, J., and C. Haynes. 1989. *Computer viruses, worms, data diddlers, killer programs, & other threats to your system*. New York: St. Martin's Press.

McWilliams, A., and D. Siegel. 1997. Event studies in management research: Theoretical and empirical issues. *Academy of Management Journal* 40 (3):626-657.

Mehta, M., and B. George. 2001. Security in today's e-world. In *Proceedings of the Seventh Americas Conference on Information Systems*, August 3-5, Boston, MA.

Mendes, S. M. 2004. Certainty, severity, and their relative deterrent effects: Questioning the implications of the role of risk in criminal deterrence policy. *The Policy Studies Journal* 32 (1):59-74.

Menon, A., S. G. Bharadwaj, P. T. Adidam, and S. W. Edison. 1999. Antecedents and consequences of marketing strategy making: A model and a test. *Journal of Marketing* 63 (2):18-40.

Mills, J., and M. Tsamenyi. 2000. Communicative action and the accounting/marketing interface in industry. *Journal of Applied Management Studies* 9 (2):257-273.

Moore, D., G.M. Voelker, and S. Savage. 2002. Inferring internet denial-of-service activity. In *Proceedings of the 10th USENIX Security Symposium*, August 13-17, Washington, D.C.

Moore, G. C., and I. Benbasat. 1991. Development of an instrument to measure perceptions of adopting an information technology innovation. *Information Systems Research* 2 (3):192-222.

Moores, T. T., and J. Chang. 2006. Ethical decision making in software piracy: Initial development and test of a four-component model. *MIS Quarterly* 30 (1): 167-180.

Moorman, C., and A. S. Miner. 1997. The impact of organizational memory on new product performance and creativity. *Journal of Marketing Research* 34 (1):91-106.

Morris, M. G., and V. Venkatesh. 2000. Age differences in technology adoption decisions. *Personnel Psychology* 83:375-403.

Munro, K. I., and J. F. Cohen. 2004. Ethical behavior and information systems codes: The effects of code communication, awareness, understanding, and enforcement. In *Proceedings of the Twenty-Fifth International Conference on Information Systems*, December 12-15, Washington, D.C.

Nachenberg, C. 1997. Computer virus - antivirus coevolution. *Communications of the ACM* 40 (1):46-51.

Nagin, D. S. 1978. General deterrence: A review of the empirical evidence. In
     *Deterrence and incapacitation: Estimating the effects of criminal
     sanctions on crime rates*, edited by A. Blumstein, J. Cohen and D. S.
     Nagin. Washington, D.C.: National Academy of Sciences.

Nagin, D. S., and G. Pogarsky. 2001. Integrating celerity, impulsivity, and
     extralegal sanction threats into a model of general deterrence and
     evidence. *Criminology* 39 (4):865-891.

Nancarrow, C., I. Brace, and L. T. Wright. 2001. Tell me lies, tell me sweet
     little lies: Dealing with socially desirable responses in market research.
     Marketing Review 2 (1):55-69.

Nance, W. D., and D. W. Straub. 1988. An investigation into the use and
     usefulness of security software in detecting computer abuse. In
     *Proceedings of the Ninth International Conference on Information
     Systems*, November 30 – December 3, Minneapolis, MN.

Newsted, P. R., W. Chin, O. Ngwenyama, and A. Lee. 1996. Resolved:
     Surveys have outlived their usefulness in IS research. In *Proceedings of
     the Seventeenth International Conference on Information Systems*,
     December 16-18, Cleveland, OH.

Niederman, F., J. C. Brancheau, and J. C. Wetherbe. 1991. Information
     systems management issues for the 1990s. *MIS Quarterly* 15 (4):475-502.

Nunnally, J. C. 1978. *Psychometric theory, second edition*. New York:
     McGraw-Hill.

Osborn, S., S. Ravi, and M. Qamar. 2000. Configuring role-based access
     control to enforce mandatory and discretionary access control policies.
     ACM Transactions on Information and System Security 3 (2):85-106.

Panko, R. R. 2003. Slammer: The first blitz worm. *Communications of the AIS*
     11 (12): 207-218.

Panko, R. R., and H. G. Beh. 2002. Monitoring for pornography and sexual
     harassment. *Communications of the ACM* 45 (1):84-87.

Paradice, D. B. 1990. Ethical attitudes of entry-level MIS personnel.
     Information & Management 18:143-151.

Parker, D. B. 1976. *Crime by computer.* New York: Charles Scribner's Sons.

Parker, D. B. 1981. *Computer security management*. Reston, VA: Reston
     Publishers.

Parker, D. B. 1992. Computer crime. In *Computer security reference book*,
     edited by K. M. Jackson and J. Hruska. Boca Raton, FL: CRC Press.

Parker, D. B. 1995. Security accountability in job performance. *Information
     Systems Security* 3 (4):16-21.

Parker, D. B. 1998. *Fighting computer crime*. New York: John Wiley & Sons.

Payne, C. 2002. On the security of open source software. *Information Systems Journal* 12 (1):61-78.

Peace, A. G., D. F. Galletta, and J. Y. L. Thong. 2003. Software piracy in the workplace: A model and empirical test. *Journal of Management Information Systems* 20 (1):153-177.

Pearlson, K. E., and C. S. Saunders. 2001. There's no place like home: Managing telecommuting paradoxes. *Academy of Management Executive* 15 (2):117-128.

Pedhazur, E. J. 1982. *Multiple regression in behavioral research*. New York, NY: Holt, Rinehart, and Winston Inc.

Pierce, M. A., and J. W. Henry. 1996. Computer ethics: The role of personal, informal, and formal codes. *Journal of Business Ethics* 15 (4):425-437.

Pierce, M. A., and J. W. Henry. 2000. Judgements about computer ethics: Do individual, co-worker, and company judgments differ? Do company codes make a difference? *Journal of Business Ethics* 28 (4):307-322.

Ping, R. A. 2004. *Testing latent variable models with survey data, second edition*: [on-line], www.wright.edu/~robert.ping/lv1/toc1.htm.

Pinsonneault, A., and K. L. Kraemer. 1993. Survey research methodology in management information systems: An assessment. *Journal of Management Information Systems* 10 (2):75-105.

Plouffe, C. R., J. S. Hulland, and M. Vandenbosch. 2001. Richness versus parsimony in modeling technology adoption decisions: Understanding merchant adoption of a smart-card payment system. *Information Systems Research* 12 (2):208-222.

Podsakoff, P. M., and D. W. Organ. 1986. Self-reports in organizational research: Problems and prospects. *Journal of Management* 12 (4):531-544.

Poore, R. S. 2003. Advances in cryptography. *Information Systems Security* 12 (4):6-11.

Post, G., and A. Kagan. 1998. The use and effectiveness of anti-virus software. *Computers & Security* 17 (7):589-606.

Postmes, T., and R. Spears. 1998. Deindividuation and antinormative behavior: A meta-analysis. *Psychological Bulletin* 123 (3):238-259.

Potter, E. E. 2003. Telecommuting: The future of work, corporate culture, and american society. *Journal of Labor Research* 24 (1):73-84.

Poulou, M. 2001. The role of vignettes in the research of emotional and behavioural difficulties. *Emotional and Behavioural Difficulties* 6 (1):50-62.

Ramsower, R. M. 1984. *Telecommuting: The organizational and behavioral effects of working at home.* Ann Arbor, MI: UMI Research Press.

Randall, D. M., and A. M. Gibson. 1990. Methodology in business ethics research: A review and critical assessment. *Journal of Business Ethics* 9 (6):457-471.

Rasmussen, G. T. 2003. Building a security awareness program - addressing the threat from within. *CyberGuard E-Newsletter*, September.

Research Institute of America. 1983. Safeguarding your business against theft and vandalism. *Computer Crime Digest*, (November):5.

Richards, P., and C. R. Tittle. 1981. Gender and perceived chances of arrest. *Social Forces* 59 (4):1182-1199.

Rindfleisch, A., and D. X. Crockett. 1999. Cigarette smoking and perceived risk: A multidimensional investigation. *Journal of Public Policy & Marketing* 18 (2):159-171.

Robin, G. D. 1969. Employees as offenders. *Journal of Research in Crime and Delinquency* 6:17-33.

Rockart, J. F., and L. S. Flannery. 1983. The management of end user computing. *Communications of the ACM* 27 (10):776-784.

Rosenthal, D. A. 2002. Intrusion detection technology: Leveraging the organization's security posture. *Information Systems Management* 19 (1):35-44.

Rubin, A. D. 2003. Wireless networking security. *Communications of the ACM* 46 (5):28-30.

Saari, J. 1987. Computer crime - numbers lie. *Computers & Security* 6 (2):111-117.

Sacco, V. F., and E. Zureik. 1990. Correlates of computer misuse: Data from a self-reporting sample. *Behaviour & Information Technology* 9 (5):353-369.

Sandhu, R., E. J. Coyne, H. L. Feinstein, and C. Youman. 1996. Role-based access control models. *IEEE Computers* 29 (2):38-47.

Sarathy, R., and K. Muralidhar. 2002. The security of confidential numerical data in databases. *Information Systems Research* 13 (4):389-403.

Savage, M. 2006. Protect what's precious: 2007 priorities survey. *Information Security Magazine* 9 (12): 22-28.

Schou, C. D., and K. Trimmer, J. 2004. Information assurance and security. *Journal of Organizational and End User Computing* 16 (3):i - vii.

Schultz, E. E. 2002. A framework for understanding and predicting insider attacks. *Computers & Security* 21 (6):526-531.

Schultz, E. E. 2004. Security training and awareness - fitting a square peg in a round hole. *Computers & Security* 23 (1):1-2.

Schweitzer, J. A. 1990. *Managing information security*. Boston: Butterworth Publishers.

Sein, M. K., R. P. Bostrom, and L. Olfman. 1987. Training end users to compute: Cognitive, motivational, and social issues. *INFOR* 25 (3):236-255.

Seyal, A. H., M. Noah, A. Rahman, and M. Rahim. 2002. Determinants of academic use of the internet: A structural equation model. *Behaviour & Information Technology* 21 (1):71-86.

Shaw, E. S., K. G. Ruby, and J. M. Post. 1998. The insider threat to information systems: The psychology of the dangerous insider. *Security Awareness Bulletin* 2:1-10.

Sheppard, B. H., J. Hartwick, and P. R. Warshaw. 1988. The theory of reasoned action: A meta-analysis of past research with recommendations for modifications and future research. *Journal of Consumer Research* 15:325-343.

Sherman, R. 1992. Biometric futures. *Computers & Security* 11 (2):128-133.

Silberman, M. 1976. Toward a theory of criminal deterrence. *American Sociological Review* 41 (3):442-461.

Simmons, G. 1994. Cryptanalysis and protocol failures. *Communications of the ACM* 37 (11):56-64.

Sims, R. R., H. K. Cheng, and H. Teegen. 1996. Toward a profile of student software piraters. *Journal of Business Ethics* 15:839-849.

Sindell, K. 2002. *Safety net: Protecting your business on the internet*. New York: John Wiley & Sons.

Siponen, M. T. 2000. A conceptual foundation for organizational information security awareness. *Information Management & Computer Security* 8 (1):31-41.

Siponen, M. T. 2000a. Critical analysis of different approaches to minimizing user-related faults in information systems security: Implications for research and practice. *Information Management & Computer Security* 8 (5):197-209.

Sitkin, S. B., and A. L. Pablo. 1992. Reconceptualizing the determinants of risk behavior. *Academy of Management Review* 17 (1):9-38.

Sitkin, S. B., and L. R. Weingart. 1995. Determinants of risky decision-making behavior: A test of the mediating role of risk perceptions and propensity. *Academy of Management Journal* 38 (6):1573-1592.

Skinner, W. F., and A. M. Fream. 1997. A social learning theory analysis of computer crime among college students. *Journal of Research in Crime and Delinquency* 34 (4):495-518.

Slovic, P. 1972. Information processing, situation specificity and the generality of risk-taking behavior. *Journal of Personality and Social Psychology* 22 (April):128-134.

Smith, M. B. 1974. *Harmonizing social psychology*. San Francisco: Josey-Bass.

Solarz, A. 1987. Computer-related embezzlement. *Computers & Security* 6 (1):49-53.

Sommer, R., and B. Sommer. 2002. *A practical guide to behavioral research: Tools and techniques, fifth edition*. New York: Oxford University Press.

Spafford, E. H. 1989. Crisis and aftermath. *Communications of the ACM* 32 (6):678-687.

Standage, T. 2002. The weakest link. *Economist*, October 26.

Stanton, J. M., C. Caldera, A. Isaac, K. R. Stam, and S. J. Marcinlowski. 2003. Behavioral information security: Defining the criterion space. In *The internet at work or not: Preventing computer deviance*, edited by P. M. Mastrangelo and W. J. Everton. Meeting of the Society for Industrial Organizational Psychology, Orlando, FL.

Stanton, J. M., K. R. Stam, P. R. Mastrangelo, and J. Jolton. 2005. An analysis of end user security behaviors. *Computers & Security* 24 (5): 124-133.

Stanton, J. M., and E. M. Weiss. 2000. Electronic monitoring in their own words: An exploratory study of employees' experiences with new types of surveillance. *Computers in Human Behavior* 16:423-440.

Straub, D. W. 1986. Deterring computer abuse: The effectiveness of deterrent countermeasures in the computer security environment. PhD diss., Indiana University.

Straub, D. W. 1989. Validating instruments in MIS research. *MIS Quarterly* 13 (2):147-169.

Straub, D. W. 1990. Effective IS security: An empirical study. *Information Systems Research* 1 (3):255-276.

Straub, D. W., M. C. Boudreau, and D. Gefen. 2004. Validation guidelines for IS positivist research. *Communications of the AIS* 13 (24):380-427.

Straub, D. W., P. J. Carlson, and E. H. Jones. 1993. Deterring cheating by student programmers: A field experiment in computer security. *Journal of Management Systems* 5 (1):33-48.

Straub, D. W., and W. D. Nance. 1990. Discovering and disciplining computer abuse in organizations: A field study. *MIS Quarterly* 14 (1):45-60.

Straub, D. W., and R. J. Welke. 1998. Coping with systems risk: Security planning models for management decision making. *MIS Quarterly* 22 (4):441-469.

Straub, D. W., and C. S. Widom. 1984. Deviancy by bits and bytes: Computer abusers and control measures. In *Proceedings of the Second IFIP International Conference on Computer Security*, September 10-12, Toronto, Ontario.

Swanson, M. 2001. Security self-assessment guide for information technology systems, NIST special publication 800-26. Washington, D.C.: National Institute of Standards and Technology.

Taylor, S., and P. A. Todd. 1995. Understanding information technology usage: A test of competing models. *Information Systems Research* 6 (2):144-176.

Thiagarajan, V., and M. Comp. 2003. Information security management BS 7799.2:2002 Audit check list. Bethesda, M.D.: SANS Institute.

Thompson, D. 1998. 1997 computer crime and security survey. *Information Management & Computer Security* 6 (2):78-101.

Thomson, M. E., and R. von Solms. 1998. Information security awareness: Educating your users effectively. *Information Management & Computer Security* 6 (4):167-173.

Tittle, C. R. 1980. *Sanctions and social deviance: The question of deterrence.* New York: Praeger.

Tittle, C. R., and C. H. Logan. 1973. Sanctions and deviance: Evidence and remaining questions. *Law and Society Review* 7:371-392.

Tittle, C. R., and A. Rowe. 1974. Moral appeal, sanction threat, and deviance: An experimental test. *Social Problems* 20 (Spring):488-498.

Tooke, W. S., and W. Ickes. 1988. A measure of adherence to conventional morality. *Journal of Social and Clinical Psychology* 6 (3/4):310-334.

Trochim, W. M. K. 2002. *The research methods knowledge base, second edition.* Cincinnati, OH: Atomic Dog Publishing.

United Nations Conference on Trade and Development. 2005. *Information economy report 2005.* Geneva, Switzerland: United Nations.

Urbaczewski, A., and L. M. Jessup. 2002. Does electronic monitoring of employee internet usage work? *Communications of the ACM* 45 (1):80-83.

Venkatesh, V., and M. G. Morris. 2000. Why don't men ever stop to ask for directions? Gender, social influence, and their role in technology acceptance and usage behavior. *MIS Quarterly* 24 (1):115-139.

Venkatesh, V., and C. Speier. 1999. Computer technology training in the workplace: A longitudinal investigation of the effect of mood. *Organizational Behavior and Human Decision Processes* 79 (1):1-28.

Venter, H. S., and J. H. P. Eloff. 2003. A taxonomy for information security technologies. *Computers & Security* 22 (4):299-307.

Vigna, G., and R. Kemmerer. 1999. Netstat: A network based intrusion detection system. *Journal of Computer Security* 7 (1):37-71.

von Solms, R., H. van de Haar, S. H. von Solms, and W. J. Caelli. 1994. A framework for information security evaluation. *Information & Management* 27 (3):143-153.

von Solms, R., and B. von Solms. 2004. From policies to culture. *Computers & Security* 23 (4):275-279.

Wang, H., and C. Wang. 2003. Taxonomy of security considerations and software quality. *Communications of the ACM* 46 (6):75-78.

Warren, M. J. 2002. Security practice: Survey evidence from three countries. *Logistics Information Management* 15 (5/6):347-351.

Wasserman, J. J. 1969. Plugging the leaks in computer security. *Harvard Business Review* 47 (5):119-129.

Watad, M. M., and F. J. DiSanzo. 2000. Case study: The synergism of telecommuting and office automation. *Sloan Management Review* 41 (2):85-97.

Weaver, F. M., and J. S. Carroll. 1985. Crime perceptions in a natural setting by expert and novice shoplifters. *Social Psychology Quarterly* 48 (4):349-359.

Wen, H. J. 1998. Internet computer virus protection policy. *Information Management & Computer Security* 6 (2):66-71.

White, G. W., and S. J. Pearson. 2001. Controlling corporate e-mail, pc use and computer security. *Computers & Security* 9 (2):88-92.

Whitman, M. E. 2003. Enemy at the gate: Threats to information security. *Communications of the ACM* 46 (8):91-95.

Whitman, M. E., A. M. Townsend, and R. J. Alberts. 2001. Information systems security and the need for policy. In *Information security management: Global challenges in the new millennium*, edited by M. Khosrowpour. Hershey, PA: Idea Group Publishing.

Wiant, T. L. 2003. Policy and its impact on medical record security. PhD diss., University of Kentucky.

Wiesenfeld, B. M., S. Raghuram, and R. Garud. 1999. Communication patterns as determinants of organizational identification in a virtual organization. *Organization Science* 10 (6):777-790.

Wiesenfeld, B. M., S. Raghuram, and R. Garud. 2001. Organizational identification among virtual workers: The role of need for affiliation and perceived work-based social support. *Journal of Management* 27 (2):213-229.

Williams, K. 1992. Social sources of marital violence and deterrence: Testing an integrated theory of assaults between partners. *Journal of Marriage and Family* 54 (3):620-629.

Willison, R. 2000. Understanding and addressing criminal opportunity: The application of situational crime prevention to IS security. *Journal of Financial Crime* 7 (3):201-210.

Wood, C. C. 1999. *Information security policies made easy*. San Rafael, CA: Baseline Software.

Woszczynski, A. B., and M. E. Whitman. 2004. The problem of common method variance in IS research. In *The handbook of information systems research*, edited by M. Khosrowpour. Hershey, PA: Idea Group Publishing.

Wyatt, G. 1990. Risk-taking and risk-avoiding behavior: The impact of some dispositional and situational variables. *The Journal of Psychology* 124 (4):437-447.

Wybo, M. D., and D. W. Straub. 1989. Protecting organizational information resources. *Information Resources Management Journal* 2 (4):1-15.

Zimbardo, P. G. 1969. The human choice: Individuation, reason, and order versus deindividuation, impulse, and chaos. In *Nebraska symposium on motivation*, edited by W. J. Arnold and D. Levine. Lincoln: University of Nebraska Press.

Zimring, F. E., and G. Hawkins. 1973. *Deterrence: The legal in crime control*. Chicago: The University of Chicago Press.

Zviran, M., and W. J. Haga. 1999. Password security: An empirical study. *Journal of Management Information Systems* 15 (4):161-185.

IS Misuse Scenarios

<u>Distribution of an inappropriate e-mail:</u> Taylor received an e-mail from a friend that contained a series of jokes. Many of the jokes poked fun at the stereotypes that people often associate with different ethnic groups. Taylor found the jokes very funny and decided to send the e-mail to several co-workers.

<u>Installation of unlicensed computer software (software piracy):</u> Jordan is given a personal computer (PC) at work. However, the new PC is missing a piece of software that Jordan believes would make her more efficient and effective on the job. Jordan requests that the company purchase the software but her request is denied. To solve the problem, Jordan obtains an unlicensed copy of the software from a friend outside of the company and installs the software on her PC at work.

<u>Password sharing:</u> Sam works in the marketing department and therefore has access to the company's customer account database. One day while at work, one of Sam's co-workers in the marketing department asked to borrow his password in order to access the customer account database. The co-worker explained to Sam that he had forgotten his own password and that the system administrator who was in charge of resetting passwords was in a meeting. Sam gave the co-worker his password to access the customer account database.

<u>Unauthorized access:</u> By chance, Alex found the password that allowed him to access the restricted computer system that contained the salary information of employees within his company. Around the same time, Alex was preparing to ask for a raise. Before meeting with his boss, Alex accessed the computer system and viewed the salaries of others in similar jobs. Alex used this information to determine how much of a salary increase to ask for.

<u>Unauthorized modification:</u> Chris prepares payroll records for his company's employees and therefore has access to the computer timekeeping and payroll systems. Periodically, Chris would increase the hours-worked records of certain employees with whom he was friends by "rounding up" their total hours for the week (for example, Chris would change 39.5 hours worked to 40 hours worked).

APPENDIX B

Survey Items

<u>IS misuse intention (modified for each scenario)</u>
INT1. If you were Taylor, what is the likelihood that you would have sent the e-mail?
INT2. What is the probability that a typical employee within your place of work would have sent the e-mail, just as Taylor did?

<u>Perceived certainty of sanctions (modified for each scenario)</u>
PC1. Taylor would probably be caught, eventually, after sending the e-mail:
PC2. The likelihood the organization would discover that Taylor sent the e-mail is:

<u>Perceived severity of sanctions (modified for each scenario)</u>
PS1. If caught sending the e-mail, Taylor would be severely reprimanded:
PS2. If caught sending the e-mail, Taylor's punishment would be:

<u>Security awareness program (* item dropped)</u>
SA1. Employees in my organization are instructed in the appropriate usage of information technologies.
SA2. My organization educates employees on their responsibilities for managing computer passwords.*
SA3. My organization provides training to help employees improve their awareness of computer and information security issues.
SA4. My organization provides employees with education on computer software copyright laws.
SA5. In my organization, employees are briefed on the consequences of modifying computerized data in an unauthorized way.

SA6. My organization educates employees on their computer security responsibilities.

SA7. My organization provides employees with education on appropriate use of e-mail.*

SA8. In my organization, employees are briefed on the consequences of accessing computer systems that they are not authorized to use.

<u>Security policies (* item dropped)</u>

P1. My organization has specific guidelines that describe acceptable use of e-mail.

P2. My organization has established rules of behavior for use of computer resources.

P3. My organization has a formal policy that forbids employees from accessing computer systems that they are not authorized to use.

P4. My organization has a formal policy that forbids employees from installing their own software on work computers.*

P5. My organization has specific guidelines that describe acceptable use of computer passwords.

P6. My organization has specific guidelines that govern what employees are allowed to do with their computers.

P7. My organization has a formal policy that forbids employees from modifying computerized data in an unauthorized way.*

<u>Monitoring practices (* item dropped)</u>

M1. I believe that my organization monitors any modification or altering of computerized data by employees.

M2. I believe that employee computing activities are monitored by my organization.

M3. I believe that my organization monitors computing activities to ensure that employees are performing only explicitly authorized tasks.

M4. I believe that my organization reviews logs of employees' computing activities on a regular basis.

M5. I believe that my organization conducts periodic audits to detect the use of unauthorized software on its computers.*

M6. I believe that my organization regularly monitors employee access to sensitive computerized information.

M7. I believe that my organization actively monitors the content of employees' e-mail messages.

<u>Preventative security software (* item dropped)</u>

PR1. In my organization, employees are forced to change their passwords periodically.*

PR2. My organization uses biometric controls (for example, voice patterns, fingerprints) to authorize employees' access to computer systems.*

PR3. My organization uses e-mail content filters to prevent employees from sending inappropriate e-mail messages.*

PR4. Employees in my organization are only able to gain access to the computer systems that they are authorized to use.

PR5. Computer systems in my organization have security controls that prevent employees from accessing sensitive information.

PR6. A password is required to gain access to any computer system in my organization.

PR7. Computers in my organization are configured with security controls that prevent employees from installing their own software.*

<u>Risk propensity (* item dropped; † reverse coded)</u>

RP1. I always try to avoid situations involving a risk of getting into trouble with my boss/supervisor.

RP2. I always play it safe even when it means occasionally losing out on a good opportunity.

RP3. I am a cautious person who generally avoids risks.

RP4. I am rather bold and fearless in my actions when I am at work†.

RP5. I am generally cautious when trying something new.

RP6. On the job, I prefer to work on a project that has problems that I know about rather than take the risks of working on a new project that has unknown problems, even if the new project offers greater potential rewards.

<u>Computer self-efficacy</u>

I could complete the job using the software package…

CSE1. …if I had seen someone else using it before trying it myself.

CSE2. …if I could call someone for help if I got stuck.

CSE3. …if someone else had helped me get started.

CSE4. …if I had a lot of time to complete the job for which the software was provided.

CSE5. …if someone showed me how to do it first.

CSE6. …if I had used similar packages like this one before to do the same job.

<u>Social desirability bias († reverse coded)</u>
SDB1. I sometimes feel resentful when I don't get my way†.
SDB2. I am always courteous even to people who are disagreeable.
SDB3. There have been occasions when I took advantage of someone†.
SDB4. No matter who I'm talking to, I'm always a good listener.
SDB5. I sometimes try to get even rather than forgive and forget†.

<u>Moral commitment († reverse coded)</u>
MC1. The problems of other people concern me deeply.
MC2. I take care of myself and don't worry too much about other people†.
MC3. I envy people who have more than I do†.
MC4. I am forgiving of others who have injured or offended me.
MC5. I like to control other people's behavior as much as I can†.
MC6. I am not willing to shift the blame to others, even if it will keep me out of trouble.
MC7. I am honest in the way I deal with people.
MC8. I make sure that I get my share of whatever rewards are available†.

<u>Virtual status</u>
VS1. Average number of days per week spent working in the office:
VS2. Average number of days per week spent working from home:
VS3. Average number of days per week spent working from neither home or office (for example, "on the road"):

Data Analysis for MBA and Industry Samples

Table C.1. Descriptive Statistics – MBA and Industry Samples

	MBA Sample				Industry Sample			
	Min	**Max**	**Mean**	**SD**	**Min**	**Max**	**Mean**	**SD**
INT	5.0	30.0	14.73	5.4	5.0	24.5	10.47	4.8
PC	6.5	33.0	18.33	5.1	6.0	35.0	20.87	5.9
PS	11.0	35.0	22.72	4.6	9.0	35.0	23.65	5.4
P	1.0	7.0	4.75	1.4	1.1	7.0	5.46	1.3
SA	1.0	7.0	4.17	1.4	1.0	7.0	4.64	1.4
M	1.0	7.0	4.19	1.3	1.3	7.0	4.63	1.3
PR	1.4	6.7	4.47	1.0	1.6	7.0	4.83	0.9
RP	1.7	6.3	4.01	0.9	1.2	6.8	3.99	0.9
CSE	2.7	7.0	5.71	1.0	1.7	7.0	5.69	1.0
SD	0.0	0.8	0.08	0.2	0.0	1.0	0.15	0.2
MC	2.9	6.9	4.55	0.6	3.0	6.4	4.81	0.6
VS	0.0	8.0	1.02	1.6	0.0	8.0	0.81	1.6

Table C.2. EFA for Endogenous, Moderator, and Control Variables – MBA Sample

Item	Factor								
	1	2	3	4	5	6	7	8	9
CSE4	.885								
CSE5	.869								
CSE3	.844								
CSE6	.837								
CSE1	.820								
CSE2	.762								
RP3		.860							
RP2		.817							
RP5		.748							
RP1		.598							
RP6		.506							
PS2			.818						
PC2			.817						
PS1			.796						
PC1			.793						
INT1				.963					
INT2				.960					
MC3*									
MC7*									

Note: Loadings less than .40 not shown

Table C.2 (continued). EFA for Endogenous, Moderator, and Control Variables – MBA Sample

Item	Factor								
	1	2	3	4	5	6	7	8	9
SDB2					**.728**				
SDB3					**.679**				
SDB4					**.607**				
SDB1					**.553**				
MC8*						.783			
MC5*						.496			
RP4*		.419				.490			
MC1*							.830		
MC2*							.691		
MC4*								.748	
SDB5								**.744**	
MC6*									.920
Eigenvalue	4.84	3.71	2.87	2.25	1.62	1.52	1.32	1.09	1.05
Variance explained (%)	15.62	11.98	9.24	7.26	5.22	4.90	4.26	3.52	3.40
Cumulative variance (%)	15.62	27.60	36.84	44.10	49.32	54.22	58.49	62.00	65.40

Note: Loadings less than .40 not shown; * Marked for deletion

Table C.3. EFA for Endogenous, Moderator, and Control Variables – Industry Sample

Item	Factor								
	1	2	3	4	5	6	7	8	9
CSE3	.850								
CSE5	.818								
CSE4	.802								
CSE2	.786								
CSE6	.781								
CSE1	.705								
PC1		.913							
PC2		.881							
PS1		.840							
PS2		.827							
RP3			.812						
RP2			.728						
RP5			.618						
RP4			.587						
RP6			.498						
RP1			.445						
SDB4				.793					
SDB2				.719					
SDB5				.591					

Note: Loadings less than .40 not shown

Table C.3 (continued). EFA for Endogenous, Moderator, and Control Variables – Industry Sample

Item	Factor								
	1	2	3	4	5	6	7	8	9
SDB3				.578					
SDB1									
INT2					.953				
INT1					.916				
MC8*						.758			
MC5*						.682			
MC3*									
MC6*							.691		
MC7*							.685		
MC1*								.844	
MC2*								.714	
MC4*									.765
Eigenvalue	4.26	4.00	2.47	2.22	1.49	1.42	1.38	1.25	1.13
Variance explained (%)	13.74	12.91	7.98	7.18	4.79	4.59	4.44	4.02	3.64
Cumulative variance (%)	13.74	26.64	34.62	41.81	46.60	51.19	55.63	59.65	63.30

Note: Loadings less than .40 not shown; * Marked for deletion

Table C.4. EFA for Security Countermeasures – MBA Sample

	Factor				
Item	**1**	**2**	**3**	**4**	**5**
P1	**.952**				
P2	**.874**				
PR1*	.809				
SA2*	.770				
SA7*	.560				
P5	**.515**				
P6	**.503**				
M7		**.833**			
M4		**.829**			
M2		.744			
M3		.726			
PR3		.475			
M1		**.453**			
M6		**.401**			
SA4			.925		
PR2*			.782		
SA5			**.665**		
SA3			**.649**		
SA6	.485		**.594**		
SA8			**.581**		
P7**			.471		
SA1					
PR7				.965	
P4				.888	
M5				.518	
PR4					**.880**
PR6					**.798**
PR5					**.783**
P3					
Eigenvalue	10.07	9.57	8.06	7.56	7.15
Variance explained (%)	15.76	14.97	12.60	11.82	11.19
Cumulative variance (%)	15.76	28.36	43.33	55.15	66.34
Note: Loadings less than .40 not shown; * Marked for deletion					

Table C.5. EFA for Security Countermeasures – Industry Sample

	Factor				
Item	1	2	3	4	5
SA4	**.882**				
SA8	.752				
SA3	.736				
SA6	**.652**				
SA5	**.643**				
PR2*	.630				
SA1	**.533**	.526			
P7*	.473				
P1		**.916**			
P2		**.903**			
SA7*		.597			
P6		**.591**			
SA2*		.534			
PR1*		.508		.491	
P3		**.406**			
P5					
M4			**.805**		
M3			.790		
M7			.774		
M2		.497	**.667**		
PR3*			.611		
PR5				**.812**	
PR4				.751	
PR6				.704	
M6			**.422**	.457	
M1			**.444**	.448	
PR7					.813
P4					.698
M5					.611
Eigenvalue	9.13	9.10	7.64	6.42	6.24
Variance explained (%)	14.40	14.36	12.05	10.13	9.85
Cumulative variance (%)	14.40	28.76	40.81	50.94	60.79

Note: Loadings less than .40 not shown; * Marked for deletion

Table C.6. Reliability of Constructs – MBA and Industry Samples

		Cronbach's Alpha	
Construct	Number of Items	MBA Sample	Industry Sample
INT	2	0.97	0.93
PC	2	0.91	0.94
PS	2	0.89	0.93
P	5	0.88	0.88
SA	6	0.87	0.89
M	6	0.88	0.86
PR	3	0.70	0.73
RP	5	0.77	0.67
CSE	6	0.91	0.88
SDB	5	0.55	0.65
MC	1	-	-
VS	1	-	-

Table C.7. Revised Descriptive Statistics and Tests for Normality – MBA Sample

			Skewedness		Kurtosis	
Construct	Mean	SD	Stat	z-score	Stat	z-score
INT	11.07	4.51	0.65	**3.89**	0.06	0.18
PC	15.61	4.30	0.23	1.43	-0.33	-1.06
PS	19.18	3.75	0.20	1.27	-0.30	-0.97
P	4.87	1.50	-0.90	**-5.68**	0.41	1.29
SA	4.05	1.38	-0.06	-0.37	-0.53	-1.68
M	4.24	1.35	-0.21	-1.34	-0.33	-1.29
PR	5.53	1.25	-1.01	**-6.37**	0.59	1.89
RP	4.00	1.03	.0.01	0.04	-0.65	**-2.07**
CSE	5.71	1.03	-0.82	**-5.17**	0.33	1.04
SDB	0.08	0.17	2.51	**15.87**	7.77	**21.53**
MC	21.88	4.01	-0.63	**-4.01**	0.34	1.07
VS	1.02	1.58	1.80	**11.39**	2.94	**9.35**
Note: Bolded z-scores indicate a significant ($p<0.025$) departure from normality.						

Table C.8. Revised Descriptive Statistics and Tests for Normality –
Industry Sample

Construct	Mean	SD	Skewedness		Kurtosis	
			Stat	z-score	Stat	z-score
INT	7.87	3.62	0.90	**6.01**	0.39	1.32
PC	17.71	4.80	0.09	0.59	-0.26	-0.89
PS	19.95	4.18	-0.34	**-2.30**	-0.18	-0.63
P	5.58	1.29	-1.28	**-8.61**	1.682	**5.66**
SA	4.47	1.46	-0.21	-1.44	-0.69	**-2.34**
M	4.62	1.29	-0.33	**-2.20**	-0.26	-0.87
PR	5.86	1.13	-1.14	**-7.65**	1.10	**3.69**
RP	4.00	0.99	-0.04	-0.23	-0.10	-0.32
CSE	5.69	1.01	-0.74	**-4.99**	0.44	1.48
SDB	0.15	0.23	1.63	**10.95**	2.24	**7.56**
MC	24.13	3.58	-0.97	**-6.52**	0.85	**2.85**
VS	0.81	1.71	2.62	**17.59**	6.83	**22.99**

Note: Bolded z-scores indicate a significant ($p<0.025$) departure
from normality.

Table C.9. Weights, Loadings, and AVEs for MBA Sample

Item	Loading	T-value	AVE	Item	Loading	T-value	AVE
INT1	.9864	396.52	0.97	M6	.7670	22.13	
INT2	.9882	548.48		M7	.7942	28.55	
PC1	.9576	137.38	0.92	PR4	.7939	20.44	0.63
PC2	.9575	123.22		PR5	.8333	29.02	
PS1	.9476	102.58	0.92	PR6	.7390	13.04	
PS2	.9547	150.19		RP1	.6463	13.99	0.54
P1	.8290	29.60	0.68	RP2	.8211	31.54	
P2	.8499	32.35		RP3	.8459	48.95	
P3	.7877	25.35		RP5	.7270	18.17	
P5	.7917	23.95		RP6	.5821	10.60	
P6	.8538	39.29		CSE1	.8240	34.60	0.71
SA1	.5917	10.24	0.60	CSE2	.7961	24.42	
SA3	.7286	16.30		CSE3	.8674	45.05	
SA4	.7232	16.83		CSE4	.8595	39.90	
SA5	.8474	46.14		CSE5	.8577	41.38	
SA6	.8621	45.15		CSE6	.8318	23.77	
SA8	.8366	38.77		SDB1	.5590	3.81	0.35
M1	.7786	29.70	0.62	SDB2	.4555	2.04	
M2	.8418	43.55		SDB3	.6672	4.26	
M3	.7800	26.93		SDB4	.1952	1.06	
M4	.7750	25.71		SDB5	.6709	5.11	

Table C.10. Weights, Loadings, and AVEs for Industry Sample

Item	Loading	T-value	AVE	Item	Loading	T-value	AVE
INT1	.5001	81.02	0.93	M6	.2671	28.80	
INT2	.5366	81.41		M7	.1973	17.16	
PC1	.5070	201.26	0.94	PR4	.3650	19.62	0.65
PC2	.5235	242.83		PR5	.5360	37.72	
PS1	.5110	194.06	0.93	PR6	.3199	9.11	
PS2	.5235	204.57		RP1	.2644	9.90	0.44
P1	.2390	33.64	0.69	RP2	.3428	20.83	
P2	.2565	39.48		RP3	.3559	22.40	
P3	.2382	22.98		RP5	.2728	10.72	
P5	.2328	25.99		RP6	.2691	8.59	
P6	.2385	29.11		CSE1	.1835	15.74	0.63
SA1	.2066	25.03	0.64	CSE2	.2074	22.08	
SA3	.1950	19.83		CSE3	.2251	34.77	
SA4	.1789	24.75		CSE4	.2154	29.36	
SA5	.2090	37.05		CSE5	.2158	27.63	
SA6	.2428	50.55		CSE6	.2068	22.26	
SA8	.2131	35.78		SDB1	.1816	3.63	0.41
M1	.2480	25.74	0.58	SDB2	.2108	4.00	
M2	.1907	24.68		SDB3	.2639	5.42	
M3	.1941	19.65		SDB4	.2846	4.94	
M4	.2119	18.39		SDB5	.5002	9.17	

Table C.11. Reliability and Inter-Construct Correlations – MBA Sample

Construct	CR	Inter-Construct Correlations										11	12
		1	2	3	4	5	7	7	8	9	10		
(1) INT	.98	.98											
(2) PC	.96	-.23	.96										
(3) PS	.95	-.36	.47	.96									
(4) SA	.90	-.23	.41	.42	.77								
(5) P	.91	-.27	.37	.48	.74	.82							
(7) M	.91	-.18	.49	.35	.64	.67	.79						
(7) PR	.84	-.20	.30	.40	.48	.59	.50	.79					
(8) RP	.85	-.10	-.07	-.01	-.09	.03	-.08	-.03	.73				
(9) CSE	.93	-.05	-.18	-.04	-.08	-.01	-.10	.16	-.14	.84			
(10) SDB	.74	-.17	.13	.18	-.08	-.07	-.02	.06	-.01	.08	.61		
(11) MC	-	-.62	.16	.26	.23	.25	.14	.26	-.03	.11	.15	-	
(12) VS	-	.08	.06	.03	.05	-.07	-.01	-.15	.02	-.18	.05	.05	-

CR = Composite reliability

Note: Shaded items are the square root of the average variance extracted (AVE). Off-diagonal elements are the correlations among constructs.

Table C.12. Reliability and Inter-Construct Correlations – Industry Sample

Construct	CR	Inter-Construct Correlations											
		1	2	3	4	5	7	7	8	9	10	11	12
(1) INT	.97	.96											
(2) PC	.97	-.26	.97										
(3) PS	.97	-.33	.59	.96									
(4) SA	.91	-.36	.44	.43	.80								
(5) P	.92	-.35	.34	.45	.70	.83							
(7) M	.90	-.16	.58	.38	.57	.59	.76						
(7) PR	.85	-.27	.33	.32	.57	.63	.45	.81					
(8) RP	.79	.01	-.01	.01	.11	-.04	-.02	-.02	.66				
(9) CSE	.91	-.03	-.13	-.01	.02	.11	-.05	.07	-.13	.79			
(10) SDB	.78	-.17	.20	.12	.13	.09	.12	.18	-.02	.03	.64		
(11) MC	-	-.47	.28	.32	.31	.29	.21	.21	-.02	-.02	.27	-	
(12) VS	-	.12	.04	.07	-.02	-.08	-.07	-.12	.03	-.01	.09	.04	-

CR = Composite reliability

Note: Shaded items are the square root of the average variance extracted (AVE). Off-diagonal elements are the correlations among constructs.

Hypotheses Tests for MBA and Industry Samples

The results of the main effects hypotheses tests for the MBA sample are depicted in figure D.1 and summarized in Table D.1. As shown in Figure D.1, the structural model explained 27 percent of the variance for perceived certainty of sanctions, 28 percent of the variance for perceived severity of sanctions, and 44 percent of the variance for IS misuse intention. These figures all exceeded 10 percent, implying a satisfactory and substantive model (Falk and Miller 1992).

Consistent with hypotheses H2a and H3a, security awareness program and monitoring practices each had significant direct effects on perceived certainty of sanctions, after controlling for age and gender. Monitoring practices had a greater effect on perceived certainty of sanctions (β = .403, p<0.01), although the influence of security awareness program was still strong (β = .190, p<0.05). Security policies and preventative security software did not have significant effects on perceived certainty of sanctions. Thus, H1a and H4a were not supported.

Consistent with hypotheses H1b – H3b, security policies, security awareness program, and preventative security software each had significant direct effects on perceived severity of sanctions, after controlling for age and gender. Security policies had the strongest effect (β = .291, p<0.01), followed by preventative security software (β = .165, p<0.05), and security awareness program (β = .136, p<0.10). Monitoring practices did not have a significant effect on perceived severity of sanctions, and therefore H4b was not supported.

Hypotheses 8a and 8b predicted that perceived certainty and severity of sanctions would be negatively associated with IS misuse intention (after controlling for moral commitment and social desirability bias). Consistent with

H8b, perceived severity of sanctions had a significant negative effect on IS misuse intention (β = -.175, p<0.01). Perceived certainty also had a negative effect on IS misuse intention. However, this relationship was not significant (β = -.055, p>0.10). A post hoc analysis found that perceived certainty of sanctions also had a strong relationship with perceived severity of sanctions (β = .358, p<0.001). Hence, perceived certainty of sanctions had a significant indirect effect on IS misuse intention through perceived severity of sanctions, and H8a was supported indirectly.

In terms of the control variables, age was a significant correlate of perceived severity of sanctions and moral commitment had a strong negative relationship with IS misuse intention. Social desirability bias was not significantly associated with IS misuse intention, suggesting that impression management concerns were not an issue for this sample.

The interaction effects predicted in H5 – H7 were examined using the PLS product-indicator procedure described in the combined sample analysis (i.e., latent interaction variables were added to the main effect models). The results of the interaction tests for the MBA sample are provided in Table D.2. Computer self-efficacy had a moderately significant negative effect on the relationship between security policies and perceived certainty of sanctions (β = -.203, p<0.10), thus providing marginal support for H5a. Virtual status had a moderately significant negative effect on the relationship between monitoring practices and perceived certainty of sanctions (β = -.148, p<0.10), providing marginal support for H7c. The only other significant interaction effects were in the opposite direction than hypothesized. Computer self-efficacy had a positive effect on the relationship between preventative security software and perceived certainty of sanctions (β = .157, p<0.10) and virtual status had a positive effect on the relationship between security awareness program and perceived certainty of sanctions (β = .221, p<0.10).

The results of the main effect hypotheses for tests for the industry sample are depicted in Figure D.2 and summarized in Table D.3. As shown in Figure D.2, the structural model explained 38 percent of the variance for perceived certainty of sanctions, 26 percent of the variance for perceived severity of sanctions, and 25 percent of the variance for IS misuse intention. These figures all exceeded 10 percent, implying a satisfactory and substantive model (Falk and Miller 1992).

Consistent with hypotheses H1a – H3a, security policies, security awareness program, and monitoring practices each had significant direct effects on perceived certainty of sanctions, after controlling for age and gender. Monitoring practices had the strongest effect (β = .537, p<0.01), followed by security awareness program ($\beta = .223$, p<0.01), and security policies ($\beta = .186$, p<0.05). The relationship between preventative security software and perceived certainty of sanctions was not significant, and therefore H4a was not supported.

Consistent with hypotheses H1b – H3b, security policies, security awareness program, and preventative security software each had significant direct effects on perceived severity of sanctions, after controlling for age and gender. Security policies had the strongest effect ($\beta = .211$, p<0.01), followed by security awareness program ($\beta = .189$, p<0.05), and monitoring practices ($\beta = .147$, p<0.05). Preventative security software did not have a significant effect on perceived severity of sanctions, and therefore H4b was not supported.

Hypotheses 8a and 8b predicted that perceived certainty and severity of sanctions would be negatively associated with IS misuse intention (after controlling for moral commitment and social desirability bias). Consistent with H8b, perceived severity of sanctions had a significant negative effect on IS misuse intention ($\beta = -.168$, p<0.01). The relationship between perceived certainty of sanctions and IS misuse intention was directionally consistent with H8b, but not significant ($\beta = -.052$, p>0.10). However, a post hoc analysis found that perceived certainty of sanctions had a significant indirect effect on IS misuse intention through perceived severity of sanctions ($\beta = .551$, p<0.001), and therefore H8a was supported indirectly.

In terms of the control variables, gender was a significant correlate of perceived severity of sanctions and moral commitment had a strong negative association with IS misuse intention. Social desirability bias was not significantly associated with IS misuse intention, suggesting that impression management concerns were not an issue for this sample.

The interaction effects were examined using the PLS product-indicator procedure described previously. The interaction results for the industry sample are provided in Table D.4. Computer self-efficacy had a moderately significant negative effect on the relationship between monitoring practices and perceived certainty of sanctions ($\beta = -.204$, p<0.10), thus providing marginal support for H5c. Virtual status had a significant negative effect on the relationship between security policies and perceived certainty of sanctions ($\beta = -.240$, p<0.05), providing support for H7a. The only other significant interaction effects were in the opposite direction than hypothesized. Virtual status had a positive effect on both the relationship between monitoring practices and perceived certainty of sanctions ($\beta = .151$, p<0.10) and the relationship between security awareness program and perceived certainty of sanctions ($\beta = .224$, p<0.10).

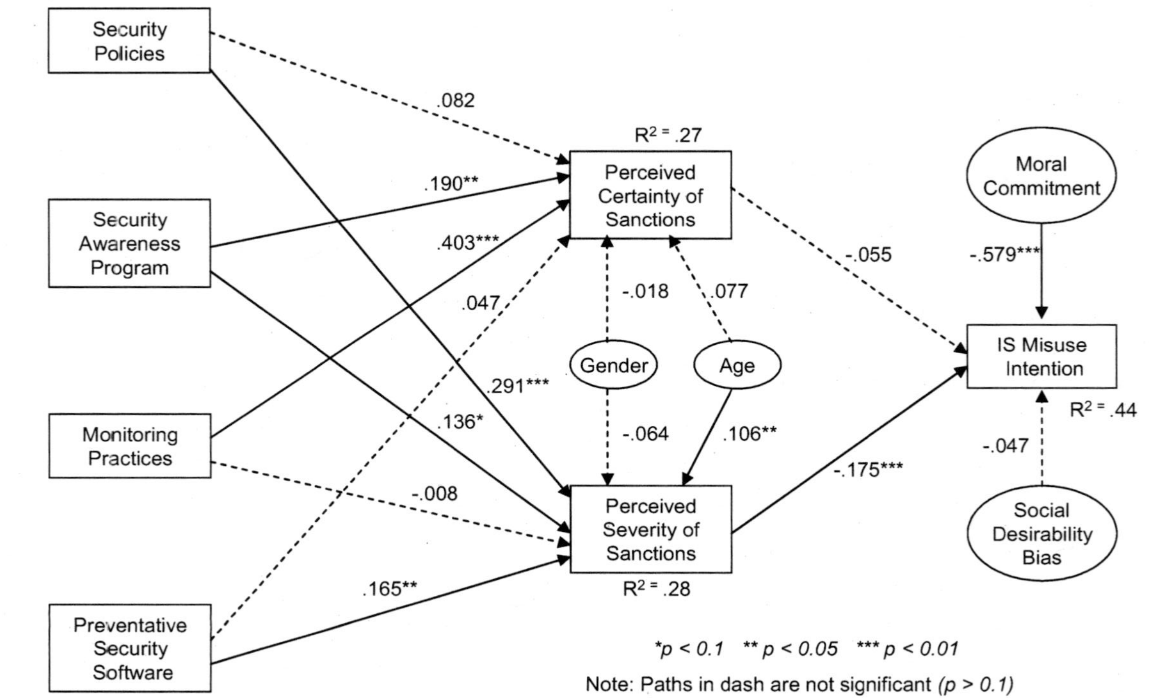

Figure D.1. PLS Analysis of Main Effects – MBA Sample

Table D.1. Main Effect Path Coefficients – MBA Sample

H#	Hypothesis (Direction)	Path Coefficient	T-value	Significance (one-tailed)	Supported?
H1a	P → PC (+)	0.116	1.589	$p < 0.10$	Yes
H1b	P → PS (+)	0.215	3.024	$p < 0.01$	Yes
H2a	SA → PC (+)	0.206	3.508	$p < 0.01$	Yes
H2b	SA → PS (+)	0.183	2.460	$p < 0.01$	Yes
H3a	M → PC (+)	0.471	8.608	$p < 0.01$	Yes
H3b	M → PS (+)	0.088	1.581	$p < 0.10$	Yes
H4a	PR → PC (+)	0.044	0.977	n.s.	No
H4b	PR → PS (+)	0.078	1.528	$p < 0.10$	Yes
H8a	PC → INT (-)	-0.080	2.198	$p < 0.05$	Yes
H8b	PS → INT (-)	-0.139	3.400	$p < 0.01$	Yes
INT = IS misuse intention; PC = Perceived certainty of sanctions; PS = Perceived severity of sanctions; P = Security policies; SA = Security awareness program; M = Monitoring practices; PR = Preventative security software					

Table D.2. Interaction Effect Path Coefficients – MBA Sample

H#	Hypothesis (Direction)	PLS Model Description	Path Coefficient	T-value	Sig.	Supported?
H5a	CSE moderates P → PC (-)	CSE*P → PC (-)	-0.203	1.400	$p < 0.10$	Yes
H5b	CSE moderates SA → PC (-)	CSE*SA → PC (-)	0.118	1.041	n.s.	No
H5c	CSE moderates M → PC (-)	CSE*M → PC (-)	0.052	0.532	n.s.	No
H5d	CSE moderates PR → PC (-)	CSE*PR → PC (-)	0.157	1.503	$p < 0.10$	No*
H5e	CSE moderates P → PS (-)	CSE*P → PS (-)	0.017	0.129	n.s.	No
H5f	CSE moderates SA → PS (-)	CSE*SA → PS (-)	-0.034	0.358	n.s.	No
H5g	CSE moderates M → PS (-)	CSE*M → PS (-)	0.057	0.486	n.s.	No
H5h	CSE moderates PR → PS (-)	CSE*PR → PS (-)	-0.017	0.187	n.s.	No
H6a	RP moderates P → PC (-)	RP*P → PC (-)	0.082	0.564	n.s.	No
H6b	RP moderates SA → PC (-)	RP*SA → PC (-)	0.024	0.197	n.s.	No
H6c	RP moderates M → PC (-)	RP*M → PC (-)	-0.008	0.066	n.s.	No
H6d	RP moderates PR → PC (-)	RP*PR → PC (-)	0.050	0.459	n.s.	No

* Significant but in opposite direction than hypothesized.

Table D.2 (continued). Interaction Effect Path Coefficients – MBA Sample

H#	Hypothesis (Direction)	PLS Model Description	Path Coefficient	T-value	Sig.	Supported?
H6e	RP moderates P → PS (-)	RP*P → PS (-)	-0.002	0.017	n.s.	No
H6f	RP moderates SA → PS (-)	RP*SA → PS (-)	0.118	0.871	n.s.	No
H6g	RP moderates M → PS (-)	RP*M → PS (-)	-0.027	0.237	n.s.	No
H6h	RP moderates PR → PS (-)	RP*PR → PS (-)	0.027	0.271	n.s.	No
H7a	VS moderates P → PC (-)	VS*P → PC (-)	-0.107	0.890	n.s.	No
H7b	VS moderates SA → PC (-)	VS*SA → PC (-)	0.221	1.312	$p < 0.10$	No
H7c	VS moderates M → PC (-)	VS*M → PC (-)	-0.148	1.353	$p < 0.10$	**Yes**
H7d	VS moderates PR → PC (-)	VS*PR → PC (-)	-0.057	0.597	n.s.	No
H7e	VS moderates P → PS (-)	VS*P → PS (-)	-0.073	0.651	n.s.	No
H7f	VS moderates SA → PS (-)	VS*SA → PS (-)	0.103	0.805	n.s.	No
H7g	VS moderates M → PS (-)	VS*M → PS (-)	0.054	0.553	n.s.	No
H7h	VS moderates PR → PS (-)	VS*PR → PS (-)	0.002	0.023	n.s.	No

* Significant but in opposite direction than hypothesized.

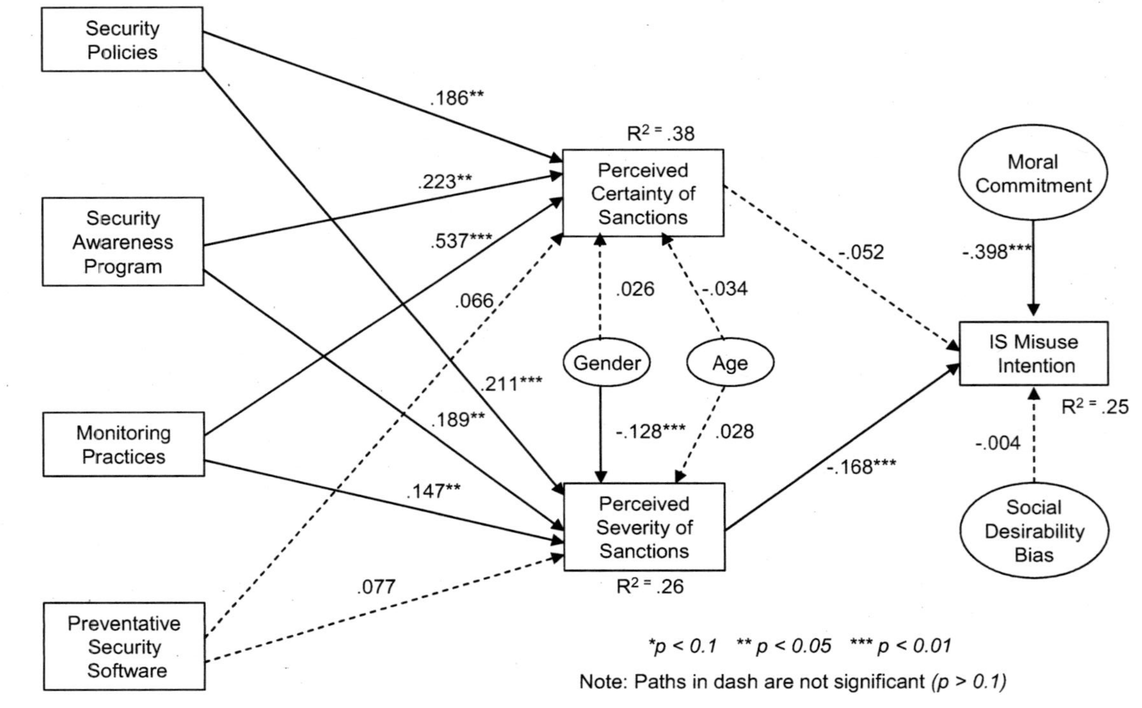

Figure D.2. PLS of Main Effects – Industry Sample

Table D.3. Main Effect Path Coefficients – Industry Sample

H#	Hypothesis (Direction)	Path Coefficient	T-value	Significance (one-tailed)	Supported?
H1a	P → PC (+)	0.186	2.228	$p < 0.05$	Yes
H1b	P → PS (+)	0.211	2.456	$p < 0.01$	Yes
H2a	SA → PC (+)	0.223	3.248	$p < 0.01$	Yes
H2b	SA → PS (+)	0.189	2.128	$p < 0.05$	Yes
H3a	M → PC (+)	0.537	8.421	$p < 0.01$	Yes
H3b	M → PS (+)	0.147	2.057	$p < 0.05$	Yes
H4a	PR → PC (+)	0.066	0.973	n.s.	No
H4b	PR → PS (+)	0.007	0.977	n.s.	No
H8a	PC → INT (-)	-0.052	0.857	n.s.	No
H8b	PS → INT (-)	-0.168	2.415	$p < 0.01$	Yes
INT = IS misuse intention; PC = Perceived certainty of sanctions; PS = Perceived severity of sanctions; P = Security policies; SA = Security awareness program; M = Monitoring practices; PR = Preventative security software					

Table D.4. Interaction Effect Path Coefficients – Industry Sample

H#	Hypothesis (Direction)	PLS Model Description	Path Coefficient	T-value	Sig.	Supported?
H5a	CSE moderates P → PC (-)	CSE*P → PC (-)	-0.076	0.568	n.s.	No
H5b	CSE moderates SA → PC (-)	CSE*SA → PC (-)	0.157	0.929	n.s.	No
H5c	CSE moderates M → PC (-)	CSE*M → PC (-)	-0.204	1.523	$p < 0.10$	**Yes**
H5d	CSE moderates PR → PC (-)	CSE*PR → PC (-)	-0.024	0.308	n.s.	No
H5e	CSE moderates P → PS (-)	CSE*P → PS (-)	-0.066	0.521	n.s.	No
H5f	CSE moderates SA → PS (-)	CSE*SA → PS (-)	0.169	0.996	n.s.	No
H5g	CSE moderates M → PS (-)	CSE*M → PS (-)	-0.139	1.010	n.s.	No
H5h	CSE moderates PR → PS (-)	CSE*PR → PS (-)	-0.060	0.681	n.s.	No
H6a	RP moderates P → PC (-)	RP*P → PC (-)	0.104	1.196	n.s.	No
H6b	RP moderates SA → PC (-)	RP*SA → PC (-)	0.153	1.159	n.s.	No
H6c	RP moderates M → PC (-)	RP*M → PC (-)	0.050	0.534	n.s.	No
H6d	RP moderates PR → PC (-)	RP*PR → PC (-)	-0.061	0.819	n.s.	No

* Significant but in opposite direction than hypothesized.

Table D.4 (continued). Interaction Effect Path Coefficients – Industry Sample

H#	Hypothesis (Direction)	PLS Model Description	Path Coefficient	T-value	Sig.	Supported?
H6e	RP moderates P → PS (-)	RP*P → PS (-)	0.025	0.244	n.s.	No
H6f	RP moderates SA → PS (-)	RP*SA → PS (-)	0.041	0.323	n.s.	No
H6g	RP moderates M → PS (-)	RP*M → PS (-)	0.039	0.416	n.s.	No
H6h	RP moderates PR → PS (-)	RP*PR → PS (-)	0.062	0.568	n.s.	No
H7a	VS moderates P → PC (-)	VS*P → PC (-)	-0.240	1.997	$p < 0.05$	**Yes**
H7b	VS moderates SA → PC (-)	VS*SA → PC (-)	0.091	1.063	n.s.	No
H7c	VS moderates M → PC (-)	VS*M → PC (-)	0.151	1.615	$p < 0.10$	No*
H7d	VS moderates PR → PC (-)	VS*PR → PC (-)	-0.089	0.144	n.s.	No
H7e	VS moderates P → PS (-)	VS*P → PS (-)	-0.186	0.913	n.s.	No
H7f	VS moderates SA → PS (-)	VS*SA → PS (-)	0.224	1.317	$p < 0.10$	No*
H7g	VS moderates M → PS (-)	VS*M → PS (-)	0.080	0.804	n.s.	No
H7h	VS moderates PR → PS (-)	VS*PR → PS (-)	-0.053	0.531	n.s.	No

* Significant but in opposite direction than hypothesized.

Index

Prologue

October in the Southern highlands is a time of leaves turning hillsides into Persian carpets of color; of chilly moon-washed nights and hot drowsy noondays; of ripeness and harvest. Corn, the succulent maize adopted by pioneers from their Indian neighbors, is gathered in bin and shock. Tobacco cures to a golden pungence. Pumpkins splash the fields with color, and orchard bees suck the sweet juices of apples that have fallen to the ground. Seeds sowed in the spring past, roots planted in long-ago decades, bring forth their yield.

In just such an October in 1780, another, quite different but no less inevitable harvest was gathered in an unlikely corner of the Southern theater of the American Revolutionary War. The place was called Kings Mountain, although it wasn't royal (named for an early settler rather than the distant resident of Windsor Castle) and, indeed, at the negligible height of only a few hundred feet above the surrounding countryside, not even much of a mountain. But there, on an early October afternoon 5 years after the beginning of the Revolution, King George and his ministers' misunderstanding of the nature and needs of their faraway rebellious colonies, and the British command's misconceptions of the American character, ripened into a confrontation that marked a turning point in the war.

If events influenced by the patriot victory at Kings Mountain reached far beyond that brief time and place, so, too, did events initiating the struggle at Kings Mountain reach far back in time and place.

The battle of Kings Mountain did not begin when a brilliant, proud young British major named

Patrick Ferguson sent a message across the wilderness barriers of the Blue Ridge to sturdy frontier mountain folk, warning that if they did not leave off opposition to British authority he would "march his army over the mountains, hang their leaders, and lay their country waste with fire and sword."

Kings Mountain did not begin when a spontaneous army of hunters, farmers, and settlers, tough as hickory, weather-beaten by sun and wind and bitten by cold, dodged from tree to tree up that rocky ridge, taking deadly aim with long squirrel rifles at their loyalist enemies.

Kings Mountain did not begin with the first shrill staccato of Patrick Ferguson's silver whistle as he spurred his horse along the crest of the ridge, rallying his men to wage the battle bravely.

The engagement at Kings Mountain began far away—in London—in the fears of a harassed Secretary of State for the Colonies named Lord George Germain, who needed to believe that there were numerous and devoted loyalists in the American colonies and that they would eventually rise and turn the tide of victory for the king.

It began long before, in the raw winter mists and grinding poverty of Ulster villages where the people who would be known in America as the Scotch-Irish nurtured fierce ideas of personal independence and property; in similar communities of French Huguenots and German Palatines; and elsewhere in Europe wherever people abandoned hopelessness and pushed their way to America.

It began with symbols, such as a royal governor's extravagant palace that became the hated token of a burdensome taxation, and with protests, peaceful and otherwise, to regulate the power and privilege of those governors and secure some semblance of law and order for the neglected western frontiers.

Kings Mountain began in the hearts and minds of people—of a king and his makers of policy, of generals, and of "rabble" who had no policy but some very firm beliefs. For the British, the message of Kings Mountain was a bitter harvest of mistaken judgment and misplaced hopes. To the Americans, it was a revelation of possible ultimate victory.

After Kings Mountain no one would claim again that there was an untapped reserve of loyalist sentiment out there in the hinterlands waiting to be gathered into the royal ranks.

After Kings Mountain no one would fail to take seriously the tenacious determination and practical democracy of the people of the western waters. They were pushing back frontiers, opening the dark and bloody ground of Kentucky, planting the seeds of permanence in the distant Cumberland settlements, reaching ever westward.

In America, in the rich interior expanses of meadow and canebrake, forest and wilderness, they had found land. Land was security such as landless people had never known; land was commitment, a sense of purpose, a sense of permanence; land was freedom such as the dispossessed had never experienced: the freedom to change, to grow, to discover alternatives and make one's own choices. Their land and their freedom had been restricted and burdened and threatened long enough by distant authority. At Kings Mountain they were ready to settle the matter once and for all.

Maj. Patrick Ferguson's Tory army enters Gilbert Town, N.C. The ultimatum he issued there set the stage for the Battle of Kings Mountain.

The patriot army of farmers, hunters, and frontiersmen crosses the mountains to find Ferguson.

After the Battle of Kings Mountain, the patriots, enraged by stories of alleged Tory atrocities, tried and executed nine of Ferguson's captured loyalists.

It is necessary to remember that at the battle of Kings Mountain every participant but one was an American. Only Maj. Patrick Ferguson of His Majesty's 71st Highlanders was a professional British soldier from the British Isles. All others were either loyalist and patriot volunteers or–and this was the vast majority–militia mustered by local governments.

Compulsory militia service had become a tradition in all the American colonies. Many a town and county seat had its "muster field" where citizen soldiers assembled at designated times to train and discharge their duties of preparedness. Muster days were serious events that frequently culminated in celebrations and free-for-alls involving hard cider and fisticuffs. The people of these colonies were hard-working and hard-playing. When necessary many could be hard fighters.

The quality of the various militia units varied widely, and many historians now agree that the militia's contribution to America's Revolutionary War has probably been underrated. At Kings Mountain the militia's unique features were brought into full use and translated into assets for the patriots. Among these were minimum organization with maximum individual responsibility; ability to attack from ambush; quick maneuverability; and capability for swift, decisive action. In other circumstances, over a lengthier period, the militia's "excessive turnover, lax discipline, and an urge to question why" could play havoc with military effectiveness; but there were occasions when these were not drawbacks but conditions which made men more determined and dauntless. No engagement demonstrated this more dramatically than Kings Mountain.

Who were these men of Kings Mountain? Except for 100 British soldiers picked from the King's American Regiment, the Queen's Rangers, and the New Jersey Volunteers, they came from the Carolinas, Virginia, Georgia, and present East Tennessee. Most of those in the loyalist forces were from the lowlands and Piedmont areas, while many of the patriots were from the upcountry, with a highly fierce and visible nucleus from the remotest corners of Virginia and North Carolina–the region known as the over-mountain country.

Geography, national origins, economics, religion, and culture shaped the primary differences within these Southern colonies and these differences impelled each person to choose his side when war with Great Britain erupted. East-West sectionalism remained the most enduring divisive reality in North Carolina and to a somewhat lesser extent in South Carolina.

Geography gave the coastal regions of these colonies certain riches: a fertile tidewater in Virginia; naval stores such as tar, pitch, turpentine, and timber in the Carolinas; and acres adaptable to indigo and rice along the South Carolina coast. Inland the country stretched westward across sand and clay, pine and palmetto, a gently rising Piedmont, and finally crested on the windswept pinnacles of the highest mountains in the Appalachian chain. This diverse landscape was pocked with swamps in the lowlands and laced with rivers from mountains to sea. Its fertility varied as widely as its accessibility.

In the east, settlement was predominantly English; along the North Carolina coast and extending inland there were significant numbers of Scottish Highlanders as well. The society established by these and other less numerous groups of Europeans was essentially aristocratic, a plantation economy based on slave labor and trade with Great Britain, Europe, and the West Indies. It favored the Anglican Church. To the west, there were Germans–most of them from the Palatine in southwestern Germany, fleeing devastating wars, religious persecution, and heavy taxes–and Swiss, English, Welsh, Irish, French Huguenots, and, above all, the Scotch-Irish. Their society of small farms, free labor, and a religious diversity that included Presbyterians, Lutherans, Dunkards, Moravians, Baptists, and Quakers, was ardently democratic, at least in its ideals.

During the two decades prior to the Revolutionary War, the western country was opened by increasing numbers of permanent settlers. With the defeat of the Cherokee Indians in 1761, the South Carolina backcountry saw an influx of settlers. In North Carolina, the hamlet of Salisbury claimed that in 1764 alone more than a thousand wagons of families immigrating to the western borders of the colony had passed through its streets. By the time of the Revolution, South Carolina's upcountry claimed 79 percent of the white inhabitants of the colony, amounting to 50 percent of its total population.

Increase of population did not increase mutual affection between the regions, however. "Those from the westward," wrote a North Carolinian some years later, "look upon the people in any of the commercial towns, as little better than swindlers; while those of the east consider the westerners as a pack of savages." The main point of contention was the fact that despite their growing numbers and their payment of inequitable taxes which favored the large landholders in the east, the westerners had little political influence. In South Carolina the people of the upcountry felt that they had too little access to government; in North Carolina they felt that the government had too much access to them, reaching into their pockets ever more deeply. But in both cases the coastal regions of the provinces dominated all branches of government.

In 1770, when North Carolina's royal governor, William Tryon, completed his palatial residence (considered by many as the finest "government house" in British America), the backcountry people were infuriated at this "visible and permanent symbol of eastern rule." And since the colonial treasury was on the brink of bankruptcy, new taxes would have to be levied to pay for the handsome brick edifices and its elegant furnishings.

One of these taxes was a poll tax, which always bore more heavily on the small farmer of the west than on the large planter in the east. Tryon, who had been given the name Great Wolf by the Indians, was increasingly seen by the citizens in the west as meriting the title in all too realistic a sense. "We want no such House, nor will we pay for it," they protested.

Such attitudes of defiance had been growing throughout South Carolina and North Carolina since the 1761 victory over the Cherokees. With law-abiding settlers and farmers, lawless adventurers and renegades, and all manner of new arrivals mingling along the western borders, the primary challenge became one of establishing an orderly society and viable government in the backcountry. In South Carolina the upcountry people felt that with all the power centralized in Charleston the formal institutions of local militia, weak justices of the peace, and small churches merely "moderated the disorder." When a wave of crime erupted along this frontier in the summer and fall of 1767, the citizens grew desperate. They formed into a group known as the Regulators and, lacking official protectors, took it upon themselves to "scourge the land of the criminal and the shiftless."

Stolen horses, abducted blacks, and kidnapped women and children were retrieved from criminal terrorists. The Regulators–who may have numbered between 5,000 and 6,000 at their peak of popularity– sealed off their region from Charleston. Organized to suppress outlaws, they acted outside the law themselves and soon encountered the ancient dilemma of their own uncontrolled power. Arson and whippings became weapons of control in the upcountry. When the South Carolina Assembly, with agreement of the Crown, finally established proper western courts, Regulator activity diminished and was finally abandoned.

While the South Carolina upcountry was seeking to correct the lack of local courts and sheriffs, the North Carolina backcountry began its own Regulator movement for exactly the opposite reason: to correct too much interference by unjust courts and venal sheriffs in local affairs. In the spring of 1768 the Regulators vowed to have officers "under a better and honester regulation."

Accusations multiplied, riots broke out, panic threatened. Governor Tryon called out the militia, marched to a creek named Alamance, and there, on May 14, 1771, after warning an assemblage of some 2,000 Regulators, only half of whom were armed, that they were "in a state of rebellion against your King, your country, and your laws," defeated and scattered them. It was a crushing blow, and Tryon, already appointed governor of New York at the time of Alamance, soon departed North Carolina for his new post. Many of the Regulators departed too, for the farthest land they knew of that was open for settlement–the area that was soon to become the Watauga country. Within a year a Baptist minister estimated that since Alamance 1,500 families, despairing of seeing better times, had left North Carolina. Most of them were of Scotch-Irish stock.

The region to which many of them removed was the overmountain country–sparse, rugged, beleaguered little settlements along the Holston, Watauga, and Nolichucky Rivers, and in Carter's Valley and dozens of other beckoning sites.

When the Wataugans, already uneasy because they were possibly encroaching on Indian land, realized that they were beyond the protection of either North Carolina or Virginia, they grew fearful that their settlement (in the region destined to become East Tennessee) would become a haven for criminals and outlaws. Displaying a clear notion of precisely what they wanted to achieve, these Wataugans adopted written articles of agreement dealing with debtors, the recording of deeds and wills, and similar "public business."

Lord Dunmore, royal governor of Virginia, called this Watauga Association "a dangerous example" and an encouragement "to the people of America of forming governments distinct from and independent of His Majesty's Authority." In a few years, many Americans would be part of a larger struggle to become "independent of His Majesty's authority," and it is significant that an initial impetus had come from a predominantly Scotch-Irish segment of the Southern frontier. For of all the national characters represented at Kings Mountain, none was more distinctive than that of the Scotch-Irish.

These were Scots, chiefly Lowlanders, who had been part of the "plantation" James I of England established in northern Ireland, chiefly in the province of Ulster. Scottish by heritage, Irish by geography, these energetic people had prospered until their woolen trade began to compete with that of Britain. Gradually but decisively their woolen industry was crippled by discriminatory laws and their Presbyterian religion was curtailed by prohibitions on worship and education. Adding to their plight was a series of crop failures. Choked by the tightening noose of poverty and religious antagonism, the Scotch-

Irish began their great migrations to America. From Pennsylvania they poured southwest into the Piedmont and down the valley of Virginia into the harsh and demanding backcountry.

No more numerous than the English, no more industrious than the Germans, no more freedom-loving than the Huguenots, the Scotch-Irish were nonetheless the group that left their image stamped indelibly on this frontier. Many of their characteristics came to be considered specific hallmarks of the American character, too. The Scotch-Irish have been described as restless and self-reliant with a love of adventure, great physical endurance, and the capacity to adapt to their surroundings. They have been called grasping, contentious, and so set in their ways that they could pray, "Lord, grant that I may always be right, for Thou knowest that I am hard to turn."

Above all, the Scotch-Irish person seems to have been paradoxical. He has been described as both "venturesome and cautious, taciturn to a fault, but speaking his mind freely when aroused." Essentially serious, he could nevertheless display a sense of humor; fondness for sports revealed his sociability. Friend and foe alike were objects of his steadfast attention and "his nature rebelled against anything that savored of injustice or deceit, nor did he take kindly to restraint of any kind."

This Scotch-Irish character—prompt to resent an affront, unrelenting to foes—was to leave an imprint on the history of the Revolutionary War at Kings Mountain.

The homegrown Tories, those loyalists who accompanied Patrick Ferguson on his marches across the Carolinas, came from a variety of backgrounds. Curiously enough, North Carolina, the first State to authorize its delegates to the Second Continental Congress to vote for independence, was one of the two States (New York being the other) considered most heavily loyalist during the war.

Among the reasons for this were the presence of large numbers of Highland Scots who had recently sworn allegiance to the king; the Regulators who still hated the Assembly so strongly that when that body urged a revolutionary cause they automatically rallied to the king; and the natural Tory sympathies of those devoted Anglicans who were fearful of the backwoods religions and whose economic and social ties bound them to London rather than to their native America.

These, then, were some of the people who played out the drama of Kings Mountain. They were neighbors and enemies, Highlanders and Lowlanders, king's men and democrats, natural leaders and reluctant followers. They were used to fighting. They had fought back in their native land at such places as Culloden. They had fought the Indians. In the summer and autumn of 1776 alone, Georgia, North and South Carolina, and Virginia sent more than 5,000 militiamen into the Cherokee country to meet Indian attacks encouraged by the larger war taking place along the coasts, and there were almost monthly forays and skirmishes between the Indians and the settlers pushing ever deeper into their domain. They had fought each other, in scattered violent episodes of the Regulator movement. So far, most of them had been preoccupied with meeting daily local challenges of survival; they had not yet taken a full-fledged role in the Revolution riving the rest of the country that would soon be called these United States of America.

But as the year 1780 approached, the country staggered under the burdens that seemed insupportable and the South reeled under defeats that seemed irreversible. It was to be an eventful, decisive year.

On a bitterly cold December 15, 1779, in Morristown, N.J., George Washington sent a report as commander in chief of the army to the Continental Congress: "Our prospects," he wrote, "are infinitely worse than they have been at any period of the War, and unless some expedient can instantly be adopted a dissolution of the Army for want of subsistence is unavoidable–A part of it has been again several days without Bread–and for the rest we have not either on the spot or within reach a supply sufficient for four days."

Valley Forge and the cruel winter of 1777-78 are fixed in the popular imagination as the season of suffering for the patriot forces under their dauntless leader; less appreciated is the agony the army experienced at Morristown in the winter of 1779-80. Snow was 4- to 6-feet deep before the rude winter huts could be built, and many soldiers slept under a single blanket on a thin bedding of straw, without shoes or adequate clothing. Half frozen and half starved they staggered from one day to the next.

Not only bread was lacking but bullets, too. Again, General Washington tried to impress the message that this crisis arose not from transportation problems or accidental circumstances such as had occurred in the past, "but from the absolute emptiness of our magazines everywhere and the total want of money or credit to replenish them."

The money Washington and his patriot forces needed was simply non-existent. Or, just the opposite, it was in too great an existence. One of the greatest failures of the Congress was in the realm of finance, where both imagination (ideas fostering fiscal responsibility) and courage (to implement this responsibility) were lacking. After printing 242 million paper dollars, Congress decided to stop the printing presses. By March 1780, the paper dollar was worth a fourth of a cent in gold. The saying "not worth a continental" came into use to reflect the ravages of inflation on citizens and soldiers alike. The United States, as James Madison observed years later, had tried to survive by pumping instead of patching the leaks.

Minus coordination and sometimes the will, groping for some effective system of organization and support, the colonies let the Continental Army sink toward starvation. On St. Patrick's Day in 1780, Washington complained that he had only enough grain to make bread for 5 days and pickled meat to last for 40 days. By late summer the commander in chief was reduced to feeding his army "by marching it from temporary camp to temporary camp, exhausting the food supply of the neighborhood instead of more properly drawing on the country as a whole. If this kept up the Army would become a horde of plunderers."

The condition of the private soldier was thus more desperate in 1780 than at any time during the whole war. Washington stated that the Army would have "dissolved long before except for patriotism, and the Congress could not rely on this cement forever."

In the South, circumstances of war and geography had wrought a situation in which the fierceness of combat was not confined to opposing armies. In the Carolinas and Georgia every crossroads and household became a potential battleground. The Revolution was not so much a struggle between British regulars in their scarlet coats and close formation opposed by patriot soldiers with such uniforms and weapons as they could muster as it was a fitful, miserable civil conflict. Guerrilla fighting raged, and both sides were afflicted with the violent passions that nullified all compassion. The number of skirmishes which took place in the interior of the lower South has been estimated as "dozens, possibly hundreds."

As accounts of lootings, burnings, and killings circulated through the countryside, fears and hatreds intensified with each embellished version. Vengeance became a way of life. When Nathanael Greene arrived in North Carolina late in 1780 to lead the patriot forces in the South, he found that "not a day passes but there are more or less who fall a sacrifice to this savage disposition. The Whigs seem determined to extirpate the Tories, and the Tories the Whigs." Greene, a Quaker who may have recoiled with more than normal dismay at the daily horrors compounded by such internecine warfare, warned: "If a stop cannot be put to these massacres, the country will be depopulated . . . as neither Whig nor Tory can live."

Hot tar and feathers became one of the rituals of punishment inflicted by vigilante groups on those suspected of Tory sympathies or accused of aiding the British forces invading the countryside. Painful as this searing public shame may have been, it was perhaps no more dreaded nor resisted than the confiscation of property which left a loyalist impoverished and homeless.

Among the most sinister and despised of all the participants in this warfare, however, were those who came to be known as "outliers," a term that would carry over into the American Civil War of 1861-65, when it would assume even larger and more dreaded connotations in the upcountry fighting of the Southern States. Outliers were simply those people who refused to support either side of the conflict. They rode and raided, often indiscriminately, and for their own profit. Much of the fear and turmoil that tore families and communities asunder during the war was a result of these plunderers for private gain and greed, who struck and disappeared and were all too seldom caught or punished by either side.

If 1780 was the nadir for the patriot cause, with colonial finances in shambles, Washington's army neglected and dispirited, and the Southern theater deteriorating into a cannibalistic kind of fury, there was still no reason for the British to indulge in self-satisfaction. Their fortunes, too, were at a low ebb. By 1779 the expense of war in America plus the burden of war with France and Spain had placed a heavy strain on King George's coffers and his subjects' patience. British agents sought new loans in Europe, despite high interest rates, to add to a national debt that already stood at £200 million sterling. Unemployment fostered deep unrest. John Wesley, the father of Methodism, in his travels across the British Isles saw the suffering firsthand and warned that thousands of idle, starving workmen gave portent of rebellion.

The war in America received a full share of blame for Britain's bankrupt conditions, and in mass meetings the freeholders of county after county denounced further pursuit of that conflict. Thus in the turbulent spring of 1780, the American Revolution might have been ended, or at least modified, by the frustrations and needs of a public outraged against king and Parliament—except for a strange occurrence which suddenly seized London.

A half-mad Scottish peer named Lord George Gordon, capitalizing on the unrest that prevailed throughout the land, indulged in the ages-old rabble-rousing device of blaming complex political and economic troubles on the wiles of a racial or religious minority. For three terrible days in June the city of London was at the mercy of a mob. Newgate Prison was set afire, the Bank of England was attacked, Catholic chapels were destroyed, and the House of Commons was threatened. Before the arson and pillage were brought under control, some 450 people had been killed or wounded and thousands had been terrorized.

Such a display of anarchy was sobering to those who had been leading legitimate protests against governmental policies. The episode stilled, for the moment, the questions and dissatisfactions that had been welling up across the British Isles. The time had long since arrived for a strategic reappraisal of the war in the American colonies, but the king and his ministers were no more willing to undertake the task now than they had been 2 years earlier when George III, pouring over maps of America, had devised the 1778 Southern campaign in which each side had failed—the British in their attempt to take Charleston and South Carolina, the Americans in their attempt to oust the British from Savannah and Georgia.

By late 1779, the British were turning South again, staking their fortunes on a choice that would be pursued to its ultimate perimeters in the crucial year of 1780. For the basis of that choice involved the fundamental error on which much British strategy had been constructed. Every step Britain made suggested belief in the myth of a dissident minority which would arise to become active loyalists "constituting one of Britain's most important potential resources."

Reliance, even in fantasy, on such tenuous support, had fostered a lack of decisiveness that frequently undermined the results of any British victory. Desultory operations that "neither completely destroyed the enemy nor restored peace to the conquered territory" simply served to keep opposition alive and led to the vicious situation which existed in the South throughout 1780.

Thus, on the drizzly, rainy day in March 1780, when Sir Henry Clinton, with a force of 8,500 soldiers (plus 5,000 seamen mustered from the fleet behind him), began a 30-mile march from John's Island toward Charleston, launching the final great British campaign in the South, he was following once again the strategy devised by King George and Lord Germain. According to that strategy, South Carolina was to be reestablished as a royal colony, after which it would be a relatively simple task to tramp through North Carolina, which was "but the road to Virginia," and then on to the Chesapeake Bay area where British forces could reassert their strength and control of the seaboard. Along the way it was expected—at least by those planning the maneuver on paper—that "large numbers of the inhabitants would flock to the King's standard."

Dependence on the loyalists was even more crucial to this campaign than to the earlier attempt to subdue the South. Now there was an aroused British public clamoring for an end to a war they believed Britain would not win; there were even those in high places who believed Britain could not win. After the British defeat at Saratoga and France's formal entry into the conflict on the patriots' side, Lord North himself had recognized that "the best we can make of the war is to get out of the dispute as soon as possible." But the King would not consider Lord North's resignation nor the war's unsatisfactory conclusion. His persistence and that of his Secretary for Colonial Affairs was reenforced by one vocal group in London: the loyalist exiles who had fled from America to spend the duration of the war in Britain. They were loud and positive in asserting that they represented a large, though muffled, body of opinion in the American colonies. Germain seized on their testimony to support beliefs he had long propounded, and finally he found himself locked into a position of using the loyalists as a cause for continuing the war. Military realities were being distorted or overridden by political considerations. The blunt and definitive action at Kings Mountain would do much to point out the fatal consequences of such distortion.

In this atmosphere of unreality, of feverish grasping for expedients, the potential of loyalist support in the Southern backcountry became primary "evidence" in arguments for continued prosecution of the war. Dissidents in the House of Commons who could not be persuaded by such arguments were now appealed to on the basis of honor. It was proclaimed that those who had remained stalwart loyalists were owed a debt of honor by Great Britain and efforts to defeat the American rebels must continue. Germain, in many ways an able and curious personality who bore much calumny and opposition throughout his life, had staked his career and the future of one segment of the proud and powerful British Empire on marshalling effective loyalist support in the South. His hope never materialized.

There was no alternative now. Britain, rent by internal division and increasing weakness of its far-flung external resources, increasingly dependent upon a surge of Southern loyalists to win its war, launched the Southern offensive of 1780.

As for the patriot cause, lacking the basic necessities to wage effective combat, it turned to the Southern theater and all the debilitating civil conflict there, depending upon Southern patriots to determine its future.

Thus, each side acutely needed the allegiance of that vast, neglected, enigmatic interior known as the backcountry–reaching from the lowlands and Piedmont up into the rugged mountains of southwestern Virginia, western North Carolina, and the area that would become East Tennessee. But the people of those landlocked coves and valleys had shown only sporadic interest in the war raging along the coast. They were preoccupied with their own dangers, one of which was continuing conflict–or threat of conflict–with the Indians, who tended, on the whole, to side with the British more than the patriots in this war. The over-mountain people were a buffer, protecting the Southern colonies from attack through their back door, either by hostile Indians or foreign powers. Beyond that, they had not thrown the full weight of their commitment to either side.

Nature did not welcome the British expedition of Sir Henry Clinton as it sailed along the fearful North Carolina coast in January 1780, en route from New York to South Carolina. Violent storms scattered transports and escort vessels, sank a shipload of cannon, and forced destruction of the fine cavalry horses that were to be essential to the Southern campaign.

But the British general remained confident. His assurance was matched only by the negligence of those tending the garrison in Charleston, Clinton's immediate objective. Mrs. St. Julien Ravenel, writing later about the dallying and delay displayed by Charlestonians toward their fortifications, remembered that a fort which was ordered in January to be built with "all expedition" was not half done when news of the coming of the British fleet was received. "At once all was bustle and activity. . . . The approach of the fleet had done more in one week to unite the people than the acts of the ministers or the eloquence of Gadsden had effected in months."

The bustle and activity came too late. On May 12, following a methodical month-long British siege, solid but ill-fated Gen. Benjamin Lincoln surrendered America's fourth largest city and the commercial capital of the South. It was the most severe defeat suffered by patriot forces during the entire war. The only patriot army in the South, 18 Continental regiments in all, including the entire South Carolina and Virginia Lines and one-third of the North Carolina Line, was lost. The British claimed 5,500 troops captured, including seven generals and 290 other Continental officers. It represented the largest total of patriot prisoners captured at any one time during the Revolution.

Precious quantities of muskets, ammunition, powder, and ordnance matériel were also lost. Most important, British hopes were momentarily revived. News of the victory at Charleston served as a welcome antidote to mounting Parliamentary opposition. And patriot spirits were plunged into ever deeper despair.

Rumors abounded that Washington was prepared to foresake the Southern colonies. Dejected patriots began to wonder if further resistance was justified or even possible. As they acknowledged their defenselessness they began to admit, reluctantly, the possibility of the return of royal government.

At this moment, official Britain's misunderstanding of the American character proved decisive to the future course of the war. Clinton had won a battle but he failed to win the peace. Soon after the fall of Charleston, he offered lenient paroles to any of the American rebels who would return to the royal fold and thenceforth remain peaceably at home. Thousands flocked in to receive such paroles. It appeared that the countryside might soon be pacified. Then, abruptly, on June 3, Sir Henry did an about-face and proposed a hard line in dealing with rebel Carolinians. By these new terms anyone who had taken the parole and withdrawn from conflict was now ordered to swear an oath of allegiance and take "an active part in settling and securing His Majesty's government."

From quiescence the Carolinians were aroused once more to resistance. They felt that their good faith had been violated. What had appeared to be initial clemency was now revised to involve an unwelcome kind of collaboration. Forced to choose sides once more, some of them openly took up arms with the patriots, while others subscribed to the oath but considered their pledge given under duress "and consequently felt no obligation to honor it."

In addition to this official reversal, which many citizens considered in fact a betrayal, there were also bloody British raids and depredations launched across the countryside. Following the fall of Charleston, Clinton thought it necessary to dispatch efficient, quick-striking bodies of soldiers into the hinterlands so that the populace would be convinced of British supremacy. Thus, patriots would be intimidated or dissuaded from their allegiance, and loyalists would be emboldened to rally and become the unified force of long-time British expectations.

Intimidation was not a wise weapon to use in seeking the fidelity of Carolinians, however. It was especially unwise when put in the hands of an officer such as Col. Banastre Tarleton, the dashing but ruthless commander of Clinton's light cavalry. Tarleton became to the South during the Revolutionary War what William Tecumseh Sherman was to the South during the Civil War: a symbol of all that was brutal in war, his name a rallying cry for retaliation.

A short, stocky redhead, Banastre Tarleton at 26 years of age was a graduate of Oxford, a hard-riding, high-living dragoon officer who bragged about his triumphal subjugation of sundry women and the victorious conquests of his Legion. When all the horses for his cavalry perished on the voyage South he vowed "to put his men on good horseflesh and to make his mark on the Southern rebels."

One of those indelible marks was struck on May 29, 1780, in the Waxhaws country near the North Carolina line where Tarleton, after a ride of 54 hours covering a distance of 105 miles, overtook a column of retreating Virginia Continentals and a detachment of William Washington's cavalry under Col. Abraham Buford. Exaggerating his force of 200 by claiming 700 men, Tarleton demanded Buford's surrender and when the latter refused, Tarleton attacked. The result was a slaughter. Dr. Robert Brownfield, a surgeon with the Continental forces, later recalled the encounter as it was to be recorded in the memory of Americans: "Not a man escaped. Poor Pearson [a lieutenant in the patriot rear guard] was inhumanely mangled on the face, as he lay on his back. . . . The demand for quarter, seldom refused to a vanquished foe, was at once found to be in vain. Not a man was spared, and it was the concurrent testimony of all the survivors that for fifteen minutes after every man was prostrate, they [the British] went over the ground, plunging their bayonets into everyone that exhibited any signs of life, and in some instances, where several had fallen one over the other, these monsters were seen to throw off on the point of the bayonet the uppermost, to come at those beneath."

In all, 113 patriots were killed and another 150 so badly maimed that they were left to die on the field. Tarleton lost five men killed and 12 wounded. With this skirmish the British had "eliminated the last organized military force in the three southern provinces" and the call to remember "Tarleton's Quarter" entered the American lexicon. The cry of "Bloody Tarleton" became part of the psychological ammunition of the Americans. Tarleton's brutality would be repaid, with interest, to future British forces.

Objective historians may or may not have decided that the brash, fierce Tarleton was a butcher. But, more important, partisans of the time believed it. Francis Marion, the "Swamp Fox," told of finding Tarleton's victims, "Women & Children," who were "Sitting in the open Air round a fire without a blanket or any Cloathing but what they had on." And the effect of such reports was what mattered in arousing public sentiment. In the Waxhaws, an influential citizen named William Hill decided, following Tarleton's victory there, that the time had come for him to join the war. A group of followers went with him and they volunteered their services to Thomas ("The Gamecock") Sumter, who was fighting his own rearguard battles in upper South Carolina. There were many similar instances of those who stirred out of their non-alliance and marched to oppose Bloody Tarleton.

These operations seemed to Sir Henry Clinton merely peripheral, however. The city of Charleston was secure. No sustained resistance seemed to be gathering in North Carolina. Grumbling about his final severe edict on loyalty oaths would subside. Triumphant and confident, Clinton prepared to return to New York. On June 8, with a substantial part of his army, he departed for the north, leaving his second in command, the able, aggressive, and controversial Charles, Earl Cornwallis, to subdue any lingering resistance and launch a successful march across North Carolina and Virginia.

Two years earlier, Cornwallis had left America because of the illness of his wife in England. In 1779 he returned because her death "had made England unendurable to him." He wished to rejoin his friends on active service. Cornwallis firmly believed that the only way to protect South Carolina was to advance northward and defeat the Continental regulars around whom hordes of militiamen rallied during every engagement. The advance on Virginia and dispersal of American regular troops thus became central to Cornwallis' plans for victory in the South.

In the summer of 1780, with 8,345 men to hold and extend British control in the South, Cornwallis found himself in a rapidly deteriorating situation. Pacification was not proceeding as planned. A series of strategic posts had been fortified across the backcountry, from Augusta on the Savannah through Camden to Georgetown on the coast. But these were not sufficient to hold the loyalists' support while civil war was intensifying. By early August Cornwallis admitted that "the whole country between Peedee and Santee" had flared into "an absolute state of rebellion." It was a terrible summer of civil war, "marked by bitterness, violence, and malevolence such as only civil wars can engender."

Patriot partisans, operating out of the tangled swamps of the Carolinas, used their knowledge of terrain, their adaptability to the weather, and their familiarity with the region's inhabitants to gain impressive advantages. Their exploits became legendary, their names gathered a mythical aura: Francis Marion, Thomas Sumter, Andrew Pickens—hardy, daring men who could assemble a small loyal band of followers and strike an enemy with the deadly speed and force of lightning.

In addition to the lowland guerrilla leaders there were three partisans who commanded other special patriot forces. One of these, Col. Charles McDowell, led North Carolina militia. With the fall of Charleston and the British forays into the countryside, McDowell notified the over-mountain men to send him all the riflemen they could spare. Col. Isaac Shelby had been in the Kentucky area surveying his claims to lands there when news of the fall of Charleston reached him. He hastened home, he said, "determined to enter the service of the Country, until her independence was secured." He responded to McDowell's call by leading 200 mounted riflemen from Sullivan County to join McDowell on Broad River. Uniting with these was Col. Elijah Clarke, a native North Carolinian who had moved to Georgia and led Georgia militia in the skirmishes that took place from the last of June until the battle on Kings Mountain.

The three major encounters of these troops took place at Thicketty Fort on July 30, at Cedar Spring on August 8, and at Musgrove's Mill on August 18. At Thicketty, one of the British posts in the South Carolina interior along the headwaters of the Pacolet River, Shelby and Clarke achieved the surrender of the fort without firing a shot. It was a heady victory. A few days later they were ordered out again to cut off foragers for the large British forces under command of Maj. Patrick Ferguson. The patriots and Tories met at Cedar Spring. The encounter concluded with a chase through the forest, which was to the liking of the mountain men who knew how to fight "Indian fashion." The British won the field but were unable to recapture prisoners the patriots had taken at the beginning of the fight. Here, for the first time, Ferguson encountered that bold and tenacious breed of men from the western waters.

At Musgrove's Mill, on the Enoree River, Shelby, Clarke, and Col. James Williams attempted a surprise attack on the provincials and Tory militia. The surprise failed, but their sharpshooting did not. The result was 63 dead, 90 wounded, and 70 prisoners among the British forces, with only 4 patriots killed and 8 wounded.

Elated by this victory the leaders turned their thoughts toward a larger goal: the post at Ninety-Six, where Major Ferguson was enjoying remarkable success raising his loyalist militia and securing public support. The officers had mounted their horses to lead the way toward Ninety-Six when they were diverted. "At that moment," Colonel Shelby remembered later, "an express [messenger] came up from McDowell in great haste with a short letter in his hand." That letter told of a major battle 2 days before the skirmish at Musgrove's Mill, a disastrous rout near Camden.

In the early morning darkness of August 16, 7 miles north of the village of Camden, S.C., the patriots under Gen. Horatio Gates, recently appointed commander of the small, newly formed Southern Army, stumbled into a British column led by Cornwallis, who was seeking to determine the whereabouts and the strength of this patriot force. Both armies fired a few shots and recoiled from the sudden confrontation until dawn could help them discover each other's location. The patriot general was at a special disadvantage. Cornwallis had long since won the devotion of his officers and men. Lord Germain's nephew had reported that the Earl was "deservedly the favourite of every person of every rank under his command." But Horatio Gates was largely unknown to the men following him across the sweltering Carolina land that night in deep summer.

Upon assuming command of what he insisted on calling "the grand army," Gates, the hero of Saratoga, had been warned by his old friend, Charles Lee: "Take care lest your Northern laurels turn to Southern willows." Gates came south after his appointment and found in the encampment at Coxe's Mill, N.C., "an army without strength, a military chest without money, a department apparently deficient in public spirit and a climate that increases despondency instead of animating the soldier's arm." Under temporary command of the remarkable Bavarian, self-styled "Baron" Johann de Kalb, the meager, largely untrained army carried its baggage on its back and foraged for its own food as it marched. There were long fasts broken by occasional summertime feasts of green apples and peaches, which played havoc with digestive systems.

Promptly upon joining this haggard, ill-supplied army Gates issued the astounding order to make ready to march. They would attack Camden. Choosing, against the advice of the shrewd and able Kalb, an unlikely route through desolate pine barrens and Tory country, Gates led his hungry men past fields of new corn. A diet of green corn, hastily wrenched from its stalks in the fields, combined with peaches scavenged along the way and "poor fresh beef without salt," increased the painful digestive disorders. Diarrhea sent men fairly reeling into the woods and slowed the march.

As they approached the vicinity of Camden, Gates decided to make a night march. When they heard his announcement, his subordinates were too confounded to protest, although one officer later wrote, "it could not be conceived that an army consisting of more than two-thirds militia, and which had never been once exercised in arms together, could form columns and perform other maneuvers in the night and in the face of the enemy." To complete the comedy, or tragedy, of errors, when Gates discovered that there was no rum available for the customary extra allowance of "spirits" which was provided before a military engagement, he ordered molasses to be dispensed as an "acceptable" substitute. Gates' adjutant general remembered afterwards that the "hasty meal of quick baked bread and fresh beef, with a dessert of molasses . . . operated so cathartically as to disorder very many of the men, who were breaking the ranks all night and were certainly much debilitated."

Suddenly, at 2 o'clock on that moonless, sultry night, the advance guards of the two armies slammed into each other–to their mutual astonishment. After some sharp firing, each withdrew and preparations were made for an engagement to begin at dawn.

That engagement was short and catastrophic for the patriot forces. Gates placed his untrained, untested militia opposite Cornwallis' regulars, some of whom belonged to such crack outfits as the 71st (Frazer's) Highlanders and the 23d Regiment of Foot (Royal Welsh Fusiliers). As the battle began, the weakened, inexperienced militiamen were suddenly confronted with firing, huzzaing redcoats descending upon them–and they broke and ran. They had bayonets, but these had been issued only the previous day and few of the militia knew how to handle them. They threw down their bayonets and their loaded muskets and fled across the fields. The Continental soldiers fought, but they were hopelessly outnumbered.

Dauntless 60-year-old Kalb led attack and counterattack. The horse on which he rode was killed and he received a saber slash on his head. Still he fought, his great frame taking cruel punishment. When at last he fell, he was bleeding from 11 wounds. He had refused to retreat until he received orders from his general. But Gates was not around to give any orders. Swept from the field in the first stampede of the militia, the general was covering the ground, "astride a charger sired by a famous racer named Fearnought," from Camden to Hillsborough, N.C. He made the 200 miles in 3½ days.

Patriot dismay at the Camden fiasco was summarized in the cutting sarcasm of Alexander Hamilton who remarked on Gates's flight: "Was there ever such an instance of a general running away . . . from his whole army? And was there ever so precipitous flight . . .? It does admirable credit to the activity of a man at his time of life." Laurels had indeed become willows.

Fellow soldiers were more tolerant of the general. The man who would become his successor, Nathanael Greene, subsequently looked at the battlefield and considered Gates's hastily assembled, inexperienced army, and decided that Gates was "unfortunate but not blameable." Wherever the blame might lie, the patriot situation in the South had been rendered even more desperate. Another army had been routed. The historian George Otto Trevelyan described the patriots' situation at this point as "a morass of trouble which seemed to have neither shore nor bottom."

As for the partisan leaders, the Camden defeat forced Shelby and Clarke to abandon their plans to attack Ninety-Six and head toward the hills. Maj. Patrick Ferguson pursued them closely.

Ferguson was halted in his pursuit near Fair Forest by a message from Cornwallis summoning him to Camden. At the Earl's temporary headquarters, Ferguson learned of the general strategy for the next stage of the Southern campaign. Cornwallis was uneasy. He would have liked to move out across North Carolina at once except for two considerations. One was the weather. The intense heat of late summer in the South increased the miserable illness of malaria and yellow fever among his men. The other deterrent was the number of rebel bands still roaming the countryside. Cornwallis had finally decided to launch a three-pronged thrust: his right wing, to the east, would secure the coast and insure a stream of supplies. He himself would command the main army in the center, driving straight up through North Carolina. His left wing would make a wide western sweep, subduing that troublesome, unknown country along the frontier.

This important left wing was placed under command of Major Ferguson. McDowell and Shelby and all the mountain militia who had been harassing the British army, along with Sevier and Campbell and Cleveland and all the backcountry men who would soon be involved in thwarting these British plans, could consider it something of a tribute that Cornwallis sent this particular officer against them. For Patrick Ferguson was one of the best that Cornwallis had.*

* In accounts of Kings Mountain, Ferguson is sometimes referred to as "major," sometimes as "lieutenant colonel." This is because word of his long-expected promotion to the latter rank did not arrive until after the battle and Ferguson's death.

The dynamic that defined Patrick Ferguson's life and character most consistently was the fact that he was a professional soldier in the best possible tradition of that term. He fought for patriotism (loyalty to his own country) and honor (loyalty to his own code of manhood), and he followed the recognized rules of war. Where his compatriot, Banastre Tarleton, killed with a relish that suggested pleasure as well as necessity, Ferguson balanced diplomacy with battle and seemed to wage war only from necessity as he evaluated a given situation.

"You must no longer look upon him as your son," Ann Ferguson's brother wrote to her from Quebec in August 1762. "He is the son of Mars and will be unworthy of his father if he does not give proofs of contempt of pain and danger." The son from whom this Scottish woman was supposed to disengage her motherhood was then 18 years old—not as tall as he would like to be, but intelligent and as personable as any mother could wish. Already he had been in the military service for 3 years. He would live up to his uncle's challenge to display only contempt for pain and danger.

Perhaps his less than commanding height—5 feet 8 inches—and an unprepossessing appearance (ordinary, dark straight hair framing a serious countenance and even, chiseled features) caused Ferguson to intensify those qualities of character which emphasized leadership. Those who knew him spoke of the intelligence, as well as the impulsiveness, of the man. In addition, he was gifted with that rare magnetism which wins the affection and loyalty of followers.

The world in which Patrick Ferguson spent his youth was that of the landed gentry of the Scottish Highlands. On his father's, Lord Pitfour's, family estate in Aberdeenshire, he and five brothers and sisters grew up in an atmosphere of physical comfort and intellectual culture. Spirited horses, riding to hounds, and the exuberance of exertion in a natural world at once harsh and beautiful was balanced with respect for education and surroundings that included the exhilaration of great books, paintings, and lively conversation. His inclination, however, was to fulfill the meaning of his Gaelic name, "Feargachus"–bold–and he chose the active life of a soldier over the contemplative life of the scholar.

When he was 15 years old a commission was purchased for him and he entered the army as a cornet in the Royal North British Dragoons. At 16 he was serving in the wars of Flanders and Germany, and in an incident at the Battle of Minden in 1760 he exhibited that coolness which would characterize him throughout his life. When his horse jumped a ditch and his pistol fell from its holster, he turned and galloped back under fire to face enemy hussars and calmly retrieved the weapon. His dragoons were later commended for "prodigies of valor" performed at that battle. Such a brilliant, ambitious teenager must have been deeply disappointed when contaminated drinking water brought on an illness so serious that he was sent home in 1762. He remained in Scotland and England for the next 4 years. This interval provided him with an experience singularly useful for his subsequent role of leadership in America. As a participant in the debate over extension of English militia laws to Scotland, Ferguson gained firsthand knowledge of some of the problems and potential of the role he would later fill as His Majesty's Inspector of Militia in the Carolinas.

In 1768, when he was 24, he became a captain and was sent to the West Indies to quell an insurrection among the Caribs. There he learned something about the fierceness of partisan fighting on the part of brave marksmen defending their homeland. The West Indies, Nova Scotia, and back to England–all this before the spring of 1777 when he was sent to America where he joined Sir Henry Clinton's army and was placed at the head of a corps of riflemen. At the battle of Brandywine in September, his "meritorious conduct was acknowledged by the whole British army."

During that same fight his conduct might have won the appreciation of the patriots had they known of a strange episode that took place on the battlefield. Captain Ferguson later wrote about it to a relative in Scotland. As he and his riflemen lay at the edge of a wood in the forefront of one of the British divisions, "a Rebel officer, remarkable by a hussar dress, passed towards our army, within a hundred yards of my right flank, not perceiving us. He was followed by another, dressed in dark green and blue, mounted on a bay horse, with a remarkably high cocked hat. I ordered three good shots to steal near to and fire at them; but the idea disgusting me, I recalled the order."

Then Ferguson continues:

The hussar, in returning, made a circuit, but the other passed within a hundred yards of us, upon which I advanced from the wood towards him. Upon my calling, he stopped; but after looking at me, he proceeded. I again drew his attention, and made signs to him to stop, levelling my piece at him; but he slowly cantered away. As I was within that distance, at which, at the quickest firing, I could have lodged half a dozen balls in or about him, before he was out of my reach, I had only to determine; but it was not pleasant to fire at the back of an unoffending individual, who was acquitting himself very coolly of his duty–so I let him alone.

Next day, Ferguson wrote, he was telling some wounded officers about his little encounter when one of the surgeons came in. The doctor had been informed that General Washington spent that morning with the light troops, attended only by a French officer in hussar dress. Descriptions of Washington's clothing and mount coincided with that of the officer Ferguson had spared. "I am not sorry that I did not know at the time who it was," Ferguson concluded.

Of course, neither he nor anyone else ever really "knew." The interesting aspect of this anecdote is Ferguson's attitude toward his most renowned enemy.

While he was still in England, Ferguson had heard of the "boasted skill of the American marksmen." As inventor of the first breechloading rifle used in the British army, he was an authority on firearms. His rifle improved on the old flintlock in a number of ways: it was loaded at the breech, without using a ramrod, which increased its rate of fire; its aim was more precise; and it proved more dependable in wet weather. Exhibition of this rifle in action impressed Great Britain's highest military dignitaries and King George himself, and Ferguson was issued patents for his rifle and improvements. The 100 select soldiers he brought to America with him were painstakingly trained by Ferguson in the use of his breechloader.

But the military, ever chary of innovations, decided against using Ferguson's rifle. This decision was made by Gen. William Howe after the battle of Brandywine, while Ferguson was incapacitated by a wound that had shattered his right elbow and permanently crippled his arm. General Howe took advantage of Ferguson's absence from the army during his painful recuperation to disband the special corps Ferguson had trained so patiently and successfully (but without Howe's personal approval) and to store the rifles Ferguson was using to such advantage (but without Howe's personal permission).

Without the use of his right arm, without his special corps of marksmen, without use of his efficient new rifle, Ferguson returned to the field. Persistent practice with his left hand led to increased skill with the sword. At Monmouth, Little Egg Harbor, N.J., and finally in the siege of Charleston he continued to win the respect of British and Americans alike for his "valor and enterprise." No wonder his fellow officers called him the "Bull Dog." He was promoted to the rank of major and finally (although he would never learn of it) to the temporary rank of lieutenant colonel. When a bayonet was thrust through his left arm during one of the skirmishes outside Charleston, a fellow officer wrote: "The whole army felt for the gallant Ferguson." Three weeks later, the tenacious Bull Dog was fully recovered, however, at least in one arm.

This was a proud, bitter, brilliant, frustrated officer who came under the command of Lord Cornwallis after the fall of Charleston. Toward each other, Cornwallis and Ferguson were correct but not cordial. At the age of 36, the latter was 10 years older and immensely more experienced than either Tarleton or Francis, Lord Rawdon, commander of the loyalist regiment known as the Volunteers of Ireland, but Cornwallis gave these two favored treatment. One reason for the distance between Cornwallis and Ferguson was Ferguson's belief that an effective loyalist militia could be formed.

As he set forth on his forays, Ferguson was mindful of the Southern summer heat which played havoc with soldiers unaccustomed to its extremes. He led the marches of his Provincial Corps (some 150 to 200 men) in the cool of the mornings. As Inspector of Militia in the Southern Provinces, Ferguson's duty seemed to Cornwallis "more that of a Justice of the Peace than a soldier." His remarkable achievement, however, was to raise about 4,000 loyalist militia and put a force of some 1,000 of these into the field. His success in this difficult task was especially apparent when contrasted with the failure of many similar efforts.

Ferguson's attitude was not that of Tarleton, whose "no quarter" repelled Ferguson and caused him to demand the execution of those dragoons who had butchered a surrendering enemy. His tactics were not those of Cornwallis, who had given orders "that all the inhabitants of this province, who have subscribed and taken part in this revolt, should be punished with the greatest rigor, and their whole property taken away from them or destroyed," and "that every militia-man, who has borne arms with us, and afterwards joined the enemy, shall be immediately hanged." Ferguson chose to pacify rather than to terrorize.

Historian Lyman C. Draper, who spent a lifetime documenting the personalities and events surrounding the battle of Kings Mountain, tells us that Ferguson would "sit down for hours, and converse with the country people on the state of public affairs, and point out to them, from his view, the ruinous effects of the disloyalty of the ring-leaders of the rebellion—erroneously supposing that it was the leaders only who gave impulse to the popular uprising throughout the Colonies. He was as indefatigable in training them to his way of thinking, as he was in instructing them in military exercises. This condescension on his part was regarded as wonderful in a King's officer, and very naturally went far to secure the respect and obedience of all who came within the sphere of his almost magic influence." He appealed to patriot wives and mothers to persuade the men in their families who were "outliers" to return home and renew allegiance to the King.

As he began his marches across the interior of the Carolinas,

Ferguson announced, "We come not to make war on women and children, but to relieve their distresses." Some households which were not sympathetic to the British cause nevertheless found a certain drama in some of their encounters with the urbane Major Ferguson. There was irony in the fact that this soldier could be less bloody and harsh in his relations with civilians than the Tory and patriot civilians were in their attacks on each other. As he sought to win their allegiance, Ferguson brought a measure of unaccustomed subtlety, even diversion, into many rude, routine lives.

Despite Ferguson's personal attitudes, many of those who joined his ranks were loyalists who had become part of the ferocious antagonism tearing the region apart during that summer and autumn of 1780, and British progress through the countryside inflicted excesses and sufferings on numbers of patriot citizens. There was plundering of "cattle, horses, beds, wearing apparel, bee-gums, and vegetables of all kinds–even wresting the rings from the fingers of the females."

Foraging parties rounded up the people's cattle and soldiers' horses were turned loose in fields of grain. Partisan leaders led attacks and counterattacks against these invasions. Colonels Charles McDowell and Isaac Shelby harassed Ferguson in engagements already described. Then, following Cornwallis' victory at Camden in August, Ferguson's Tory militia and his Provincial Corps of American loyalists joined ranks to secure the backcountry and protect Cornwallis' rear and western flank as he marched across South Carolina and into North Carolina.

There was one vast area that remained an unknown factor, however. That was the country to the west, across the Blue Ridge. From his headquarters at Gilbert Town, Ferguson now issued an ultimatum to the people and their leaders in this wild mountain country. He paroled one of his prisoners, Samuel Phillips, who had been captured at the Musgrove's Mill engagement, and sent him to Col. Isaac Shelby with a message. Shelby and his fellow mountain men were to "desist from their opposition to the British arms, and take protection under his standard," and if they did not Ferguson would "march his army over the mountains, hang their leaders, and lay their country waste with fire and sword."

No strategy could have been better devised to unify the patriots scattered along the frontier and set them on the long march across the mountains. Maj. Patrick Ferguson had made the first of two mistakes disastrous to his campaign: he misjudged the men he would face in forthcoming battle, as he would soon misjudge the place where he chose to wage that battle.

Britain's Lord Rawdon wrote in his report of Kings Mountain that "A numerous Army now appeared on the Frontiers drawn from Nolachucki and other Settlements beyond the mountains whose very names had been unknown to us." Not only the very names but the essential history and character of the men who made up this army were unknown to the British leaders.

An accepted attitude was probably reflected in an estimate written by Maj. George Hanger, a swashbuckling soldier briefly attached to Ferguson's Legion, with which he was more compatible. "This distinguished race of men," he sarcastically observed of the dwellers in the backcountry, "are more savage than the Indians, and possess every one of their vices, but not one of their virtues. I have known one of these fellows [to] travel two hundred miles through the woods never keeping any road or path, guided by the sun by day, and the stars by night, to kill a particular person belonging to the opposite party. He would shoot him before his own door, and ride away to boast of what he had done on his return."

Hanger made the mistake that many observers of mountain civilization would repeat during coming generations, enlarging—perhaps exaggerating—a single instance into a stereotype by which to describe a large and varied group of people. The men who received and responded to Ferguson's ultimatum were not savages. They might more accurately have been likened to members of Scottish clans, momentarily subjecting their cherished individuality to demands of the common good—in fact, their common survival. Their leaders exemplified much of the natural authority, unhesitating militancy, and tactical skill shown by ancient chieftains.

The first of these leaders, sought out at Ferguson's command by his distant kinsman and neighbor, Samuel Phillips, was Isaac Shelby who lived on the lower settlements of the Holston River. A large man whose size belied his agility, Isaac resembled his father, Evan Shelby, who had emigrated from Wales at the age of 15 and become a community leader in Maryland and then in the Holston settlements, "a man of commanding appearance, stout and stern."

Young Isaac had been a cattle herder in the mountains, an Indian fighter, and, during Lord Dunmore's war, a soldier who distinguished himself at the battle of Point Pleasant in western Virginia in October 1774. When the Transylvania Company was formed with a vast acreage embracing much of the country that would become Middle Tennessee and the State of Kentucky, he served with several surveying parties in the vast new domain. Although he became captain of a company of Virginia minutemen in 1776, and helped supply various frontier garrisons, he was not deeply engaged in the Revolution until July 1780, when Col. Charles McDowell called upon him for help in resisting Ferguson's thrusts toward the western waters. Isaac Shelby left off surveying lands to which he had laid claim on earlier expeditions and returned to take part in encounters at Thicketty Fort and elsewhere, until Gates' defeat at Camden had driven the patriots back across the mountains.

When they had returned home the latter part of August, Shelby's men were suffering from exhaustion and malnutrition. Their terms of enlistment were ready to expire. And now Isaac Shelby received this threat borne by Samuel Phillips from the arrogant Ferguson. He saddled his horse and rode some 40 miles to talk with the fiery commander of the Washington County militia, embracing the Watauga and Nolichucky settlements. His name was John Sevier.

No man on that frontier was more popular or widely known than this descendant of French Huguenots. It was typical that Shelby should find Sevier and his family and friends enjoying a "jollification" complete with horse-racing and barbecue. The contrast between the two friends was apparent in their response to each other. Shelby was deeply disturbed by the message he carried and the apparently carefree merriment by which he found himself surrounded on Sevier's place seemed inappropriate. He spoke abruptly to his friend, saying that it was no time for fun-making. When Shelby explained his plans for a campaign, Sevier was as enthusiastic as he had been a moment before in the frolic. John Sevier's love of pleasure provided welcome relief in a border country where daily life was laborious and relentless. Sevier could dance all night or fight all day, pursuing each with equal skill and enthusiasm.

As Shelby and Sevier talked during that day and the next, considering every aspect of their situation and that of their communities, isolated on the westernmost boundaries of States that took little interest in their welfare and provided scant protection, the two militia leaders resolved that their only defense must be an immediate offense.

No other decision could have been expected of John Sevier. He had not yet won the reputation of being a scourge of the Indians, and he was only at the beginning of a career of leadership for his district and, in the future, his new State. But the qualities described by his biographer, Carl Driver, were already plain: "All characteristics of the pioneers blended in the personality of John Sevier. He was settler and speculator, adventurer and trader, Indian fighter and law-maker." He married his first wife, Sarah Hawkins, when he was 17 years old. They had 10 children. His second wife, "Bonny Kate" Sherrill, bore him eight children. This, too, was typical of the pioneer.

Physically, Sevier and Ferguson may have been the shortest of the leaders engaged at Kings Mountain; Sevier, too, was some 3 or 4 inches under 6 feet in height. Also like Ferguson, he was well-proportioned, hard-muscled, and lithe. He could assume the manners of a cavalier as well as the authority of a militia leader, and his fellow Westerners liked the reputation that "he could out-ride and outshoot—and, it is said, outswear—the best and the worst of the men who followed him."

John Sevier, soon to be popularly known as "Chucky Jack," after his home on the Nolichucky River, would lead no more men and fight no more steadfastly than a number of other participants in the battle of Kings Mountain, yet more than any other he would become the legendary hero and personification of that victory. One reason for this lies perhaps in another particular quality he shared with his opponent, Patrick Ferguson: his charisma as a leader. It posed no small challenge to be a leader of frontiersmen, many of whom had sought out their place and way of life precisely because they wished to be free of all authority. But Sevier followed the course that could prove successful in welding prickly individualists into an effective single force: "He gave his commands as to equals, and, because these orders appealed to his men as being wise and practical, they gave unquestioned obedience. This loyalty of his friends formed one of the outstanding features of his success throughout his whole career."

The jollification at Sevier's farm was ended as he and the judicious Isaac Shelby laid their plans to surprise Ferguson and his Tories. Neighbors hurried to their own homes to await a call to action. There were several pressing needs to be met.

The first was for men. Quickly, without delay, an effective force must be assembled and marched across the mountains to answer the British threat of invasion. Sevier and Shelby needed the help of Col. William Campbell of the Virginia settlements on the Clinch River and Col. Charles McDowell's troops from North Carolina's Burke County, and they sent communications to these two leaders. Disappointed by Campbell's initial response–he thought it better to keep their positions on the frontier strong and let Ferguson come to them, increasing Ferguson's distance from Cornwallis–Shelby wrote a second urgent message, pointing out that without Campbell and his men there could be no force sufficient to undertake the task of challenging the British provincials and militia. The Virginian reconsidered and agreed to join his friends, as did McDowell. A call was issued for a general rendezvous at the Sycamore Shoals on the Watauga River near the present Elizabethton, Tenn., on the 25th of September.

McDowell and his North Carolina refugees from the skirmishes with Ferguson's troops were already encamped at or near Sycamore Shoals. The accounts these refugees told of Tory atrocities in the Piedmont and lowcountry had stoked the anger of the over-mountain people and assured their resistance to any threat of invasion.

The second necessity for such an expedition was funds. An early historian of the Tennessee country, J. G. M. Ramsey, has left us an account of how this problem was met:

Colonel Sevier tried to borrow money on his own responsibility, to fit out and furnish the expedition. But every inhabitant had expended the last dollar in taking up his land, and all the money of the country was thus in the hands of the Entry-taker. Sevier waited upon that officer and represented to him that the want of means was likely to retard, and in some measure to frustrate, his exertions, to carry out the expedition, and suggested to him the use of the public money in his hands.

John Adair, Esq., late of Knox County, was the Entry-taker, and his reply was worthy of the times and worthy of the man. 'Col. Sevier, I have no authority by law to make that disposition of this money. It belongs to the impoverished treasury of North Carolina, and I dare not appropriate a cent of it to any purpose. But, if the country is overrun by the British, liberty is gone. Let the money go, too. Take it. If the enemy, by its use, is driven from the country, I can trust that country to justify and vindicate my conduct. Take it.'

Sevier and Shelby personally pledged repayment of the $12,000 or $13,000 received for ammunition and supplies to outfit the gathering troops.

In response to the need for supplies, there was a surge of activity throughout the mountains. At the grist mill near Matthew Talbot's home in the Watauga settlement, corn fresh from the autumn harvest was ground into meal for an army's bread. On a little branch of Buffalo Creek, a woman named Mary Patton was in charge of a small powder mill which supplied some of the needs of the riflemen. In a mineral-rich cove of the hills near John Sevier's home, lead was mined for balls to add to the ammunition supply. And on almost every farm beeves and horses were rounded up for the march. At every household clothing was prepared for the marchers.

Word of the call to arms spread like a leaf-fire among the settlements. On September 25th the flats at the Sycamore Shoals began to fill with rough-skinned, sharp-eyed, resolute men accompanied by women whose hands were calloused and whose courage was likewise evident. Six years before, there had been another historic gathering at this site. At that time, some 1,200 Cherokee Indians and their chiefs had treated with Judge Richard Henderson of North Carolina and several hundred eager white settlers for purchase of approximately 20 million acres of land that would become the State of Kentucky and part of Tennessee. It was at that time and place that the dissident chief, Dragging Canoe, had leaped into the circle of treaty makers and warned the white men that they had purchased a fair land but in its settlement it would be a dark and bloody ground.

For all the grimness of their purpose, an air of excitement bordering on revival fervor animated this crowd. They dwelt in rude little forts and isolated cabins huddled among virgin forests of towering trees and trackless mountain ranges. Loneliness and hard labor were their daily fare. Any event that drew them together provided an opportunity to exchange news, to savor the fellowship of those enduring challenges similar to their own, to relish exchanges of wit and humor, sympathy and grief. As they assembled–more than 1,000 strong, the largest gathering of settlers that had ever been seen in that part of the country–they built their campfires, smelled the bitter pungence of wood smoke in the evening air and the welcome aromas of food, watched their horses picking at grassy patches in the meadows, and tended the beeves they were taking along for a ready food supply. The men talked and planned and prepared. And the women cooked, made last-minute patchings or polishings on clothing or equipment, and they talked and worried over the dangers of the battlefield and made plans to meet the dangers of their scantily protected homefront.

They were an army without uniforms. Many of their hunting shirts were of fringed buckskin while others were of homespun linsey-woolsey, "clumsily made, blouse fashion, reaching to the knees and, gathered up, tied around the waist. In the fulth [fullness] was often carried heavy burdens, as much as a bushel of corn at one time." Their breeches and gaiters were of rough, home-dyed cloth. Long hair was tied back in a queue beneath their wide-brimmed hats.

They were an army little encumbered with baggage, unaccompanied by any supply train. Each man had a blanket, a cup, and "a wallet of provisions, the latter principally of parched corn meal, mixed, as it generally was, with maple sugar." There was an occasional skillet in which to stir up the meal in hot water or cook whatever game they might find along the way.

The pride of many a participant was his long rifle. Remarkable for the precision and distance of its shot, this weapon was also known as the Deckard or Dickert rifle, after its maker in Lancaster, Pa. The owner of one of these long, heavy rifles "rejoiced in its possession." Powder was carried in the powderhorns the men wore slung around their necks. Some of the horns bore carvings which their owners had whittled out during long winter nights, just as most of the rifles bore names given them by owners who had found them to be their nearest companions in the endless search for food, safety, entertainment—and now freedom.

They were an army without staff or quartermaster, without commissary or surgeon or chaplain. In fact, all they had to offer was themselves and their fierce determination to render Ferguson's ultimatum futile.

On the broad open spaces by the swift-flowing Watauga, surrounded by distant mountains where the headwaters of the river were born in dozens of hidden springs and clear rivulets, the people of the western waters assembled. John Sevier brought 240 men from Washington County (then North Carolina, later Tennessee). Isaac Shelby commanded a like number from Sullivan County. And the initially reluctant William Campbell caused rejoicing as he led 400 Virginians into the camp. Charles McDowell's 160 Burke and Rutherford County patriots, who had already fought Ferguson's forces, swelled the numbers at Sycamore Shoals. As they left this rendezvous and moved across the mountains they would be joined by other leaders and their militia. Like smaller streams feeding into a swelling river, Benjamin Cleveland and Joseph Winston would join with 350 men from Wilkes and Surry Counties, James Williams would bring 400 South Carolinians. Swiftly and surely they became an army. In the final count, the over-mountain men made up less than half of the total patriot force that finally faced Ferguson at Kings Mountain.

Actually this army would be properly described as "composed of patriot riflemen of the farmer, hunter, and Indian fighting class from the frontiers of the two Carolinas and Virginia." But it was the over-mountain leaders who had kindled the spirit, initiated the plans, and raised the funds for the march against Ferguson. Their image would dominate the popular memory of that western response that began with the assembly at Sycamore Shoals.

In the dewy autumn dawn of September 26th, the camp was an anthill of activity as horses were saddled, cattle were rounded up, and families made ready for parting. The horses were precious; many had been lost in Indian raids. Amidst the tumult of humans and animals, shouts and tears, military orders and whispered farewells, there was an interval of quiet. Doughty Scotch-Irish clergyman Samuel Doak–graduate of the institution that would become Princeton University, founder of the first regular school west of the Alleghenies, who had brought the first books into the Tennessee country on his horse's back, while he walked–was ready to pronounce a prayer for the expedition. Leaning on their rifles, the mountain men listened to the preacher's rhetoric as he likened their cause to that of Gideon's people, in the Bible, opposing the Midianites. Doak prayed for the victory he confidently predicted, and then in an upswelling confidence he offered the little army its battle cry:

"The sword of the Lord and of Gideon!" he thundered.

They echoed the words. "The sword of the Lord and of Gideon!"

Then they swung into their saddles and began the long ride to find Ferguson and confront the British threat to their freedom.

Their cattle delayed the mountain men's progress during the first day of their march. Their way was also made difficult because the route followed obscure Indian trails and the terrain was as rugged as that in any part of eastern America. That Tuesday, September 26th, they ate their first midday meal at Matthew Talbot's Mill, only 3 miles from Sycamore Shoals where they had started. Then they followed Gap Creek to its head, crossed Little Doe River, and made camp for the night at a landmark known as the Shelving Rock, on Big Doe River. They had covered 20 miles. Near their encampment they found a blacksmith named Miller who shod several of their horses.

The next day there was more trouble with the cattle. After a small stampede, the impatient men butchered several beeves for a temporary supply of meat and left the rest behind as they hurried on their way, relieved to be no longer encumbered with a drove of livestock. They followed Bright's Trace, named ironically enough for a rogue who was reputedly sympathetic to the Tories and whose wife was one of the first persons to be convicted of stealing in that part of North Carolina. Later, there were those who preferred to call it Yellow Mountain Road for the route that led through the gap between Yellow and Roan mountains.

As they left the fertile Crab Orchard Valley behind, the marchers encountered snow "shoe-mouth deep" on the mountain slopes. Despite this early calling-card of winter in the high altitudes, the country was stunningly beautiful. On the summit of the mountain there was a great grassy bald which would pose a continuing puzzle for later generations of botanists. Natural gardens of rhododendron suggested the blanket of rose and purple that would cover these heights in early summer. On this tableland, watered by an abundant clear spring, the army encamped, paraded, and made a disturbing discovery. Two of John Sevier's men had deserted, and he suspected that they had gone to warn Ferguson of the over-mountain men's approach.

According to one account, "Two problems now confronted the mountaineers. They must increase the speed of their march, so that Ferguson should not have time to get reinforcements from Cornwallis; and they must make that extra speed by another trail than they had intended taking so that they themselves could not be intercepted before they had picked up the Back Country militia under Colonels Cleveland, Hambright, Chronicle, and Williams, who were moving to join them. We are not told who took the lead when they left the known trail, but we may suppose it was Sevier and his Wataugans, for the making of new warpaths and wild riding were two of the things that distinguished Nolichucky Jack's leadership. Down the steep side of the mountain, finding their way as they plunged, went the over-hill men. They crossed the Blue Ridge at Gillespie's Gap and pushed on to Quaker Meadow."

It had been a hard 5 days' march to the McDowells' plantation at Quaker Meadows, near the present Morganton, N.C. But there they were so welcome that Maj. Joseph McDowell exceeded all bounds of hospitality by inviting the army to use his fencerails for the campfires!

North and South Carolina reinforcements swelled the ranks of the patriot army to just under 1,400 men. They were now within striking distance of Ferguson. The fair weather which had marked the days of their marches through the mountains took a turn for the worse, however. After a half-day's march from Quaker Meadows, the men were marooned in camp by rains that began on Sunday afternoon, the first of October, and continued through the following day. Unaccustomed to discipline and restraint, the volunteers grew uneasy and irascible. Their leaders would now be put to the test.

And who were these leaders? In addition to the Welshman, Isaac Shelby, and the French Huguenot, John Sevier, there was William Campbell, the quintessential Scotch-Irishman, ruddy-complexioned, a veritable giant of a man standing 6 feet 6 inches tall. His physical

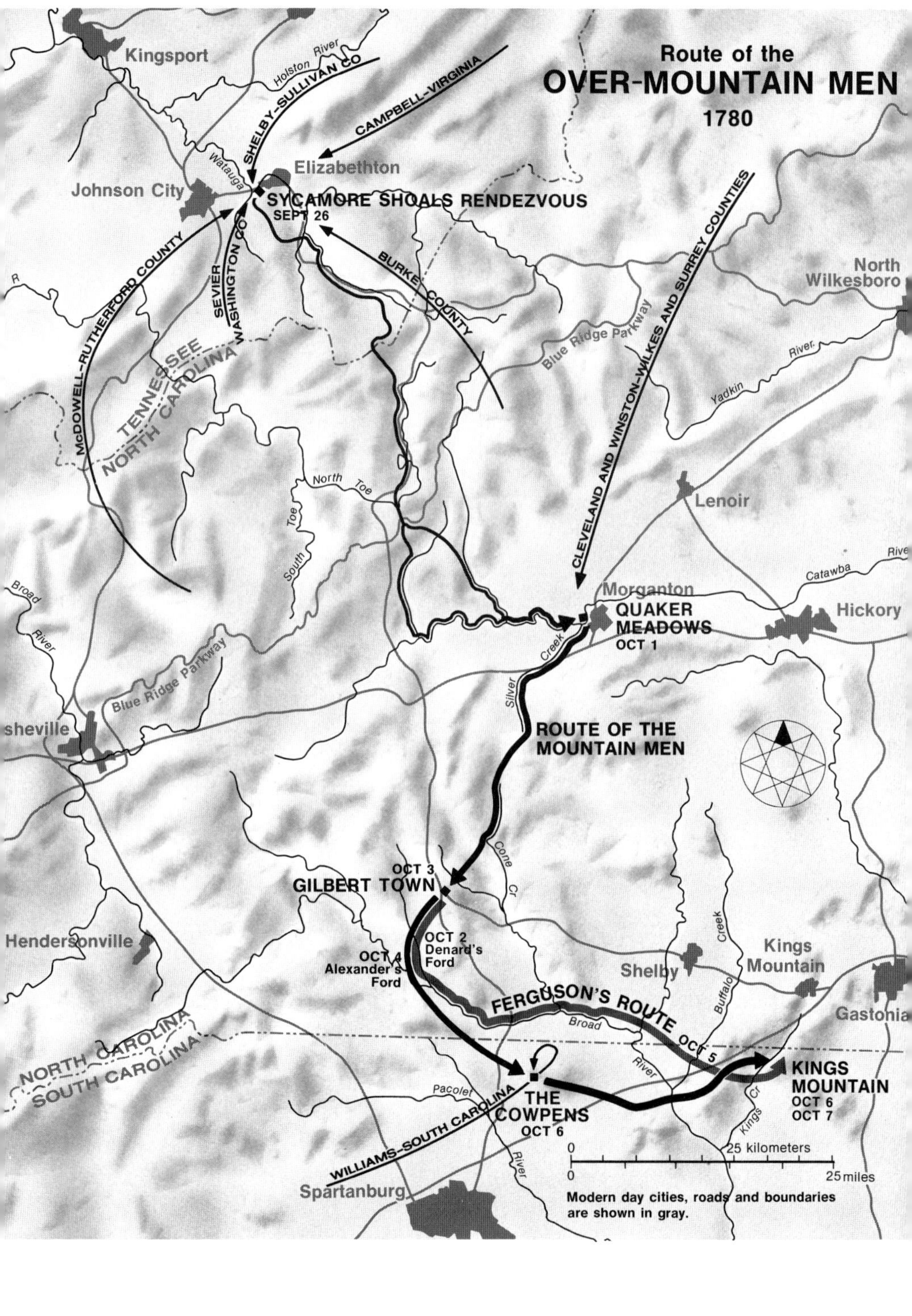

Route of the
OVER-MOUNTAIN MEN
1780
Kingsport
Holston River
SHELBY-SULLIVAN CO
CAMPBELL-VIRGINIA
Watauga
Elizabethton
Johnson City
SYCAMORE SHOALS RENDEZVOUS
SEPT 26
McDOWELL-RUTHERFORD COUNTY
SEVIER WASHINGTON CO
BURKE COUNTY
North Wilkesboro
R
TENNESSEE
NORTH CAROLINA
Blue Ridge Parkway
Yadkin River
CLEVELAND AND WINSTON-WILKES AND SURREY COUNTIES
North Toe
Toe
South
Lenoir
Catawba River
Broad
River
Morganton
QUAKER MEADOWS
OCT 1
Hickory
sheville
Blue Ridge Parkway
Creek
Silver
ROUTE OF THE
MOUNTAIN MEN
Cone Cr
OCT 3
GILBERT TOWN
Creek
Hendersonville
OCT 2
Denard's Ford
Kings Mountain
OCT 4
Alexander's Ford
Shelby
Buffalo
Gastonia
FERGUSON'S ROUTE OCT 5
Broad
River
NORTH CAROLINA
SOUTH CAROLINA
Pacolet
KINGS MOUNTAIN
OCT 6
OCT 7
Kings Cr
THE COWPENS
OCT 6
WILLIAMS-SOUTH CAROLINA
River
Spartanburg
0   25 kilometers
0   25 miles
Modern day cities, roads and boundaries
are shown in gray.

strength and endurance, his quick temper and impeccable honor were known to all. His wife was a sister of Patrick Henry. Campbell had been a militia leader since Lord Dunmore's War of 1774, and he had served in the Virginia House of Delegates.

Other leaders gathered on this venture were Joseph McDowell, a Virginian who had foresaken the easy life to move to the Carolina Piedmont, and Benjamin Cleveland, another Virginian, who had moved west and built his reputation as an Indian fighter. These would soon be joined by other outstanding fighters: James Williams, a long-time Tory hater who had served as a delegate to the provincial legislature of South Carolina; William Chronicle, a veteran of the 1780 skirmishes and a resident of the south fork of the Catawba; Joseph Winston, a leather-tough frontiersman who had been fighting Indians since he was 17; and Edward Lacey, a onetime Pennsylvanian who, at the age of 13, had served with Edward Braddock's army in the Indian campaigns.

Now, however, the leaders needed a leader. They sent Charles McDowell, the senior officer among them, to ask General Gates–still in command of the Southern forces despite the Camden debacle–to assign them a general. They closed their request with this sentence: "All our Troops being Militia and but little acquainted with discipline, we could wish him [the general officer] to be a Gentleman of address, and able to keep up a proper discipline without disgusting the soldiery."

Gates did not respond. The colonels were in no mood to wait for anything less than a prompt reply. Shelby, rejecting any proposal of delay, suggested that Campbell was the only officer not from North Carolina and could therefore serve without arousing any jealousy. Thus William Campbell became commander of the combined forces.

They took up the march again and on October 2 camped 16 miles north of Gilbert Town, where they looked forward to finding Ferguson and his army. As they broke camp the next morning Cleveland requested the troops to form a circle so that he could "tell them the news."

A blunt, corpulent man weighing at least 250 pounds, Cleveland in all his rudeness knew how to appeal to frontiersmen. He used that knowledge now. "The enemy is at hand," he said, "and we must up and at them. Now is the time for every man of you to do his country a priceless service—such as shall lead your children to exult in the fact that their fathers were the conquerors of Ferguson."

Cleveland made an offer, and Shelby repeated it, that anyone who wished to "back out" should take advantage of this opportunity and "step three paces in the rear." They could then part company with their companions and return to the safety of home—and, it was implied, permanent ignominy. No one moved.

There was a murmur of approval. And then Shelby issued a directive which summarized the spirit and the reality of the entire Kings Mountain engagement. The nugget of his message was contained in these two sentences: "When we encounter the enemy, don't wait for the word of command. Let each one of you be your own officer, and do the very best you can, taking every care you can of yourselves, and availing yourselves of every advantage that chance may throw in your way." At Kings Mountain every man in the patriot force was, in a very real sense, his own officer. Leaders and followers meshed their efforts in a kind of concentrated fury as they searched for Patrick Ferguson.

Ferguson was not in Gilbert Town when the patriots arrived there. He had left several days before. On the first day of October, he was encamped at Denard's Ford on Broad River. He had sent a message of some urgency to Col. J. H. Cruger, commander of the British post at Ninety-Six, requesting 100 men as reinforcements. He received the brief reply that such help was out of the question—the garrison at Ninety-Six totaled only half that number. He had directed an appeal for assistance to Cornwallis but he had received no answer. (Cornwallis, in fact, did not receive the message until the morning of the battle of Kings Mountain.) Deserters from the patriot forces brought news of the approach of the over-mountain men and their swelling ranks.

Ferguson's natural confidence was being eroded by a sense of growing unease. He longed to engage these backcountry rebels in a fair fight, but he needed some assurance of more support than he now enjoyed. Aware of his past successes in winning people of the countryside to the king's cause, he issued a new proclamation. Its exaggeration and bravado suggested a mounting desperation.

> *Denard's Ford, Broad River,*
> *Tyron County, October 1, 1780.*
>
> Gentlemen: Unless you wish to be eat up by an inundation of barbarians, who have begun by murdering an unarmed son before his aged father, and afterwards lopped off his arms, and who by their shocking cruelties and irregularities, give the best proof of their cowardice and want of discipline; I say, if you want to be pinioned, robbed, and murdered, and see your wives and daughters, in four days, abused by the dregs of mankind—in short, if you wish to deserve to live, and bear the name of men, grasp your arms in a moment and run to camp.
>
> The Back Water men have crossed the mountains; McDowell, Hampton, Shelby, and Cleveland are at their head, so that you know what you have to depend upon. If you choose to be degraded forever and ever by a set of mongrels, say so at once, and let your women turn their backs upon you, and look out for real men to protect them.
> *Pat Ferguson,*
> Major 71st Regiment.

Ferguson's actions during the next 5 days appear erratic and puzzling. He was awaiting the return of furloughed loyalists who had been called back into the ranks. In addition, he did not know at what point along any road or river he might meet an enemy detachment. Elijah Clarke and his Georgia patriots were supposed to be marching to join the over-mountain men and Ferguson had been ordered to intercept them. So far his searches had proved fruitless. He had also been informed by Cornwallis that patriot cavalry was riding from the east and might attack him.

There was more than uncertainty of enemy locations behind Ferguson's dallying, however. His almost aimless marches, his casual frittering away of precious time, suggest that a number of contradictory impulses and conflicting hopes were at war within him. As a shrewd and experienced soldier he knew that only these 100 Rangers of his Provincial Corps, chosen from the King's American Regiment, the Queen's Rangers, and the New Jersey Volunteers, could be absolutely depended upon when the fighting grew fierce.

However, as a self-confident and enthusiastic recruiter of his force of some 1,000 Tory militia, many of whom he had patiently trained and drilled, he anticipated an opportunity to prove his superior, Cornwallis, wrong in the latter's disdain for the militia.

As an able tactician who realized the danger of facing superior numbers on unfamiliar terrain without any promise of reinforcements, Ferguson finally directed his route toward Cornwallis' headquarters. But as a proud man whose vanity had been wounded by dismissal of his excellent rifle without a fair trial and by Cornwallis' coolness and favored treatment of the brutal Tarleton, Ferguson longed to lead this force under his command to a glorious victory. Only 3 months earlier, in mid-summer, he had considered resigning from the army; the Secretary of State for the Colonies, Lord Germain himself, had written to Sir Henry Clinton asking that Ferguson be dissuaded from quitting.

Burning with ambitious hopes, nagged by logistical realities, Ferguson did not leave Denard's Ford until 4 o'clock Monday afternoon, the 2d of October, and then he marched only 4 miles. His army slept in the open that night, their arms at the ready.

Next day, Tuesday, brought an opposite experience, with the march beginning at 4 o'clock in the dark of the morning. After fording Second Broad River, Sandy Run, and Buffalo Creek, and after covering about 20 miles, they reached the plantation of a loyalist named Tate, 1 mile from Buffalo Creek. For two full days, Wednesday and Thursday, Ferguson and his men loitered in camp at Tate's, awaiting news on the whereabout of his pursuers, still hoping for reinforcements. He was also waiting for his wagon train, which had taken a different and less-exposed route from the camp near Denard's Ford.

Where was the dashing Tarleton, who pleasured in pursuit of the enemy? Where was George Hanger, Tarleton's second in command, who held such disdain for the backcountry men and enjoyed the gore and glory of combat? Where was Cornwallis, who realized the debilitating effect upon an army of such prolonged encounters in this interior country, draining away men and time whether they resulted in Pyrrhic victories or niggling defeats?

Oddly enough, the three who might have extended help to Ferguson were each brought low by the greatest enemies of all: the weather and illness. By the time Ferguson wrote Cornwallis his final appeal, Tarleton had been desperately ill with fever for 2 weeks.

Hanger had managed to bring the Legion into Charlotte before he succumbed to malaria, too. And a "feverish cold" was racking Cornwallis' portly frame.

Ferguson's unavailing plea, written on Thursday, the 5th, to his commander-in-chief, was brief, at once pointed and pathetic in its brevity: "I am on my march towards you, by a road leading from Cherokee Ford, north of King's Mountain. Three or four hundred good soldiers, part dragoons, would finish the business. *Something must be done soon.* This is their last push in this quarter and they are extremely desolate and [c]owed."

This dispatch suggests that Ferguson had decided to move directly to join Cornwallis. On Friday his army was on the march from Tate's plantation once more by 4 o'clock in the morning. They followed the old Cherokee Ford road between Buffalo and Kings creeks, crossed a branch of the latter creek near a mill site, continued along the ridge road, and turned into Battleground Road. They forded Kings Creek, went through Stony Gap, and approached a rocky ridge of upland which was a sort of spur of a larger range known as Kings Mountain. Instead of continuing on toward Charlotte and the security of Cornwallis' army only 35 miles away, the column was directed to climb the wooded slopes of the ridge toward its rocky summit. Patrick Ferguson had found the site where he would stand and turn and meet his pursuers.

Atop the ridge, in his command quarters, Ferguson wrote Cornwallis one final message: "I arrived today at King's Mountain & have taken a post where I do not think I can be forced by a stronger enemy than that against us." The site was bountifully supplied with water from a spring on the northwest side of the ridge; forage in the surrounding countryside was scant, but Ferguson's men had become adept at discovering whatever was available.

Capt. Abraham DePeyster of the King's American Regiment was second in command. Member of an old and influential New York family, he was an able leader who had encountered some of the patriot militia in earlier forays with Ferguson–from the siege of Charleston through Musgrove's Mill to the present situation. And Captain DePeyster was not happy with the choice of Kings Mountain as a battleground. Loyalty to his commander-in-chief had led to the nickname "the Bull Dog's Pup," however, and this correct, aristocratic young officer would not carry his unease into an open dispute with Ferguson.

Other officers were from New Jersey as well as New York. One of these, Lt. Anthony Allaire, of Huguenot descent, was keeping a diary of the campaign in the Carolinas. His entry that Friday concluded with the arrival at "Little King's Mountain, where we took up our ground." Ferguson and his officers and men settled in to wait for the rebel army. They did not have to wait long.

After their disappointment in missing Ferguson at Gilbert Town, the patriot force engaged in a tracking exercise following the elusive loyalists. Baffled by the meandering, indecisive route, the patriots lost the trail, recovered it, and began to grow discouraged. Finally, on Thursday evening, the 5th, encamped at Alexander's Ford on Green River, Campbell and his colonels held a council and decided to select the best mounted riflemen among them to speed up the pursuit. At dawn the next morning, those who had good horses, some 700 in all, set out after Ferguson.

After covering 21 miles they reached The Cowpens on Friday evening. Here, several miles southwest of where the roads intersected, was a famous cattle range with a few pens for the livestock herded there; the owner, it was recalled years later, was a wealthy Tory named Hiram Saunders. When the weary riders found Saunders in bed, they hauled him out unceremoniously but were unsuccessful in their attempt to secure information about Ferguson and his men. Silas McBee, a patriot lad in that campaign, gave an account in his old age of the slaughter of several of Saunders' cattle to feed the hungry soldiers: "The bright camp fires were everywhere seen lighting up the gloomy surroundings, and strips of beef were quickly roasted upon the coals and embers; while fifty acres of corn found there were harvested in about ten minutes."

If farmer Saunders' spirits were downcast by the sudden destruction which had been visited upon him, the army's spirits at The Cowpens were gladdened by two developments. The first was the arrival of Col. James Williams with his 400 men. The second was the report of a spy, a crippled man named Joseph Kerr, who had gained access to Ferguson's camp by pretending to seek protection for his lame condition. The Tories were at that time halted for their noon meal only 6 or 7 miles from Kings Mountain. Kerr learned of the plans to march up the ridge and encamp later that day.

The patriots made another selection of the fittest, fastest mounted men. These more than 900 horsemen were to be followed by about 85 foot soldiers. They set forth from The Cowpens about 9 o'clock on Friday night, the 6th, in their final push to confront Ferguson. The night was dark as tar from Carolina pines as they followed the route taken by Ferguson only the day before. The march along rough country roads was made more difficult by a steady drizzle of rain. Campbell's Virginians became separated from the main group and were not set on the right road and reunited until after daylight the next morning. Flintlocks of the long rifles were kept dry by being wrapped in knapsacks, blankets, and hunting shirts. All else was sacrificed to the well-being of those rifles.

About sunrise the marchers forded the deep rushing waters of Broad River. Now the officers rode at a slow gait ahead of their men, many of whom were growing weary of the pursuit. If they were going to fight a battle, they said between curses, they would just as soon fight it now and get it over with. During short halts they ate whatever their wallets and saddlebags provided, or pulled corn from the fields as they passed by. They cut some of the hard dry kernels from the cobs for their own nourishment and they fed some of the corn to their nearly exhausted horses.

Saturday morning's dawn was gray and gloomy. The drizzle had changed to rain. Colonels Campbell, Sevier, and Cleveland agreed that the weary men and beasts needed a rest. They rode up to Shelby to tell him of their decision. They met the full force of his tenacious determination. With an oath he informed them, "I will not stop until night, if I follow Ferguson into Cornwallis' lines."

The men rode on. They had gone only a mile when they learned from one Solomon Beason (who lived up to his name for balanced judgment and "was half-Whig, half-loyalist, as occasion required") that Ferguson was only 8 miles ahead of them. Five miles farther, one of their scouts encountered a Tory girl who said that "she had been in Ferguson's camp that very morning, which was only about three miles away, and had carried the British commander some chickens; that he was posted on a ridge between two branches where some deer hunters had a camp the previous autumn."

As they came closer to the ridge, the patriots captured a boy named John Ponder who was carrying Ferguson's last message to Lord Cornwallis. They read the dispatch. Then they asked Ponder how they would recognize Ferguson when they saw him. From the boy they learned that "while that officer was the best uniformed man on the mountain, they could not see his military suit, as he wore a checked shirt, or duster over it." They would be alert for a checked shirt. They already knew that the right arm of that shirt would be dangling, useless, because of the wound suffered at the Brandywine.

By 3 o'clock on Saturday afternoon the patriot army was in the woods at the base of Kings Mountain. The rain had stopped. A shimmer of October's rich light spread over the brilliantly colored leaves and the drenched landscape.

Kings Mountain: Harvest of Death

Kings Mountain was a battle of ultimate simplicity.

Ferguson and his Tory militia, some of them arrayed in red coats and uniforms, intended to hold the crest of this mountain spur and by soundly defeating the patriot assailants break decisively any spirit of resistance that remained in the backcountry.

The ridge they had chosen was shaped roughly like a human footprint or the paddle of a canoe. It extended northeast some 600 yards and varied in width from 60 to 120 feet. Its heavily wooded slopes, seamed with occasional ravines, led to a rocky, almost treeless summit. The Scottish major obviously considered such rough, boulder-strewn terrain to be ideal fortifications, for he issued no orders for breastworks or redoubts to be constructed.

The patriot colonels and their men, on the other hand, intended to dislodge the defenders from this ridge and end forever the Tory threat to their homes and freedom. And like Bre'r Rabbit in the briar patch, they welcomed the rugged terrain. Trees and rocks could provide cover for their ascent. The open crest would expose their enemy to the deadly aim of the long rifles. Squirrel hunters, Indian fighters, marksmen of remarkable accuracy, they were at home among woods and ledges.

When they were about a mile from the ridge, the patriots halted, hitched their steaming horses and formed themselves into two lines of two columns each, led by Campbell, Sevier, Shelby, and Cleveland. Proceeding on foot, they were to encircle Ferguson's force by taking up preassigned positions around the ridge. At the right center was

Campbell and his Virginians, followed by Shelby. On the right flank were detachments under Sevier, McDowell, and Winston. The latter was to make a wide sweep to the south of Ferguson to cut off the possibility of retreat by this most likely route. The left flank detachments were led by Williams, Chronicle, and Cleveland, with their Carolinians.

Before his men marched, William Campbell made the rounds of each corps. His message was plain. Anyone who did not wish to fight should immediately head for home; as for himself, he would "fight the enemy a week, if need be, to gain the victory." It was agreed "that when the center columns were ready for the attack, they were to give the signal by raising a regular frontier war-whoop, after the Indian style, and rush forward, doing the enemy all the injury possible."

The frustration of the past few days had evaporated; the weariness and contentiousness of the long rainy night's and morning's march had disappeared. With nerves stretched taut as bow-strings, eyes and ears alert to every detail of the danger confronting them, the volunteers followed orders for every man to attend to his rifle: "throw the priming out of his pan, pick his touchhole, prime anew, examine bullets and see that everything was in readiness for battle." Within a few minutes, such details could mean the difference between a man's survival—or death. They adopted as their countersign the word "Buford," a reminder of the men Tarleton and his legion had slaughtered in vicious disregard of Buford's attempt to surrender and his call for quarter. As a final preparation, 16-year-old James Collins, in Chronicle's regiment, followed the example of the men around him and crammed "four or five balls in his mouth to prevent thirst, also to be in readiness to reload quick." Nervous and sweating, but less fearful of the enemy than of being called a coward, he faced toward the ridge.

Their approach was so rapid that Ferguson was caught by surprise. Country men were well aware that the best time to hunt squirrels was after a rain when the fallen autumn leaves would cushion all sounds and footfalls. Capt. Alexander Chesney, a South Carolina loyalist, had been on reconnaissance for Ferguson and was just dismounting to report "that all was quiet and the pickets on the alert," when he heard sudden firing about a half-mile in the distance. He hastily called up his officers and men.

The first shots were fired by Tories who had sighted Shelby's approaching column. Shelby would not let his men immediately return the fire, however. He firmly answered their impatience: when they had reached their assigned position, their fire would not be in vain.

Shelby's men were not yet in place when Campbell stripped off his coat and called on his men to attack. He ordered them to *shout like hell, and fight like devils!*" Their whoops were taken up by Shelby's corps and then by those along the other wings. Atop the ridge, Capt. Abraham DePeyster was reminded of his former encounter with Shelby and these frontiersmen at Musgrove's Mill. He warned Ferguson that these were "the damned yelling boys!"

To one of those boys "the mountain appeared volcanic; there flashed along its summit, and around its base, and up its sides, one long sulphurous blaze." The patriots' attack was being answered with a burst of trained volley firing. And above all the din and uproar there resounded the shrill staccato of Patrick Ferguson's famous silver whistle–ranging from the main camp at the northeastern end of the ridge along the rocky crest to the southwestern rim.

The forces of Campbell and Shelby advanced up the craggy slope, their men moving Indian fashion to take advantage of every tree or rock, shrub or log. It was their fire that brought Ferguson's first order for a bayonet charge. At close quarters the Virginians could not withstand such an attack and they broke and ran down the mountain. Ferguson's Lieutenant Allaire, on horseback, overtook a tall patriot officer on foot and felled him with a single blow of his sword.

This was a critical moment in the battle. The first repulse had been sharp and bloody. In their retreat the patriots had run not only to the bottom of the ridge but across a ravine and part-way up an adjoining slope. At the battle of Camden, such a repulse and such a moment had turned into a rout of the patriot forces. Now "everything depended upon successfully rallying the men when first driven down

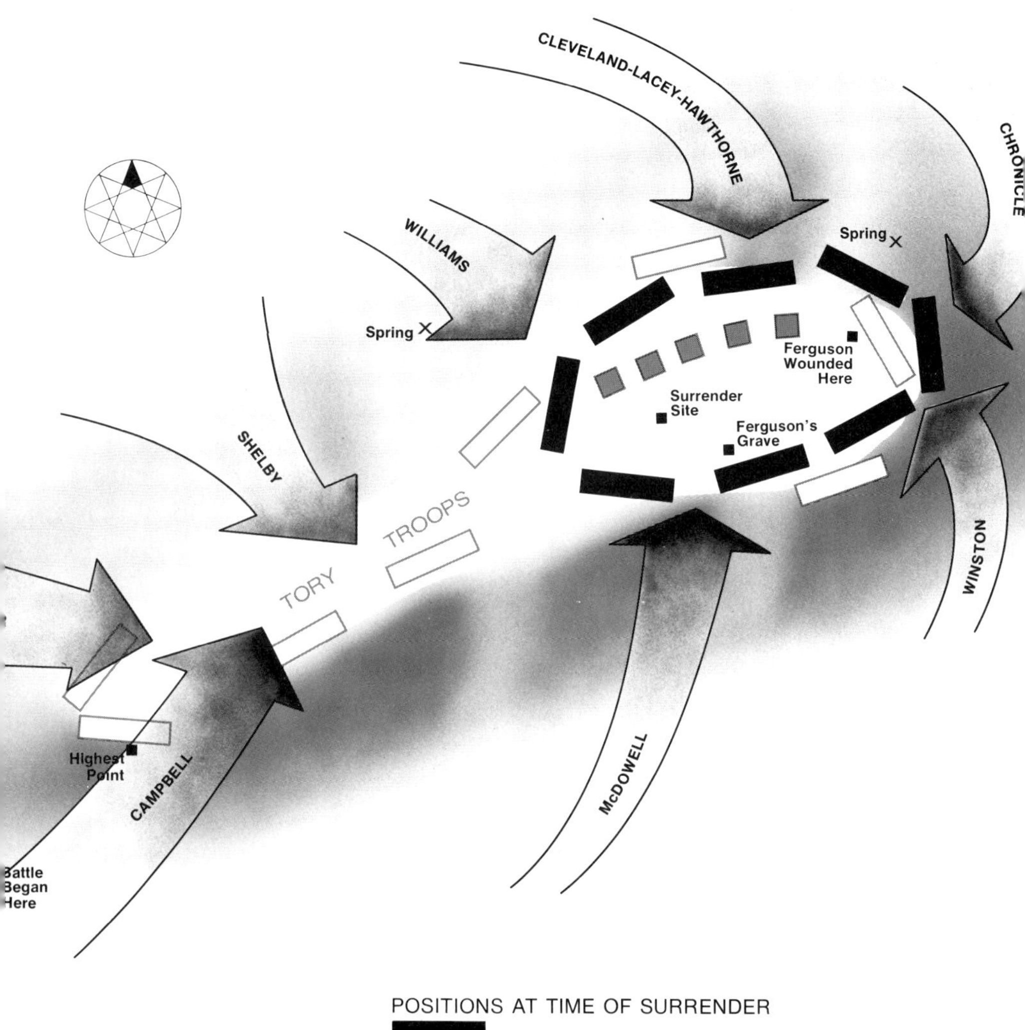

OCTOBER 7, 1780
BATTLE OF KINGS MOUNTAIN

the mountain." And this was what red-haired, energetic William Campbell was able to do. He called upon his men to halt and return to the ridge and drive the enemy before them. They heard and turned and followed his orders—and his example—reloaded their rifles, and went back to charge up the mountainside again.

The battle had become dozens of smaller fights. Three times the patriot forces of Campbell and Shelby attacked and were driven back down the mountain. But it was becoming apparent that the volleys of Ferguson's muskets were ineffective; they passed over the heads of the attackers. And the fire from the patriots' rifles was reaping an ever deadlier toll. A similar situation existed all around the mountain where the rebel riflemen could shoot and dodge for cover while the Tories and provincials on the ridge were exposed to fire from both sides.

The consequences of the day's strangest and most ironic turn of events now became increasingly evident. The inventor of the Ferguson rifle, the man who was one of the finest marksmen in the British army, had no choice but to defend Kings Mountain with the bayonet rather than the musket! When Ferguson had ordered his sergeants to inspect arms on Friday evening and Saturday morning, he directed the men who did not have bayonets to whittle down the handles of their hunting knives so they could be fitted into the muzzles of their muskets. Considerable time and energy had already gone into training the loyalist militia in skillful use of the bayonet. But on this hillside, facing these frontiersmen, the bayonet was proving a disaster. In fact, the most succinct and familiar evaluation of the military confrontation at Kings Mountain would summarize this contest between blade and bullet: the light cavalryman, Henry "Lighthorse Harry" Lee (future father of Robert E. Lee), observed that Kings Mountain proved to be "more assailable by the rifle than defensible with the bayonet."

The contest was bloody. Thomas Young, a 16-year-old private who fought his way up the northwest slope with Colonel Williams, afterward recalled that "Ben Hollingworth and myself took right up the side of the mountain, and fought our way from tree to tree, up to the summit. I recollect I stood behind one tree and fired until the bark was nearly all knocked off, and my eyes pretty well filled with it. One fellow shaved me pretty close, for his bullet took a piece out of my gun stock. Before I was aware of it, I found myself apparently between my own regiment and the enemy, as I judged from seeing the paper the Whigs wore in their hats, and the pine twigs the Tories wore in their, these being the badges of distinction."

Ferguson's men launched their third charge down among the boulders and trees where Campbell's and Shelby's sharpshooters took cover while they picked off their opponents outlined in clear relief along the brow of the hill. Flame and smoke increased as the very mountain reverberated with the clamor of battle. A South Carolina loyalist named Drury Mathis was severely wounded. As he lay flat against the rough slope the balls from the patriot rifles fell around him like hail while the shots from his fellow loyalists consistently passed above the heads of their targets. Playing possum, he hugged the ground while watching the mountaineers swarm up the ridge: men "not over-burdened with fat, but tall, raw-boned, and sinewy."

Then the loyalists discovered that they were under attack by other patriot detachments, those who had climbed the ridge along the northeastern slopes. Whirling to meet this menace from their rear, Ferguson's men left Campbell's, Shelby's, and Sevier's sharpshooters to reach and hold the crest of their segment of the ridge.

And the defenders' ground was dwindling. Each thrust by the "yelling boys" pushed the Tories and provincials into a narrower space along the ridge-top. They were shrinking toward that north-eastern bulge of the ridge-top where the headquarters of the camp stood. On the slopes here were Williams and his South Carolinians, as well as Cleveland's men, who had been delayed briefly in taking up their position because of a swampy stretch of ground grown miry under the heavy rains and because their hefty leader had taken off afoot to lead them when his fine horse, "Roebuck," was wounded. There were William Chronicle and Frederick Hambright, who faced terrain more sharp and forbidding than Campbell's men had climbed. At the base of the ridge, the Carolina-born Chronicle rushed 10 paces ahead of his men and waved them on with his military hat, shouting, "Face to the hill!" The words died in his throat as he was struck by a ball. At 25, the young major who had shown great promise and won wide popularity among his companions, was dead.

The battle raged on. German-born Colonel Hambright, severely wounded in his thigh, refused to dismount although his boot was filling with blood. "Huzza, my brave poys," his accent from the old country rang out, "fight on a few minutes more, and the battle will be over!"

Winston's and McDowell's men were among those tightening the noose at the end of the ridge. As the tide of patriot success swelled, however, Thomas Young saw his friend and leader, Col. James Williams, fall before the enemy's attack. Although Williams did not die until the following day, this "rough, rash and fearless" South Carolinian was already mourned by the youthful neighbor who had gone with him into the battle.

On top of the mountain [Young wrote] in the thickest of the fight, I saw Colonel Williams fall, and a braver or better man never died upon the field of battle. I had seen him fall but once before that day—it was in the beginning of the action, as he charged by me at full speed around the mountain. Toward the summit a ball struck his horse just under the jaw, when he commenced stamping as if he were in a nest of yellow jackets. Colonel Williams threw his reins over the animal's neck, sprang to the ground, and dashed onward.

The moment I heard the cry that Colonel Williams was shot, I ran to his assistance, for I loved him as a father, he had ever been so kind to me, almost always carrying a cake in his pocket for me and his little son, Joseph. They carried him into a tent, and sprinkled some water in his face. As he revived, his first words were, 'For God's sake, boys, don't give up the hill!' I left him in the arms of his son Daniel, and returned to the field to revenge his fall.

Suddenly word spread among Sevier's troops that the hated Tarleton and his dragoons had arrived to aid Ferguson and were even at that moment on the mountain. Sevier rode among his men, re-assuring them: Bloody Tarleton was not there, "and if he were, they could make him, like Ferguson's Rangers, turn their backs and flee up the mountain." The over-mountain men readied another attack on their enemy.

The noise of rifles, the shouts, the crashing of men and horses through the brush and among the boulders, intensified as the struggle tightened. The threshing about of wounded animals and the groans of wounded men mingled with the general din. Sixteen-year-old

Robert Henry, of Chronicle's command, had an encounter with a Tory:

I was preparing to fire when one of the British advancing, I stepped back and was in the act of cocking my gun when his bayonet was running along the barrel of my gun, and gave me a thrust through my hand and into my thigh. My antagonist and I both fell. The Fork boys retreated and loaded their guns. I was then lying under the smoke and it appeared that some of them were not more than a gun's length in front of the bayonets, and the farthest could not have been more than 20 feet in front when they discharged their rifles. It was said that every one dropped his man. The British then retreated in great haste, and were pursued by the Fork boys.

William Caldwell saw my condition, and pulled the bayonet out of my thigh, but it hung to my hand; he gave my hand a kick and it went out. The thrust gave me much pain, but the pulling of it was much more severe. With my well hand I picked up my gun and found her discharged. I suppose that when the soldier made the thrust, I gripped the trigger and discharged her; the load must have passed through his bladder and cut a main artery at his back, as he bled profusely.

The patriots were closing in but Ferguson did not flinch. He seemed to be everywhere, attended by the high sustained call of his silver whistle rallying Tory militia to resist and give battle. White flags of surrender appeared among his forces; he slashed them down with sweeping strokes as he galloped to and fro. Two horses were shot down as he rode them. He cruelly spurred a third to carry him ever faster from one threatened area to another. Several of his officers suggested that it was useless to continue the fight. Captain DePeyster believed that they might all be slaughtered like "ducks in a coop." But their commander in chief was not to be persuaded. Never, he told them, would he yield "to such a damned banditti."

And he did not yield. Cutting and slashing with his weapon in a last desperate assault, Ferguson and a handful of his officers flung themselves forward in a final attempt to break through the rebel lines. His sword broke. He spurred his horse savagely and came to the place in front of Sevier's column. Along the mountainside shots rang out. Six or eight found their mark. One penetrated Ferguson's head. He slumped in the saddle, both arms broken, hat and clothing tattered by shot. Then he dropped from his horse, one foot yet caught in the stirrup. Four of his loyalists loosed the foot, laid him on a blanket, and carried him out of the line of fire. As he lay propped up with rocks and blankets, his life ebbing away, soldiers from both sides came to gaze upon the dying chieftain whose inventions and adventures had become legendary.

DePeyster assumed command of the provincials and Tories, and the fierce combat continued for a brief interval as the patriots tightened their encirclement. But with Ferguson's whistle and encouragements silenced, the mountain's defenders panicked. White flags of surrender fluttered among the smoke and confusion. One of the soldiers on horseback waved a white handkerchief and was shot down by a grief-stricken patriot who had just learned that his brother was killed. A second man bearing a surrender token was also shot down. At last a third rider reached Maj. Evan Shelby, brother to Col. Isaac Shelby, and handed him the token of surrender.

But the battle had generated a momentum that was difficult to halt. The over-mountain men and the Piedmont patriots had sought this battle. They were not professional soldiers following military rules and protocol as much as aroused citizens following the instinct for survival. There were probably some–if not as many as later justification claimed–who did not recognize the meaning of the white handkerchiefs blossoming on muskets and ramrods.

Others knew the message well but ignored it. "Give them Buford's play!" was the shout, a reminder of Tarleton's lack of mercy to Colonel Buford and his men almost 5 months before. All the fierce hate and revenge of recent civil strife in the South seemed concentrated on that bloody battlefield at that moment. It was later recorded that "the slaughter continued until the Americans were weary of killing."

"Quarter! Quarter!" the provincials and Tories cried.

"Damn you, if you want quarter, throw down your arms!" Colonel Shelby ordered those before him.

Young Joseph Sevier, told that his father was killed in action, continued firing. Tears coursed down his cheeks as he loaded, fired, re-loaded. "The damned rascals have killed my father, and I'll keep loading and shooting till I kill every son of a bitch of them!" When John Sevier himself appeared presently, very much alive, on horseback, his son could lay aside the rifle.

A soldier of the Virginia regiment was startled to have his rifle knocked aside while he was taking aim. Colonel Campbell, striding among the various commands, pled, "For God's sake, don't shoot! It is murder to kill them now, for they have raised the flag."

Captain DePeyster, erect on his gray horse, informed Campbell what he thought of such behavior. "It's damned unfair, damned unfair." But Campbell did not pause for discussion. He ordered the men under DePeyster: "Officers, rank by yourselves; prisoners, take off your hats and sit down."

As the vanquished Tories collected in one dejected huddle on the brow of the ridge, they were surrounded by the victors who finally stood four deep around their quarry. At a cost of only 28 killed and 62 wounded, their victory was total. Ferguson's detachment of 1,100 men was annihilated; Cornwallis' left flank no longer existed.

Led by Campbell, the American patriots gave three loud *"huzzas for Liberty."*

In one brief hour the tide of war had shifted in the South. Never again would the British, boasting invincibility, be able to recruit an easy following of loyalists. Never again would the patriot Americans fear that their cause was hopeless. As imperceptibly and surely as the ocean's reversal from ebb to flow and vice versa, the morale and destiny of opponents engaging each other in the Southern theater had altered.

In the mellow light of late afternoon, surrounded by the bloody devastation they had wrought, the men of both sides turned from fighting to assessing their situation. Patrick Ferguson's corpse was wrapped in a raw beef hide and buried in a shallow ravine just below the crest of the ridge. A cairn would later be erected at this site.

Legends would also arise. The most persistent concerned two women attached to the loyalist camp. Virginia Sal and Virginia Paul were pretty enough to win the attention of the British officer, and Ferguson was charming enough to attract the allegiance of the young women. Virginia Sal was reputedly one of the first to be killed when the firing began; her red hair may have made her a special target. When Ferguson was buried, some recalled, they brought her body to lie in the earth beside his.

Virginia Paul, on the other hand, seemed immune to attack. There were those who vowed they saw her coolly riding across the battlefield during the engagement, apparently oblivious to danger. After the battle, as the patriots discussed the disposition of their prisoners, Campbell argued that Virginia Paul should be paroled. His logic was a curious combination of chauvinism and chivalry: "She is only a woman," he explained to his weary, sweaty, jubilant crowd of men, "our mothers were women. We must let her go." And the pretty woman on horseback was probably sent with other prisoners to Burke Court House (present-day Morganton, N.C.) and from there to Cornwallis' army in Charlotte.

There was one quite remarkable surgeon present to treat the wounded on both sides. Dr. Uzal Johnson was not the only doctor present at Kings Mountain, but he was the one whose ministrations lived in the memories of patriots and loyalists alike. Johnson was a native of Newark, N.J., where he began practicing medicine at the age of 19, the same year he joined the New Jersey Volunteers. In 1780 he was 23 and serving with Ferguson's corps. At Kings Mountain he could not begin to meet the demands for his attention and skills.

The injured and the dying, sprawled along the slopes and ridge, were propped against trees and boulders. A lieutenant severely wounded in the abdomen was saved from death mainly by the fact that he had had so little to eat for 3 days that his stomach was practically empty. A dauntless Irishman whose windpipe was injured confiscated the rest of the rum with which his wound was being bathed and drank it, explaining: "A little *in* is as good as *out*."

Capt. Robert Sevier, John's brother, was among the most critically wounded, struck by buckshot near his kidney when he stooped to pick up his ramrod. Dr. Johnson tried unsuccessfully to remove the shot and ended finally by dressing the wound and warning that if Sevier undertook the long trip home before the shot could be removed, his kidneys would become fatally inflamed. But Robert Sevier shared the impatience of his fellow over-mountain men to be on their way, and by the time they broke camp the next day, he was with them. The doctor's diagnosis proved correct, however, and at Bright's Place on Yellow Mountain, on his ninth day toward home and cared for by his nephew James, Capt. Robert Sevier died.

The countryside around Kings Mountain was poor, plundered, and sparsely settled, but noise of the battle had reverberated far and wide. Before nightfall men and women were making their way to the ridge to learn the outcome of the fight. Some of the women immediately turned to nursing the wounded. Some of the curiosity seekers scavenged for treasure on the dead bodies.

The prisoners–virtually an entire army by 18th-century standards–were placed under guard while food was being prepared for the hungry victors, who had scarcely rested or eaten for 24 hours. There were trophies to be divided, too, such as Ferguson's famous silver whistles–a large one and a small one, as it turned out–the former given to Shelby, the latter to a soldier named Elias Powell. Joseph McDowell received china dinner plates and a coffee cup and saucer from Ferguson's official table service, while Sevier took the silk sash and Captain DePeyster's sword. The white horse went to Cleveland, who had lost his mount, and Ferguson's correspondence became Campbell's property. Two of the men who were nearby when Ferguson fell had already appropriated his pistol and large silver watch, "as round as a turnip."

During the days to follow, someone searching the battle site reportedly found a necklace of glass beads. Quite commonplace beads they were. But whether they had belonged to Virginia Sal or Virginia Paul, the necklace was a memento of some sentiment or romance alien to this bloody battleground.

The morning after the battle, Sunday, dawned brightly. The autumn landscape became once more benign and warm with sunlight on brilliant foliage. The dead were hastily buried in shallow graves. The boy, James Collins, helped at the grisly task and later remembered:

. . . the scene became really distressing. The wives and children of the poor Tories came in, in great numbers. Their husbands, fathers and brothers lay dead in heaps, while others lay wounded or dying, a melancholy sight indeed! . . .
We proceeded to bury the dead, but it was badly done. They were thrown

into convenient piles and covered with old logs, the bark of old trees, and rocks, yet not so as to secure them from becoming a prey to the beasts of the forests, or the vultures of the air. And the wolves became so plenty, that it was dangerous for anyone to be out at night, for several miles around. The hogs in the neighborhood gathered into the place to devour the flesh of man, inasmuch as numbers chose to live on little meat rather than eat their hogs, though they were fat. Half the dogs in the country were said to be mad, and were put to death. . . .

In the evening, there was a distribution made of the plunder, and we were dismissed. My father and myself drew two fine horses, two guns, and some articles of clothing, with a share of powder and lead.

The troops claimed their own spoils as they had claimed their own responsibilities for the battle. No order of Congress or of their States had brought them here. "It was entirely a volunteer movement—no baggage-wagons, no commissaries, no pay, and no supplies." Swords were particularly sought after by poor militia officers who had never possessed one before. Other "plunder" was divided among the patriots.

Seventeen baggage wagons in Ferguson's camp were drawn across the campfires and burned. To have taken them would prove cumbersome—and the patriots were in a hurry. They expected Tarleton, who was still rumored to be on his way to reinforce Ferguson. The weary fighters were content with their present success; they did not anticipate another battle immediately.

The prisoners were lined up for the march toward North Carolina and were forced to carry their own arms. Lyman C. Draper has evoked that scene from manuscripts and memories shared by the participants:

The flints were taken from the locks; and, to the more strong and healthy Tories, two guns each were assigned for conveyance. When ready to start on the day's journey, the prisoners were marched, in single file, by the spot where the rifles and muskets were stacked, and each was directed to shoulder and carry the arms allotted to him. Colonel Shelby, with his sword drawn, stood by, among others, to see that the order was strictly obeyed. One old fellow came toddling by, and evinced a determination not to encumber himself with a gun. Shelby sternly ordered him to shoulder one without delay. The old man demurred, declaring he was not able to carry it. Shelby told him, with a curse, that he was able to bring one there, and he should carry one away; and, at the same time gave him a smart slap across his shoulders with the flat side of his sword-blade. The old fellow, discovering that he could not trifle with such a man as Shelby, jumped at the gun-pile, shouldered one, and marched away in double-quick time.

The wounded were transported on hastily improvised horse-litters made by "fastening two long poles on either side of two horses at tandem, leaving a space of six or eight feet between them, stretching tent-cloth or blankets between the poles, on which to place a disabled officer or soldier."

While some of the patriots and prisoners remained on the ridge to complete disposal of the corpses, the main army–with its more than 600 captives and its litters of wounded and dying–left the battle site. Departure began about 10 o'clock in the morning. They moved slowly. Early in the afternoon the wounded Colonel Williams died. The marchers had covered 12 miles when they made camp near the Broad River at the deserted plantation of a Tory whose dry rails fueled the evening campfires and whose sweet potato patch provided tasty provision for an army which had eaten little for 2 days and nights.

They marched sluggishly during the following days. Most of the October fields, long since stripped by raiders from both armies, offered scanty forage. Thomas Young feared that they were all near starvation. Green pumpkin, sliced and fried, came to be "about the sweetest eating" he had ever known. The prisoners' fare was even more meager: raw corn on the ear and pumpkins were thrown into their midst as if they were "farmer's swine." They devoured them greedily. Weakened by hunger, encumbered by the wounded and the captured, the Kings Mountain patriots, after a week on the road had covered only about 40 miles.

The going was rough in every way. Physical hardship rendered tempers raw and violent. Impatient to arrive home, citizen-soldiers chafed under the delays of military or legal procedures. By Wednesday, the fourth day after the battle, Colonel Campbell felt it necessary to include in his General Order a revealing statement: "I must request the officers of all ranks in the army to endeavor to restrain the disorderly manner of slaughtering and disturbing the prisoners."

On Saturday, the 14th, the smouldering hatreds flared into a final bloody epilogue to Kings Mountain. Encamped about 10 miles northeast of Gilbert Town at a site known as Bickerstaff's Old Fields–or Red Chimneys, marking the location of the crumbled plantation house–the patriots held a court to try a number of Tory prisoners in their custody. Recent memories of Cornwallis' orders following the patriot defeat at Camden, Tarleton's massacre, and individual Tory retaliations against patriot sympathizers in many communities, were recounted and circulated throughout the camp.

Citizens along the way had also added their stories of continuing hostilities. Shelby wrote that when he and others arrived at Gilbert Town "they were informed by a paroled officer that he had seen eleven patriots hung at Ninety Six a few days before, for being Rebels. Similar cruel and unjustifiable acts had been committed before. In the opinion of the patriots, it required retaliatory measures to put a stop to these atrocities. A copy of the law of North Carolina was obtained, which authorized two magistrates to summon a jury, and forthwith to try, and, if found guilty, to execute persons who had violated its precepts."

Since most of the North Carolina officers were also magistrates at home, it was no problem to find a jury of 12 who qualified under these regulations. Thirty-six of the prisoners were rounded up and brought before the grim court. They were accused, tried, and found guilty of "breaking open houses, killing the men, turning the women and children out of doors, and burning the houses." The sentence was death. Among those sitting in judgment, it appeared that "Colonel Cleveland was probably more active and determined than any other officer in bringing about these severe measures."

By the time a great old oak was found and preparations for the executions were completed, it was late at night. Pine-knot torches were lit as the over-mountain men and their companions gathered four deep around the condemned prisoners. Three at a time the Tories were swung from limbs of the giant oak. After the ninth hanging, a halt was called. Not all the patriots were ready to grant a reprieve. One bitter Tory-hater pointed to the limp bodies and voiced satisfaction: "Would to God every tree in the wilderness bore such fruit as that!"

But the next trio, already bound for execution, were untied. The remaining condemned men were pardoned. Those nine already dead were left dangling from the tree. They would serve as warning to other loyalists in the vicinity. Throughout the region that tree became known as the Gallows Oak.

The patriots broke camp before daylight the following morning. It was Sunday, the 15th of October. A heavy rain fell all day. But Shelby had received a secret warning during the night that Tarleton was on his way and might even reach Gilbert Town that morning. The over-mountain men were anxious to put the swollen waters of the Catawba River between themselves and the hated Tarleton.

Ironically, while they were fleeing from Tarleton, he was also fleeing from them. Accompanying Cornwallis' main army on the retreat from Charlotte back into South Carolina, the loyalists were fearful of the 3,000 victorious mountaineers rumored to be in pursuit of them.

Throughout that soggy day the patriots with their prisoners pushed on. They covered some 32 miles. Ferguson's Lieutenant Allaire, a prisoner, later recalled that "several of the militia that were worn out with fatigue, and not being able to keep up, were cut down and trodden to death in the mire." Late that night they reached the familiar haven of Quaker Meadows, home of Major McDowell, where they had camped on their way to Kings Mountain. Once again, Joseph McDowell shared the hospitality of his home and farm, offering the chilled men, still wet from fording the Catawba river, free use of rails from his fences to build campfires and warm themselves. Several of the loyalist officers, including Lieutenant Allaire, were even taken into the house for lodging.

The patriot army began to disperse: Lacey and his men went back to South Carolina; Shelby and Sevier and the Virginia footmen headed across their mountains to the backcountry; and the mounted Virginians, Cleveland's and Winston's troops, with some of McDowell's and a few over-mountain boys who wished to stay with the army, escorted the prisoners northward under instructions from General Gates, still the American commander in the South. Eventually the prisoners were delivered to Hillsborough, N.C., where they were exchanged for patriot prisoners of war. So many had escaped along the way, however—100 during one day, that miserable rainy Sunday after the hangings—that only an estimated 130 captives, Tories and provincials combined, remained at last to be exchanged. General Greene, when he arrived in the South to relieve Gates of the command in December, "lamented the loss of so many of the Kings Mountain prisoners."

The two forces which had faced each other atop the rocky ridge had swiftly disintegrated. The 100-odd provincials among whom Ferguson had aroused such loyalty, and the estimated 1,000 militia in whom he placed such high confidence, lay dead atop Kings Mountain or scattered like grain before the whirlwind across the ravaged countryside. The patriot army, an estimated 1,500 to 1,800 strong, which had welled up like a natural force at Sycamore Shoals and gathered tributaries from among the mountains and lowlands as it surged toward Kings Mountain, dissolved back into the countryside. Atop Kings Mountain the wild hogs scavenged, the predators gorged, and wolves became so numerous that hunters found the site a favorite place for their sport. Yet this place of death had made its significant contribution toward bringing a new nation to life.

Epilogue

News of Kings Mountain reached Cornwallis on Saturday, October 14th. Rumor could hardly magnify the defeat–Ferguson dead and his entire force killed or captured–but it enlarged the patriot army to 3,000 and placed it on the march toward British headquarters.

Cornwallis was appalled, and the effect on his plans was decisive. The thrust into North Carolina was abandoned and amid torrents of rain, on red clay roads churned to a heavy porridge, Cornwallis turned his army back toward South Carolina. About 20 wagons loaded with supplies were destroyed or abandoned in the wretched mud. The British commander in chief, sick with a bilious fever, riding in a jolting wagon, led his dispirited troops into Winnsboro and temporary encampment. The British offensive in the South was momentarily stalled. British Adj. Gen. Edward Harvey had long since warned that "Our army will be destroyed by damned driblets." Kings Mountain had been a driblet that released a flood.

Sir Henry Clinton, with the 20/20 vision of hindsight, later claimed: "The instant I heard of Major Ferguson's defeat, I foresaw most of the consequences likely to result from it. The check so encouraged the spirit of rebellion in the Carolinas that it could never afterward be humbled." And he pronounced it "the first link in a chain of evils that followed each other in regular succession until they at last ended in the total loss of America."

George Washington did not hear of Kings Mountain until October 26th, and then the report was garbled. But when the result was finally clear, he spoke in his General Orders of that "important object gained" as a "proof of the spirit and resources of the country."

On November 7, a full month after the battle, the Congress received a complete account of the engagement at Kings Mountain. Members expressed their approval of the spirited conduct which won "complete victory."

British headquarters in New York tried to dismiss the battle as one of little consequence and for a brief interval even denied that it had occurred at all. But British supporters in the Southern colonies had long since learned the battle's message, and strategists in New York and London would soon comprehend it, too: the anticipated number of loyalists waiting to enlist under Cornwallis had not and would not materialize. It was apparent that much of the Southern campaign had been founded on a delusion.

In addition, there had been a significant misunderstanding of the backcountry. Swaggering Tarleton had thought he could subdue it through terror. Proud Ferguson had believed he could win it by threat. Cornwallis had tried to impress it by force. Their force and threat and terror achieved what edicts and oratory, summonses and pleas, had not accomplished: unity among a group of tenacious individualists. If British strategists had wondered what the result might be if enough patriot bands united to form a small army, their answer came at Kings Mountain.

Kings Mountain was the greatest victory of the Southern militia. It has been considered a special achievement of the leaders, men who were able to mount an attack, coordinate it with skill, and inspire the participants to feats of courage and final victory. But more than leadership was involved in that success. When Isaac Shelby informed his men that each one of them was to consider himself an officer, he struck the keynote of the venture—from the zeal of its voluntary beginning to the excesses of its violent conclusion, both the best and the worst of the expedition grew out of the fact that each patriot considered himself leader and follower.

Between the crushing defeat of Horatio Gates by Cornwallis at Camden on August 16th and the rousing victory of Daniel Morgan over Tarleton at The Cowpens on January 17th looms Kings Mountain—a watershed of the Revolution. Cornwallis never regained the full momentum of initiative again. The patriots never completely lost confidence in their strength again. Nathanael Greene, arriving in the Carolinas to replace Gates, announced he would "recover this country or die in the attempt." Cornwallis, ill and momentarily shaken, complained of refugees and uprisings which taxed his resources and called for "the assistance of regular troops everywhere." Increasingly those "damned driblets" took their toll.

Years later, Thomas Jefferson called "that memorable victory" at Kings Mountain "the joyful annunciation of that turn of the tide of success, which terminated the Revolutionary war with the seal of independence."

Of all the patriot leaders, none received more political benefit from participation in the battle than John Sevier. His biographer, Carl S. Driver, points out that "his place in the hearts of his neighbors had been definitely established before Kings Mountain, but his participation in this spectacular victory greatly enhanced his prestige as a frontier leader. . . . This engagement introduced him to the country at large and made him a respected character in all parts of the nation." Six times he would be elected governor of Tennessee, which did not come into existence until 16 years after Kings Mountain. Four times he would represent his State in Congress. His neighbors continued to remember that he and Isaac Shelby had issued the first summons to muster at Sycamore Shoals and turn back the British threat.

Isaac Shelby returned to his interest in the Kentucky lands following the Revolution, and made important contributions toward establishment of that State. He became its first governor.

William Campbell, following Kings Mountain, represented Washington County in the Virginia House of Delegates before being recalled to duty under General Lafayette. He died on August 22, 1781, the summer after Kings Mountain, before the final victory of the patriot forces to which he had given such memorable service.

Among the other leaders who figured prominently in the Kings Mountain action, Joseph McDowell participated in the subsequent victory at The Cowpens and went on to become influential in North Carolina politics. Benjamin Cleveland eventually served as a justice in North Carolina, but his chief claim to fame was the 450-pound size he reputedly attained. Joseph Winston served in the North Carolina legislature and in the United States Congress, while Frederick Hambright bought a home in the vicinity of Kings Mountain, where he died at the age of 90.

And what happened to those loyalist leaders who were at Kings Mountain? Abraham DePeyster, whose life had been saved that day when a rifle ball was stopped by a dubloon in his vest pocket, retired following the British surrender at Yorktown and lived in New Brunswick, Canada. Others of the provincial soldiers—Capt. Samuel Ryerson and Lt. John Taylor, both from New Jersey, along with Lts. Anthony Allaire, William Stevens, and Duncan Fletcher—also found haven for retirement in Canada. Dr. Uzal Johnson, who served the wounded of patriot and loyalist forces with equal care after the battle, who endured insults during the wretched march following the battle, returned to his native Newark, N.J., where he continued practicing medicine until he died at the age of 70.

Perhaps Patrick Ferguson, writing from America early in his service there to his anxious mother in the British Isles, unwittingly provided the most concise and accurate memorial for those who died on the ridge at Kings Mountain on October 7, 1780: "The length of our lives is not at our command, however much the manner of them may be. If our Creator enable us to act the part of honour, and to conduct ourselves with spirit, probity, and humanity, the change to another world whether now or fifty years hence, will not be for the worse."

The battle in which he lost his life was a portent of another kind of change in worlds. An old world was being challenged; a new world was in birth. That birth, at Kings Mountain as elsewhere throughout the colonies, was bloody and dearly bought. It brought out the worst and best in the human beings involved. It also bore the pangs and satisfactions of that stretch toward freedom, toward fulfillment, which was part of a new people's self-discovery and self-government. Those new people would be called Americans.